LEGENDARY LOCALS

OF

PEORIA

ILLINOIS

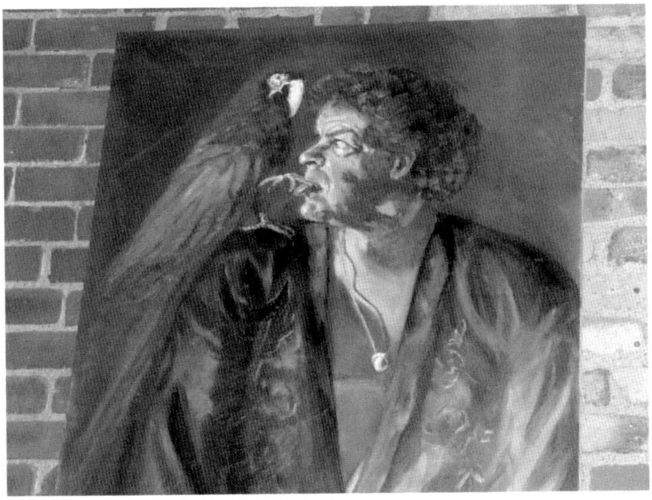

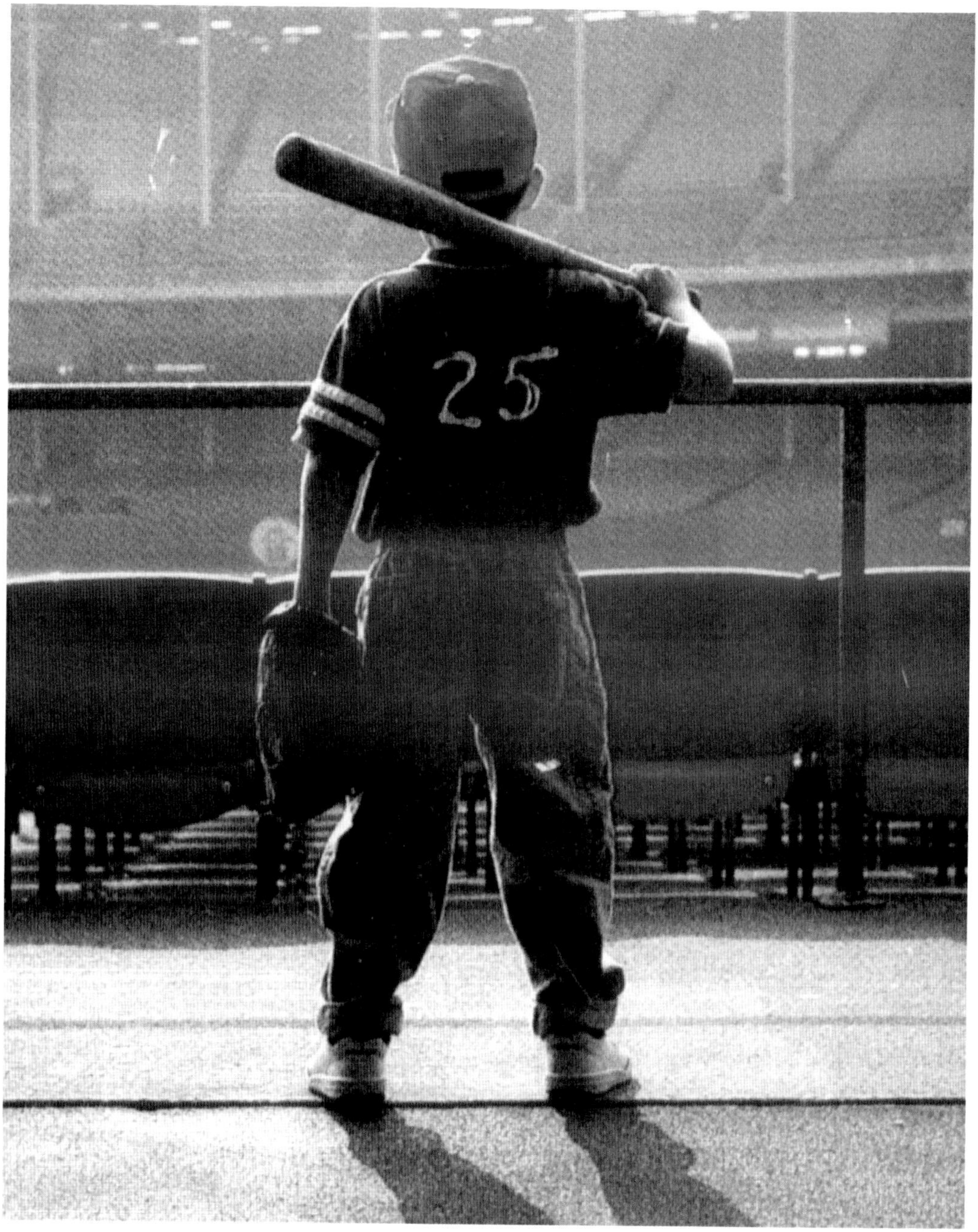

Peoria Daydreamin'
A boy daydreams of being Jim Thome (No. 25), the humble Heartland homer hero. (Courtesy of Chuck Thome Jr.)

Page 1: **The River City Rowdy**
Gary Sandberg and Jelly Bean rock the Peoria City Council Horseshoe. (Courtesy of Pat Sullivan.)

LEGENDARY LOCALS

OF

PEORIA

ILLINOIS

GREG WAHL, DDS

LEGENDARY LOCALS

ISBN 978-1-4671-0173-8

Legendary Locals is an imprint of Arcadia Publishing
Charleston, South Carolina

Printed in the United States of America

Library of Congress Control Number: 2014934850

For all general information, please contact Arcadia Publishing:
Telephone 843-853-2070
Fax 843-853-0044
E-mail sales@arcadiapublishing.com
For customer service and orders:
Toll-Free 1-888-313-2665

Visit us on the Internet at www.arcadiapublishing.com

Dedication
To my mom, Margaret, and my wife, Carole, you're always there . . . and always loved.

On the Front Cover: Clockwise from top left:
Preston Jackson, artist (courtesy of Karen Camper; see pages 34), Steve Bobbitt, entertainer (courtesy of Jeff McSweeney; see pages 58); Allene Jeanes, scientist extraordinaire (courtesy of Katie O'Hara and the National Center for Agricultural Utilization Research, Peoria, Illinois; see page 24), Jimmy Spears, pub owner (author's collection; see page 79), George Manias, celebrated shoeshine man (courtesy of Karen Camper; see page 69), Bob Humbles, athlete (courtesy of Bob Humbles; see page 94), Janet Roth, education advocate (courtesy of Karen Camper; see page 48), Spig Wead, screenwriter (courtesy of Library of Congress; see page 125), G. John Parker, Peoria fire chief (courtesy of John Parker; see page 46).

On the Back Cover: From left to right:
Col. Bill Robertson, James Robertson, and Corky Robertson, three generations of fabled coach A.J. Robertson (author's collection; see page 97), Frank Abdnour, Spotted Cow owner (courtesy of Karen Camper; see page 54).

CONTENTS

ACKNOWLEDGMENTS

Books are rarely written in a vacuum, and this one is no exception. Throughout the process, a score of people gave generously of their time and energy, and for that, I am very grateful. I cannot thank Linda Aylward, of Bradley's Special Collection, enough for her expertise in Peoria history and her ability to find obscure photographs. I also value the assistance of the Peoria Public Library's local history department, particularly Deb Bier and Ellie Nielsen. While at the US Department of Agriculture (USDA) Northern Regional Research Laboratory, researching for the penicillin story, I relied on the expertise of Kathy Warner, Larry Nakamura, Kate O'Hara, Dr. Cletus Kurtzman, and Dr. Stephen Peterson. I thank Bob Humbles for the story about his friend Dana Davis. Likewise, Leo Jordan added much. I want to thank Corky Robertson and Col. William Robertson for finer points to the story of the coach. Same goes for Rob Mueller about WEEK air. Jerry Zinn provided a lot about his brother Ron. I appreciate the time of Tim Carey, Sister Lea, and Sister Ann of the Peoria Diocese Museum. Gary Fyke is the guy to see about anything Zorro.

Thanks are also given to Pat O'Donnell, Randy Simmons, and Peoria Civic Center's Jim Wetherington and Ashlee Franken. Joy Kessler and Pat Spears provided terrific assistance. Audra Russo was most helpful. A special thank-you goes to Jim Heldman, General Downing's best friend and former US Military Academy roommate, for his insight. South Side Bank's Samantha Peitzmeier and Emma Vandeveer gave valuable time to the project.

I would like to thank Mike Johnson for everything he's done for Peorialand.

I marvel at the book that elevated brevity to an art form: *Everything I Know about Flying* by Col. Lloyd Prevett (Ret.).

Remembering early prompts Steven A. Stott and Dr. John Conlee of William and Mary College helped a lot. I owe my gratitude to my great editor Erin Vosgien for her cheerful patience and superior guidance. Throughout, Karen Camper has been a camera whiz. Bob Camper was as awesome with scanning photographs. Tim McGowan's artistry shines throughout. To Susan, "the savior," a special thank-you is bestowed for keeping the practice going.

And to Carole—I give a heartfelt thanks and my deepest love always.

INTRODUCTION

Located in the heart of the country, Peoria *is* Small-Town America. It is famed for its people who have come to embody Middle American values and achievement in every aspect of life, including the arts, sciences, and innovation.

It is, perhaps, the most famous city with a population of 100,000 in the nation, possibly the world.

For over 10,000 years, the area had been the home to the vast Illini Confederacy, drawn to the rich wildlife and fish supply of Pimiteoui ("Fat Lake"), before the European influx that began in 1673 with the French superstar voyageurs Jacques (Pere) Marquette and Louis Joliet. Henri de Tonti planted the first permanent European stake in 1691, making Peoria the most ancient of Illinois settlements. With more French rule than New Orleans, the future Chicago founder, the wandering Jean Baptiste Point DuSable, put his deepest roots anywhere on earth in Old Peoria in 1773.

Blessed with a central location, rich soil and artesian underground water springs, farming, the liquor industries, and railroads led to sizzling growth throughout the 1800s. J.B. Greenhut, the "King of the Whiskey Barons," led the Peoria domination of world trade, calling 85 percent of the globe's shots and making little River City the highest tax payer in the country. (Unfortunately, Prohibition chopped the town's booze trade at the knees.) Yet, in the mid-1920s, Caterpillar Tractor, future earth-moving equipment world leader, was gearing up as an able replacement. The Duryea Brothers invented the nation's first car, launched an entire industry, and saved the country from its 1890s worry of too much pony poo piling on city streets.

In entertainment, the city that once set the standard for America's Vaudeville, starting in the late 1800s, hit the national airwaves at radio's inception with full force. Charles Correll (*Amos 'n' Andy*), Marion and Jim Jordan (*Fibber McGee and Molly*), and Father Fulton Sheen (*The Catholic Hour*) were the biggest stars during the Golden Age of Radio (1920s–1950s) and had most of the country's ears listening for decades. Frank "Spig" Wead became a Hollywood screenwriter extraordinaire in the 1930s–1940s, while songwriter hall of famer Richard Whiting also added melodies to movies. Fiery comedians Richard Pryor and Sam Kinison blazed new trails and reached dizzying heights in the latter part of the 20th century. Singer Dan Fogelberg defined the rock balladeer in the 1970s. Renowned science-fiction maverick Philip José Farmer launched gems from River City into the cosmos. And Johnston McCulley, a one-time Peoria reporter, cut a big swath with his rogue creation—Zorro.

Peoria has produced awesome talent in all areas sports-wise, including in Major League Baseball where Jim Thome, seventh all-time in homers, has blasted more dingers than any player born and/or raised in the Midwest. Herb Jamison led the Peoria High School track team to the first-ever Illinois state championships and was a medalist at the first-ever Olympic games. Coach A.J. Robertson put Bradley University on the national map with his powerhouse basketball teams of the 1930s and 1940s. Radio/television big-pipe hall of famers Jack Brickhouse and Chick Hearn first "mic'd up" in Peoria.

Rev. C.T. Vivian in 1947 predated most civil rights leaders in the use of nonviolence when he stoically integrated Peoria lunch counters and became a prominent leader during the 1960s civil rights movement. Bradley University professor Dr. Romeo Garrett taught the virtue of tolerance toward all. Local NAACP president John Gwynn Jr. showed strong leadership throughout the latter half of the 20th century. Betty Friedan kickstarted the 1960s women's movement with her book *The Feminine Mystique*.

Then, there are those who show the true core spirit of America without the glare of the klieg lights. Bill Rutherford was an environmentalist not only locally but also globally. City councilman Gary Sandberg fought loud for the city and against ignorance. Perceptive teacher Juliette Whittaker was the first to see and inspire young Richard Pryor, as well as many others at Carver Community Center. In the 1970s, Barb and Dick Hammond saw the wretched welfare of Haitians and selflessly worked to improve the health of the poorest nation of the western hemisphere with Friends of the Children of Haiti. During World War II, the USDA Northern Regional Research Laboratory ushered in the antibiotic era by discovering the technique for the mass-production of penicillin. In the mid-1800s, Dr. Elias Cooper, surgeon and grave robber, opened Peoria's first hospital but left for San Francisco to open the West Coast's first medical school, which later became Stanford University School of Medicine. Showing towering determination that inspires others, Kevin Harmon, a quadriplegic after an accident in his teens, became a writer despite physical drawbacks. Similarly, quadriplegic Bob Cleary refused to give up and became a nationally recognized teacher and then principal at Bergan High. Unsung but a solid shoulder to everyone, Bill Noel has had weekly tragedies befall friends, family, and clergy for a decade without being crushed himself.

Militarily, Peoria has had a lot of stars. First, there is the incomparable four-star general Wayne Downing, the master of Special Forces. Four-star general John Shali, in the mid-1990s, became the Pentagon's chairman of the Joint Chiefs of Staff via the most improbable path imaginable.

The pages that follow will highlight some of the many extraordinary people of Peoria. These are individuals who exemplify and define America. The town has been exceptionally blessed with talent, with many who are internationally renowned. A number are less celebrated and perhaps unsung but are no less deserving of tribute, just as four-time All-American City winner Peoria—America's hometown.

CHAPTER ONE

Way Back

For over 10,000 years, the area had been the home to the vast Illini Confederacy before the European incursion that began in 1673 with French paddlers Jacques (Pere) Marquette and Louis Joliet. Peoria, earlier named Pimiteoui ("Fat Lake"), offered an abundant stock of wildlife and fishing in the fertile Illinois River that filled in the riverbed of the Ancient Mississippi River that had been displaced some 60 miles west to its current location by the rolling-thunder glaciers. The glaciers also softened the craggy canyons of Peoria. Once the Europeans moved in, the Illini Confederacy, including the Peoria Tribe, was also displaced at a faster-than-glacial pace.

First came Fort Crevecoeur ("Broken Heart") in 1680, the first mid-continent garrison, established by Robert de LaSalle and entrusted to his lieutenant Henri de Tonti. However, during a de Tonti foray into the hinterlands, his men mutinied, trashed the fort, and scattered, leaving behind an unfinished boat with a plank etched with a saying that has had much longer legs than "Will it play in Peoria?"—"*Nous sommes tous sauvages*" ("We're all savages"). Unfazed, de Tonti continued building forts along the Illinois River with his next upriver at Starved Rock—the first Fort St. Louis—and then, in 1691, the second Fort St. Louis at Fat Lake. This one held and made de Tonti the founder of Peoria.

Peoria's tether with Chicago is a strong one, especially at the start. Nomadic Jean Baptiste Pointe DuSable settled in Old Peoria, a French village, in 1773 and prospered with his trading post. Yet he left years later to the northeast and settled along what is now Chicago's Michigan Avenue and placed stakes, becoming the founder of Chicago. The Windy City was first under Peoria County control from 1825 to 1831.

Peoria Area Tricentennial 1691-1991

Play explores African-American part in early Peori

By Francis Duren
for the Peoria 1691 Foundation —
Peoria Area Tricentennial

A black man from the 1800's is talking to a white youth from the 1990's. They're in Peoria.

The black man says his name is Jeff Nash. He says he was an indentured servant in Peoria — until he ran away in 1810.

The youth, Bertram, asks Jeff, "So, are you free?"

"You don't understand, do you boy?" says Nash. "It's hard to say you're free when you've been a slave for so long."

This is a scene from the new play, "Black to the Future," written and directed by Channel 25 news reporter Garry Moore. The play attempts to depict Peoria's history through the eyes of its African-American citizens. Jeff Nash is one of several African-American historical characters who come to life in the play.

A company of players, called the DuSable Theatre Ensemble, is performing the one-and-a-half hour play at various locations in the Peoria area over the coming months. Methodist Medical Center is sponsoring and underwriting the project.

Moore said he wrote the play after he was approached by Mollye Bright, a French teacher at Peoria's Washington School.

"She asked me to co-chair a newly formed group that sought to fuse a Black perspective into the Peoria TriCentennial Celebration," he said.

"Our group was initially formed as a sub-committee of the Foundation's history and research committee," said Bright,

"Given the vitally important role played in Peoria by our African-American ancestors, said.

Moore says that "The Negro in Peoria," a book by Dr. Romeo B. Garrett, was a primary source for the material used in the play. He also reviewed and expanded upon "Why Did They Come," a WCBU Radio documentary, which gave characterizations to Garrett's work. Moore said WCBU Program Director Frank Thomas gave him permission to draw from the work.

"Several months of researching characters, coming up with the plot, consulting other historians, recruiting appropriate talent, securing props, etc. have gone into the project," Moore said.

He is enthusiastic about the players in the ensemble. Donawa Fowler and John Firlder, two students from Peoria Manual High School, play leading roles. In the play, they are two students (one white and one African-American) who encounter the historical people.

Playing major roles in the production are:

Nyoka McKinney plays the teacher.

Hosaia Brown plays DuSable, a well educated black man of French heritage who, in 1773, purchased land at Peoria and farmed and traded here for about 10 years. (DuSable later was the first permanent settler in what is now Chicago.)

Michael Hurt plays Mash and also Frederick Douglass, the famous Abolitionist who visited the city during the 1800's. Hurt is also in charge of costumes and make up.

Dan Allar portrays Moses Pettengill, a Peoria resident who was active in the Underground Railroad during the slave era.

Jim Barnett, weather man at Channel 25, acts the part of Abraham Lincoln, who was in Peoria on several occasions.

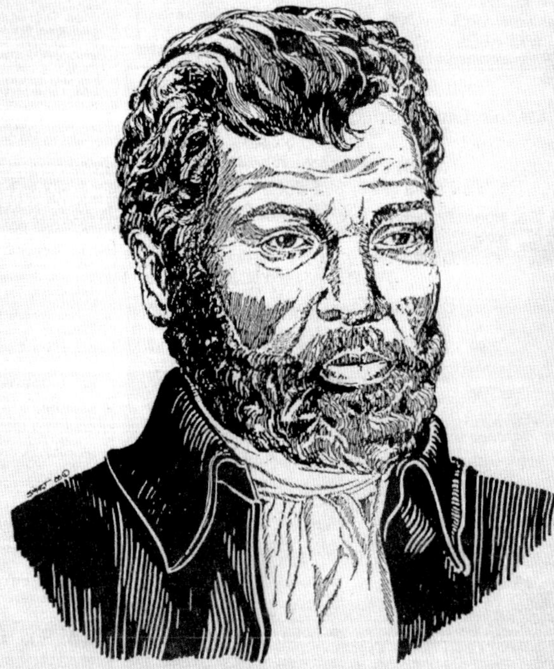

EARLY SETTLER: Jean Baptiste DuSable is believed to be the first black resident of

Eschikagou, Who's Your Daddy? (ABOVE AND OPPOSITE PAGE)

He was the son of a Caribbean love between a French sailor and a freed slave named Suzanne in Hispaniola. His birth year was not memorable; however, most believed it was 1745. His name was Jean Baptiste Point DuSable.

At 10 years old, he and his father left for France after pirates killed his mother.

He returned to the New World, educated and a wanderer. In 1773, he placed his stakes in Old Peoria, started a trading post, joined the local tribe, and married Kittihawa. He called her Catherine; they had a daughter and a son. Despite domestic harmony, DuSable left Peoria for Eschikagou ("Bad Smells") around 1779–1784. After establishing Chicago's first European outpost, he headed back to Peoria in 1800.

DuSable left for St. Charles, Missouri, to care for his granddaughter and died in 1818.

Preston Jackson created the DuSable statue pictured opposite. (Above, courtesy of the Local History and Genealogy Collection, Peoria Public Library; opposite page, courtesy of Karen Camper.)

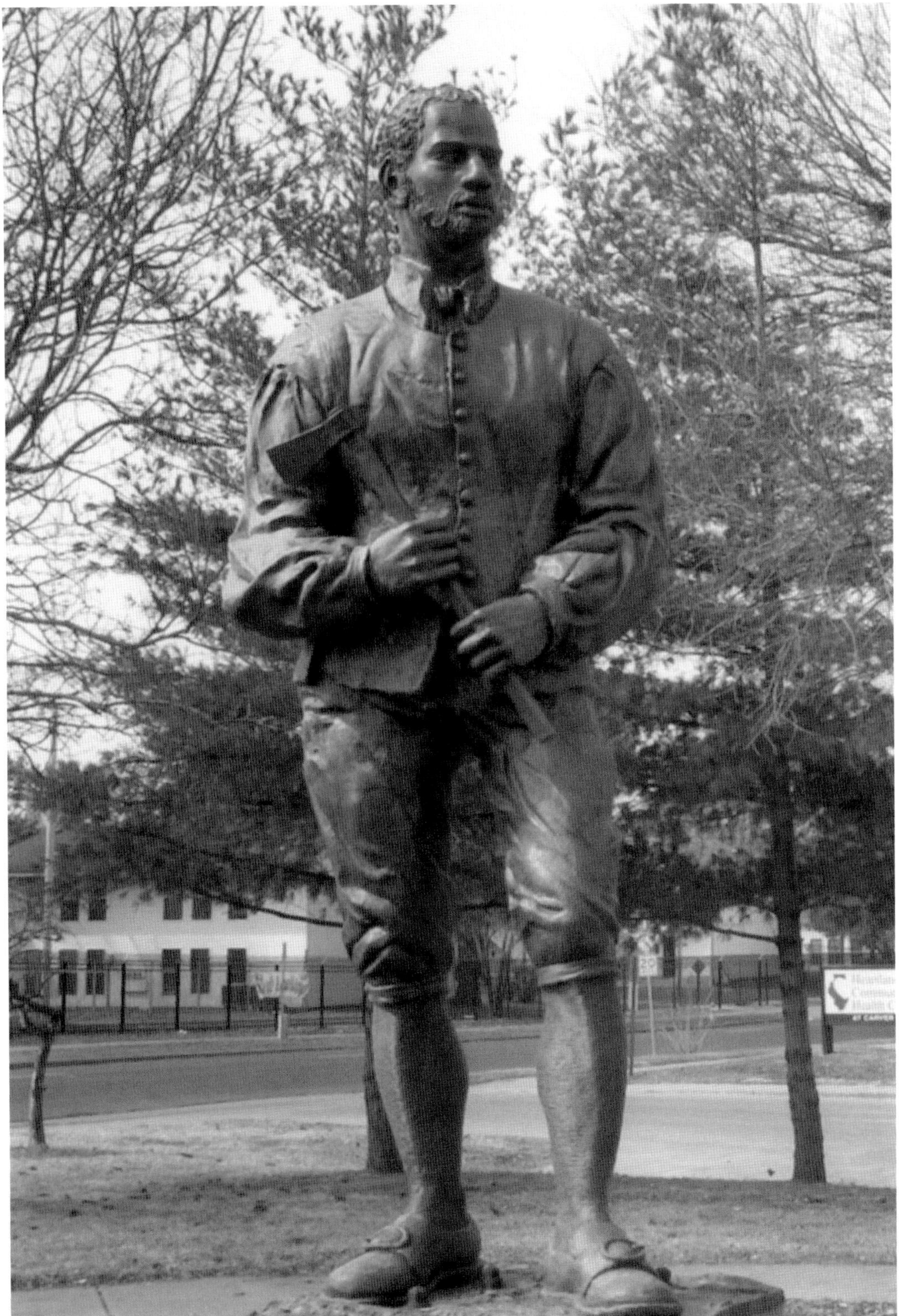

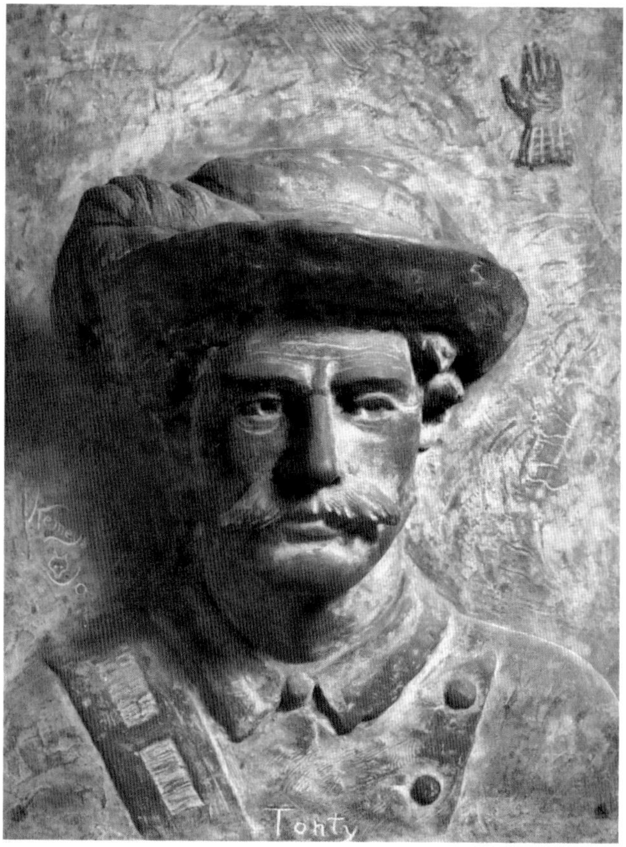

Fat Lake City, Who's Your Daddy?

Henri de Tonti (1649?–1704) was the Italian-born French lieutenant of New World explorer Robert de LaSalle. As a youth, he lost his right hand fighting and later wore a gloved iron casing. In 1680, de LaSalle settled on the eastern shore of Pimiteoui ("Fat Lake"), establishing Fort Crevecoeur ("Broken Heart")—the mid-continent's first European outpost. While de Tonti was exploring elsewhere, the men at the garrison deserted, leaving the timeless remark "We're all savages" on an unfinished boat plank.

In 1691, after fleeing Iroquois attacks at Starved Rock, de Tonti returned south to the western shore of Lake Pimiteoui and built a second Fort St. Louis, which held, and thus, River City's Iron Hand founded Peoria. (Left, courtesy of the Local History and Genealogy Collection, Peoria Public Library; below, courtesy of Tim McGowan.)

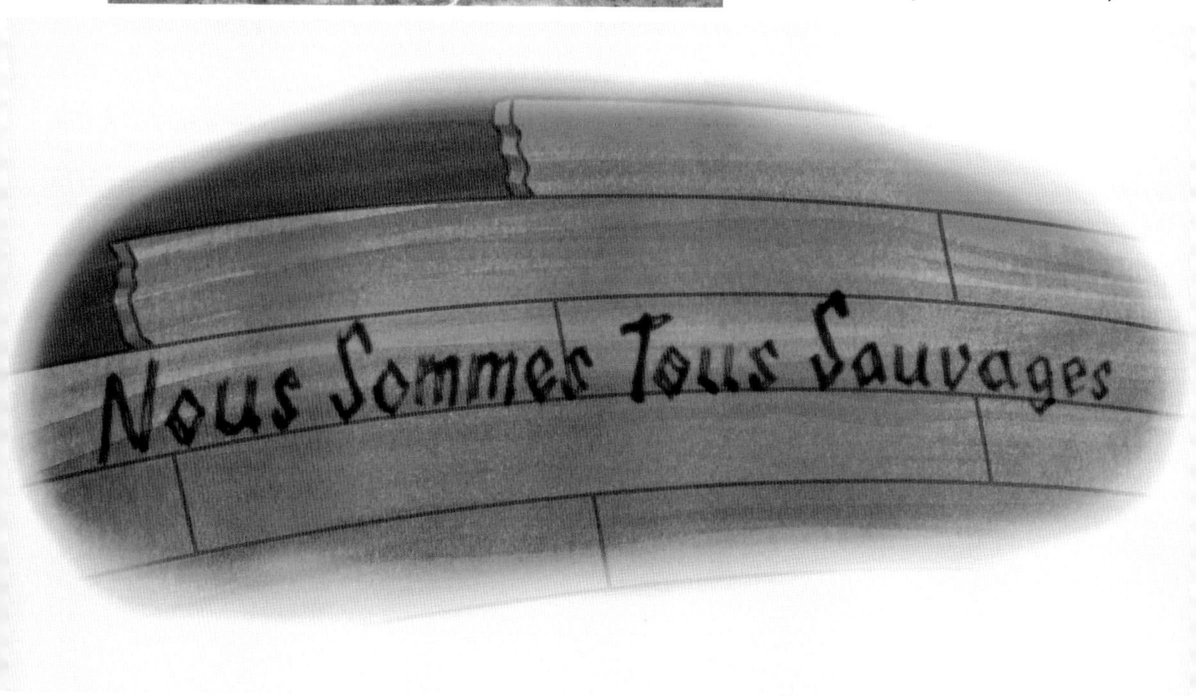

CHAPTER TWO

Health, Education, and Welfare

There exists a link between mid-1800s Peoria and the renowned Stanford University School of Medicine, and it is the dirt-caked shovel of Dr. Elias Cooper, a Peoria-steeled surgeon and grave robber. Much later, in the late 20th century, Barb and Dick Hammond dedicated themselves to improve the health of one of the poorest countries on earth; surgeon Dr. Jaime Cercone helped their cause. The USDA Northern Regional Research Laboratory in Peoria, through the World War II efforts of Andrew Moyer, Moldy Mary, and an unidentified Peoria housewife, ushered in the world's antibiotic era by developing the process of mass-producing penicillin. The lab's Dr. Allene Jeanes has saved innumerable lives with her 1950 discovery of dextran, a blood expander to offset blood loss on the battlefield. Dr. Jasti Rao continued Peoria's rarified research pedigree with groundbreaking cancer work.

Farmer Washington Corrington, though he failed to establish a namesake university in Peoria, was an early vigorous supporter for education, though not for football. Midstate College, the area's oldest college, remains strong thanks to Pres. Meredith Bunch, who continues the leadership legacy of her grandmother. Brian "Fox" Ellis uses storytelling to educate, as does Preston Jackson through his artwork. Innovative Janet Roth started *Look. It's My Book!* to distribute books to every child in the public grade schools as a way to improve reading scores, and it worked. And Dr. Kevin Stein, Bradley professor and the Illinois poet laureate, has dynamically spread the appreciation of poetry throughout the state.

Park district's Bonnie Noble has made the town one of the most park-like towns in the country. Gail Leiby has spent decades enriching those with disabilities. Dr. Romeo Garrett, Bradley professor, exhorted the virtue of tolerance, while John Gwynn Jr. fought tough against racial intolerance as Peoria chapter president of the NAACP.

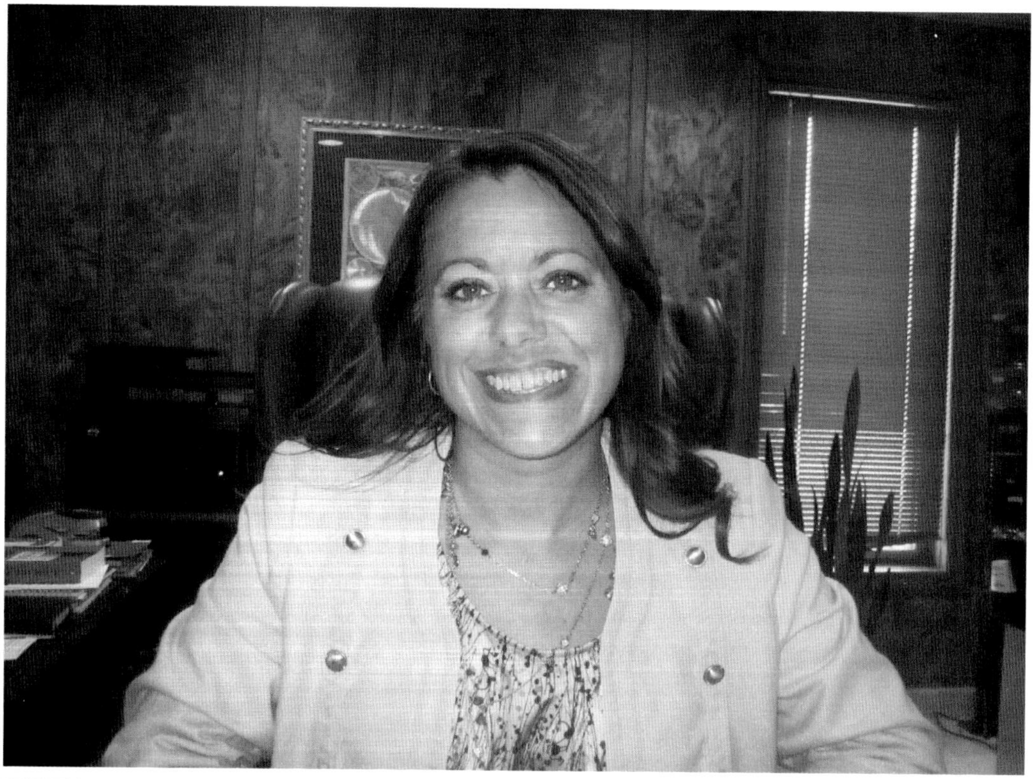

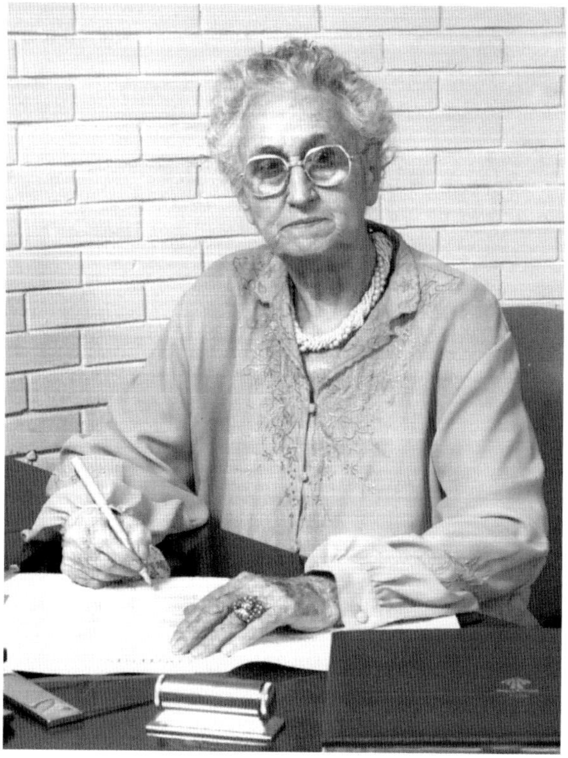

Female Leads

Starting in 1961, Arline Bunch was the driving force in the evolution of Brown's Business College of Commerce, the late-1800s pride of the 20-plus schools owned by George W. "Dubya" Brown, to today's Midstate College with its current president, Arline's granddaughter Meredith Bunch.

Arline was Midstate's matriarch, and in 1970, she named her son R. Dale Bunch college president. When Arline died in 1988, her vision of a four-year degree-granting institution had become a reality.

Meredith Bunch, most akin to her grandmother Arline, has a Bradley University Spanish education degree (1995) and a University of Phoenix master's of business administration and moved through the ranks, succeeding her father as president in 2010. As her grandmother had done, she leads by dynamic example. In her spare time, she practices Reiki, the Japanese healing art. (Above, author's collection; right, courtesy of Meredith Bunch.)

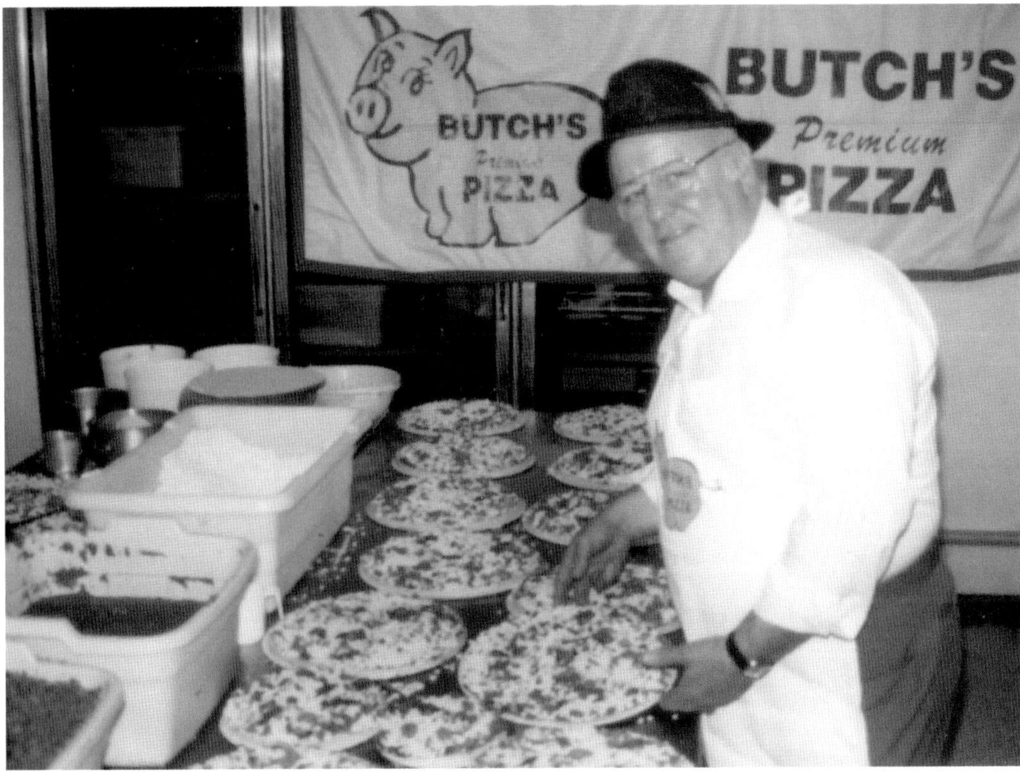

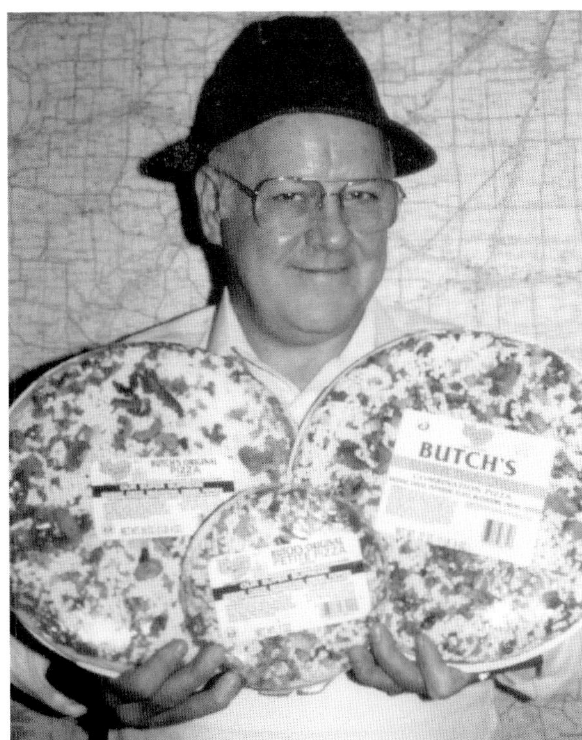

Pig On
Gordon "Butch" Carey, the Bartonville-born son of a barber, saw a break in the clouds during Peoria's dark days of the early 1980s and took the entire family with him on a lifetime adventure. The former steamfitter only asked that his wife, Barb, and their three sons, Steve, Greg, and Tim, make a full commitment to a wholesale pizza-making business that would sell pies to local eateries. From a South Adams Street shop in 1982, using the finest products and powered by their own sweat, the family added special seasonings to the mix, and Butch's Pizza was born, even hitting a national first with its white pizza topped with garlic sauce.

Nowadays Butch's, with 30 pizza varieties, has expanded to 30 employees who produce 5,000 pies daily for the continental United States. (Both, courtesy of Tim Carey.)

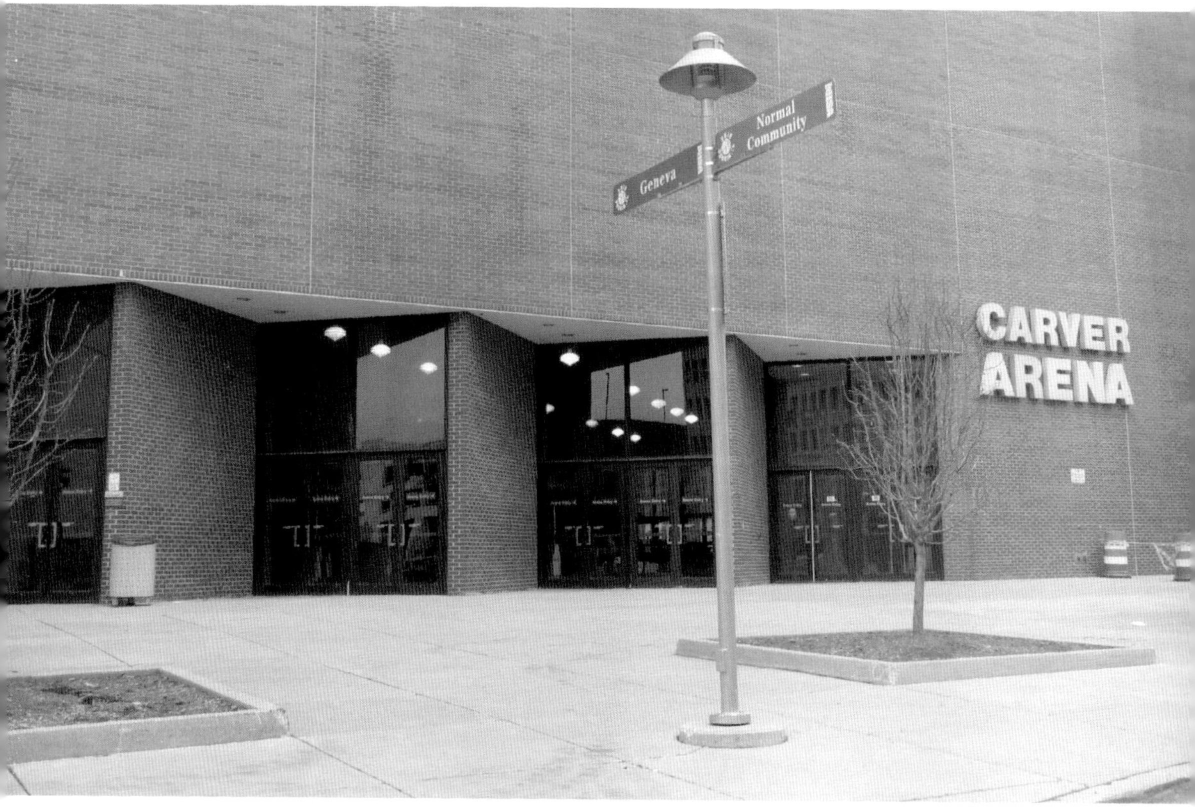

Aimed Higher: Richard E. Carver

Born in Des Moines, Iowa, in 1937, Richard "Dick" Carver received his bachelor's degree in business administration from Bradley University in 1959 and soon opened Carver Lumber in Peoria. He served on the city council from 1969 to 1973 and then as mayor for three terms from 1973 to 1984. His tenure's lasting achievement was the creation of the multipurpose Peoria Civic Center, and with it, the return of Peoria as an entertainment lodestone in central Illinois. President Reagan in 1984 tapped him as assistant secretary of the Air Force (financial management and comptroller), a post he held until 1988. Since then, Carver has been president of a number of private sector firms while keeping the reins of ownership of Carver Lumber. Peoria Civic Center's Carver Arena stands as a testament to his vision. (Above, courtesy of Karen Camper; right, courtesy of the Local History and Genealogy Collection, Peoria Public Library.)

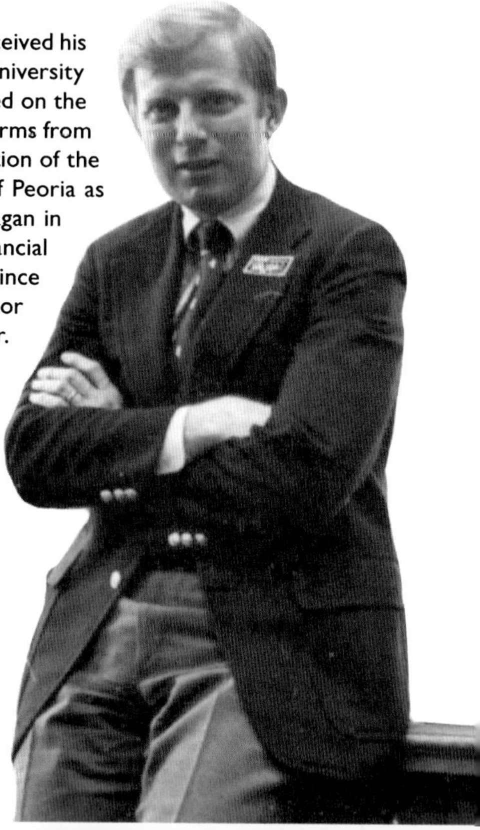

"Do you know the way from San José?"

Costa Rican Jaime Cercone was a young man on a religious mission that followed the beck of missionaries from the United States to head *norte* to America for college. Being a driver for world-famous Rev. Billy Graham, who was in Costa Rica for a series of revival meetings, sealed the deal; he would go to the same school as the reverend—Wheaton College. As long as he wrote home every week, Jaime's Italian father, Maggi, who owned a San José pasta factory, and mother, Odilie (Segura), supported his choice, and in June 1961, Jaime made landfall in America.

He graduated with a biology degree in 1965 while slogging part-time with the Lombard Sanitation Department. He continued his studies at Northern Illinois University as a microbiology graduate student. He then worked in the Department of Pharmacology at the Chicago Medical School to support his family, which, by then, included two sons, James (1968) and Justin (1971). Through his contact with medical students, he realized that he was as smart as they were and that he needed to expand his American Dream. Now wanting to become a doctor, he enrolled at the Chicago Medical School in 1971, intent on a general practice. Yet, in keeping with his free spirit, he discovered his passion for general surgery. He received his doctorate of medicine in 1975 and finished his Chicago Mount Sinai general surgery residency in 1980.

After his schooling and residency in Chicago, Dr. Cercone returned to central Illinois as a doctor who could do it all, from family practice to surgery.

In 1986, he thanked the country that let him aim high by joining the Peoria Air Guard clinic. He rose through the ranks, topping at clinic commander. Under Colonel Cercone's hands-on leadership, the clinic received an outstanding rating in a 1996 Air Force–wide inspection. He also continued his academics, earning a University of St. Francis master's in health care administration. He left his Lewistown family practice in 1988 to become Western Illinois University's Student Health Center's medical director (1988–1991).

He retired from medicine in 2003; however, he then volunteered his medical expertise throughout the world. He largely volunteered with the Peoria-based Friends of the Children of Haiti. Dr. Cercone's career was hallmarked by his keen-eyed judgment, compassion, and decisive care for all. (Courtesy of Jaime Cercone.)

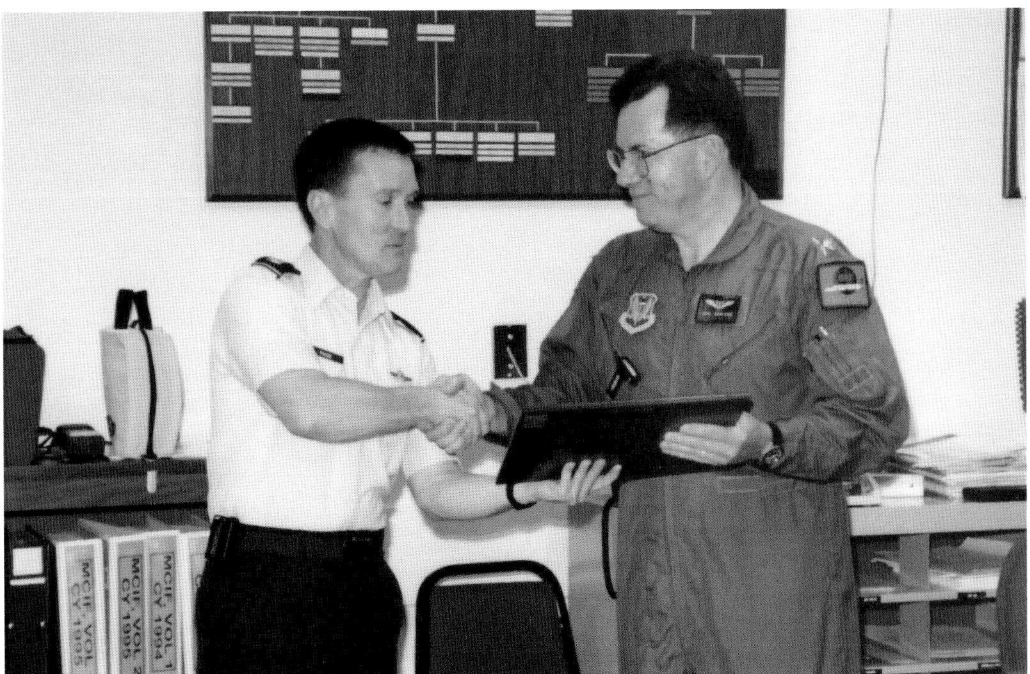

Boundless

Eighteen-year-old Bob Cleary's late-night dive into Indiana's Lake Shafer in July 1956 changed his world from carefree in a nanosecond. Unaware of the dark water's depth of only two feet, he dove headfirst and suffered an instantly paralyzing lower cervical spinal injury. And he would have died underwater if Steve O'Donnell and another friend hadn't saved him. Over time, he came to accept his quadriplegia but not its limitations. He went to the University of Illinois and graduated in 1972 with a degree in English education. Later, he earned his master's degree from Bradley University.

He taught at Bergen High (1973–1983), and in 1978, the nation honored him as one of its top teachers. Cleary became Bergen's principal in 1983. He died in 1987. (Courtesy of Peoria Notre Dame High School.)

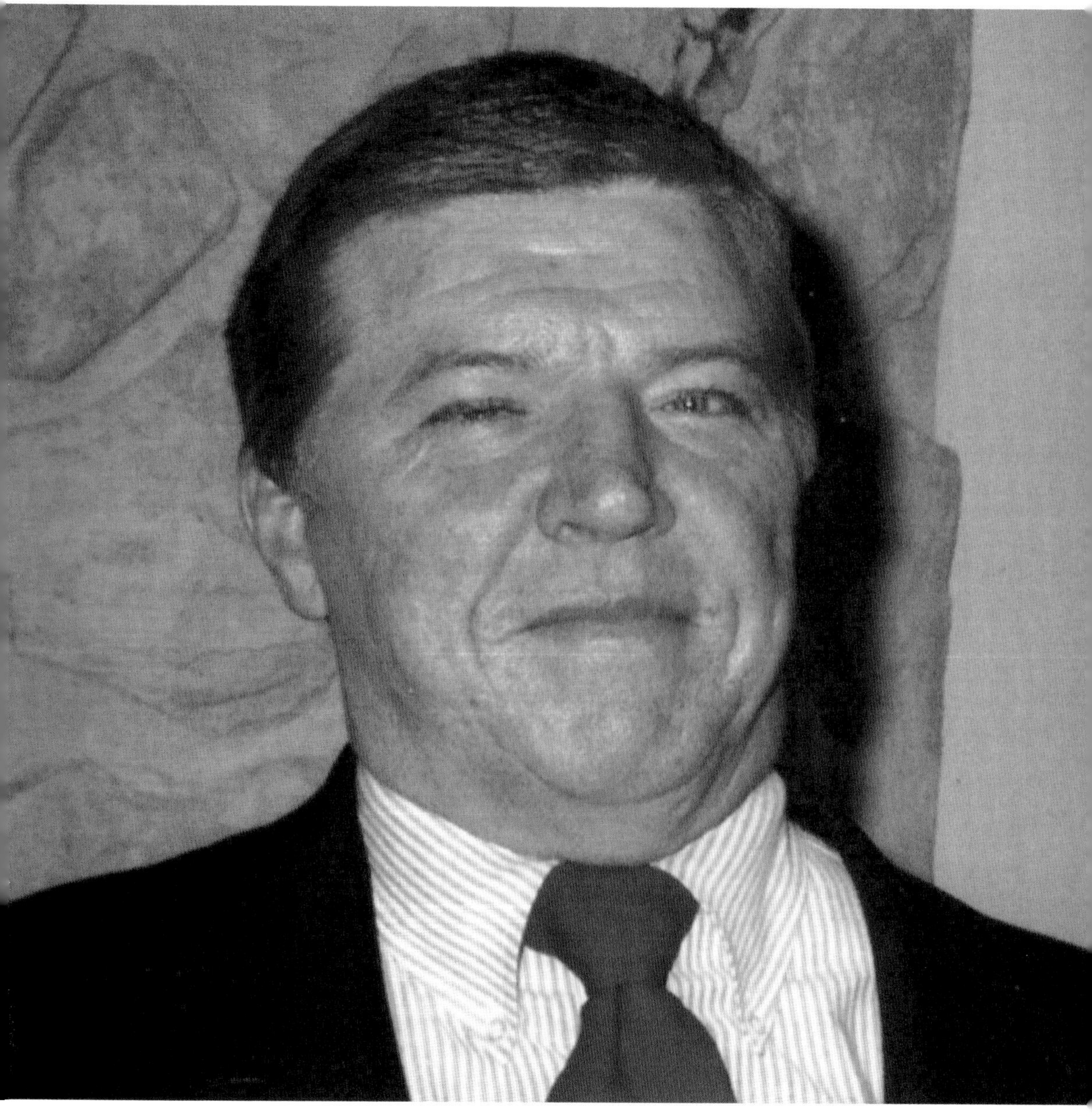

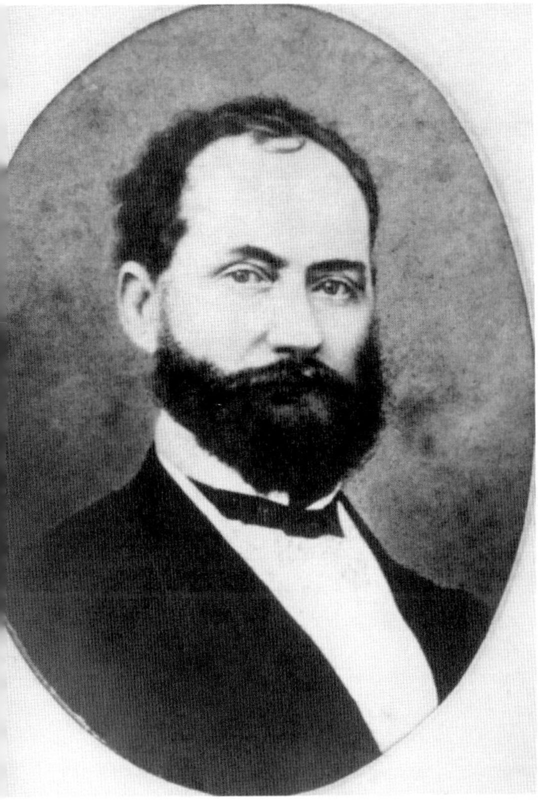

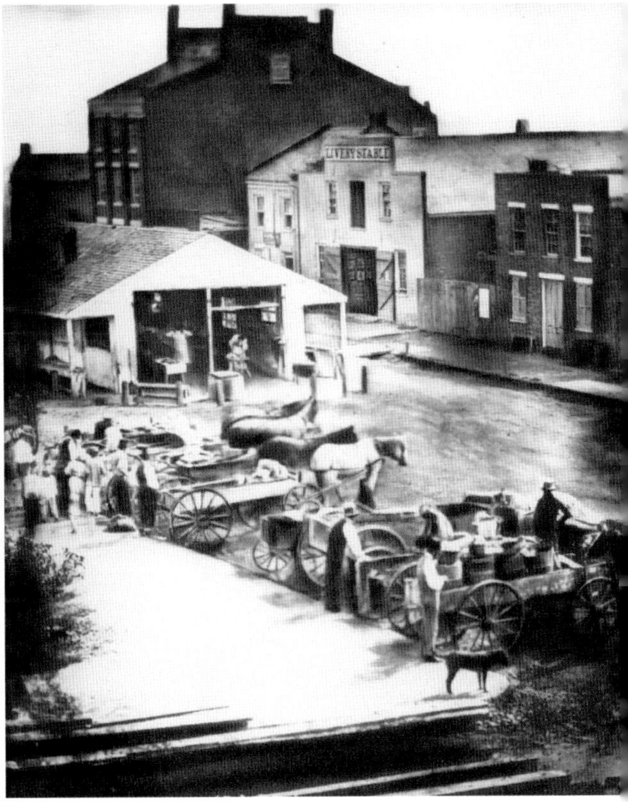

A Grave Doc's Restless Quest

As a youth, Ohio-born Dr. Elias Samuel Cooper (1820–1862) always looked Westward. A fanatic learner, he became a doctor at age 19 in Indiana. He came to Peoria in 1844, and in time, opened Peoria's first hospital in 1851. (Peoria as it appeared in the 1840s, during Cooper's time here, is illustrated at right above.) As a rabid anatomist, he also heard the shrieks of the local docs about his boneyard diggings.

In 1855, armed with his shovel, he left Peoria for San Francisco and opened the first medical school on the West Coast, which is present-day Stanford University School of Medicine.

Before he died in 1862, Cooper's last surgery was on himself; afterwards, he said he felt "much excitement" during the operation.

Ironically, in 1979, a jar with Cooper's heart and brain went missing from the Stanford Medical Library belfry. (Left, courtesy of the Lane Medical Library, Stanford University School of Medicine; right, courtesy of the Local History and Genealogy Collection, Peoria Public Library.)

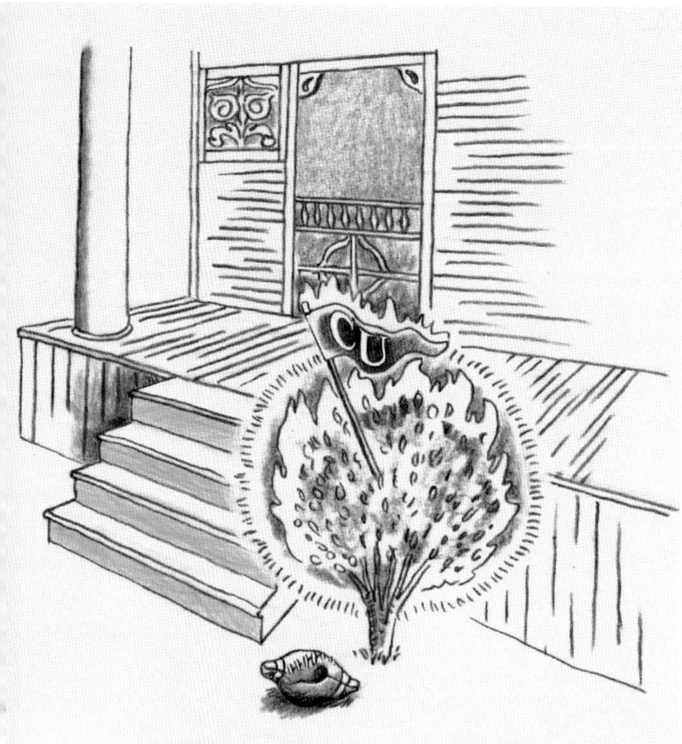

The Prairie Moses

Washington Corrington was a Peoria sodbuster in Richwoods Township. There, he raised crops and seven children. Later, the wealthy farmer decided to learn how to read and went on a reading bender.

In the late 1890s, the overjoyed reader filed a will to exclude his heirs and have all monies go to an educational institution, but not a football team, which was to be named after him.

When he died in 1903, the Corrington children contested the will, using the "dotage card." They claimed their father thought "oxygen is God" and that he would exclaim that a sunset's glow to the bushes was "God's Spirit"—the old "Prairie Moses and the Burning Shrub" routine.

In the end, the court sided with the children.

Below is Washington Corrington's last plat of land, his Springdale cemetery gravesite. (Left, courtesy of Tim McGowan; below, courtesy of Karen Camper.)

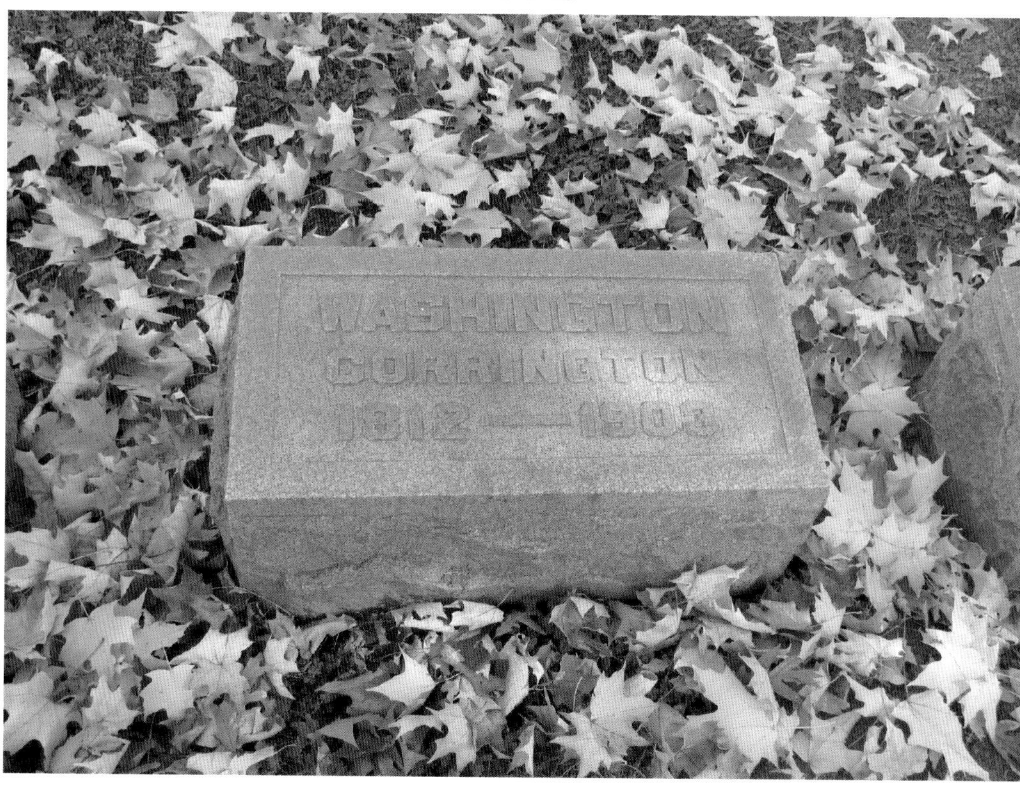

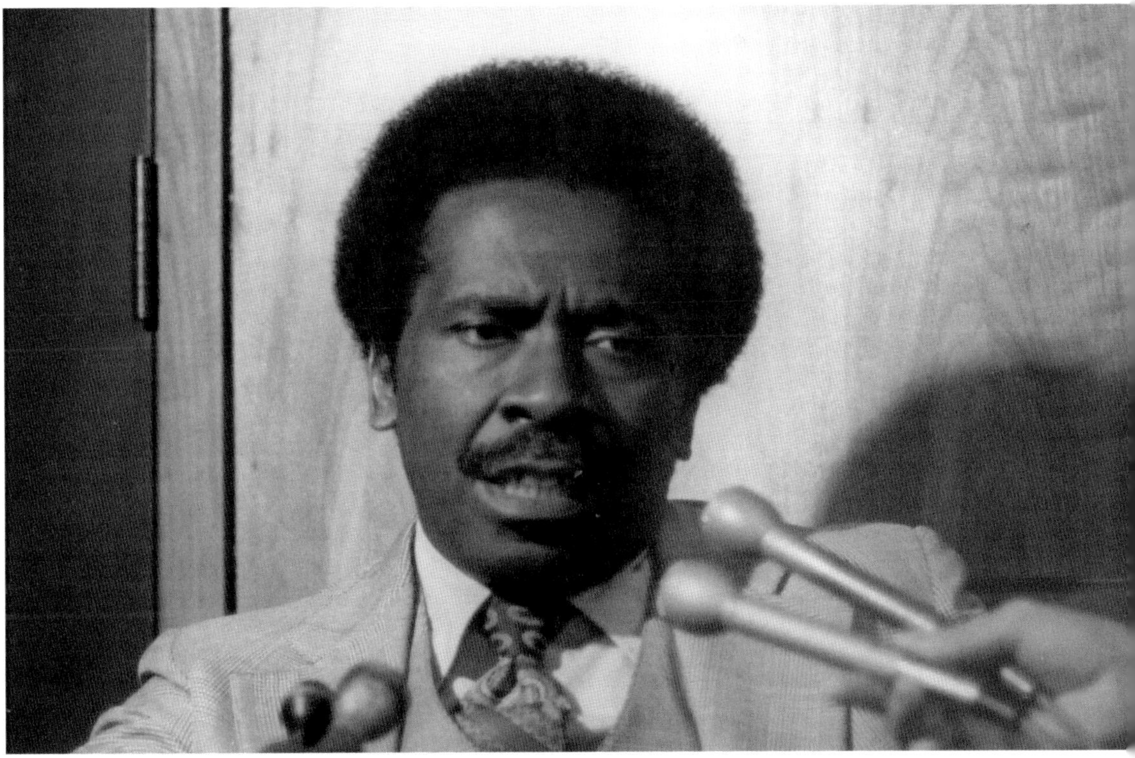

The Fire *This* Time

John H. Gwynn Jr. (1929–1996) was born and raised in Ripley, Tennessee, a segregated, mostly white town of 5,000 some 50 miles north of music-hub Memphis. And he might have pursued a singing career if he had not moved to Peoria in 1953 after his discharge from the Army. Certainly, he had the talent, having sung in a Lane College traveling quartet.

Yet, the 1951 college graduate with a bachelor's degree in secondary education with a voice minor would become Peoria's fiercest advocate for racial equality.

After college, he first worked at the post office. In 1954, he married Cozetter, whom he had met several years earlier when his college quartet had sung at Peoria's Mount Zion Baptist Church; they had a son and a daughter who went on to become lawyers. John also joined the Peoria branch of the NAACP, and it was a fateful pairing. Within seven years, he was the chapter's president. His rousing 32-year stint (1961–1993) shook River City to its core. He was an assertive president and defied city leaders who shied away from racial problems. He knew civil rights needed to jolt the establishment in order for real advancement to be made. He saw a 1950s–1960s Peoria that denied its de facto segregation and rammed that unpleasant reality home. Though mild-mannered by nature, Gwynn would meet injustice with ferocity; those who looked into his eyes couldn't deny the intensity of his commitment to civil rights. His dedication would lead to throttling discrimination in Peoria housing, local government, schools, restaurants, unions, and in workplaces, such as Caterpillar and utility companies. At times he found himself jailed, a small price he gladly paid for the cause.

Besides his Peoria NAACP presidency, Gwynn served several years as president of the Illinois branch of the NAACP and was later elected to the national board of directors of the NAACP.

When Gwynn died in 1996, he left a legacy of a River City better steeped in fairness for all. (Courtesy of Special Collections Center, Bradley University Library.)

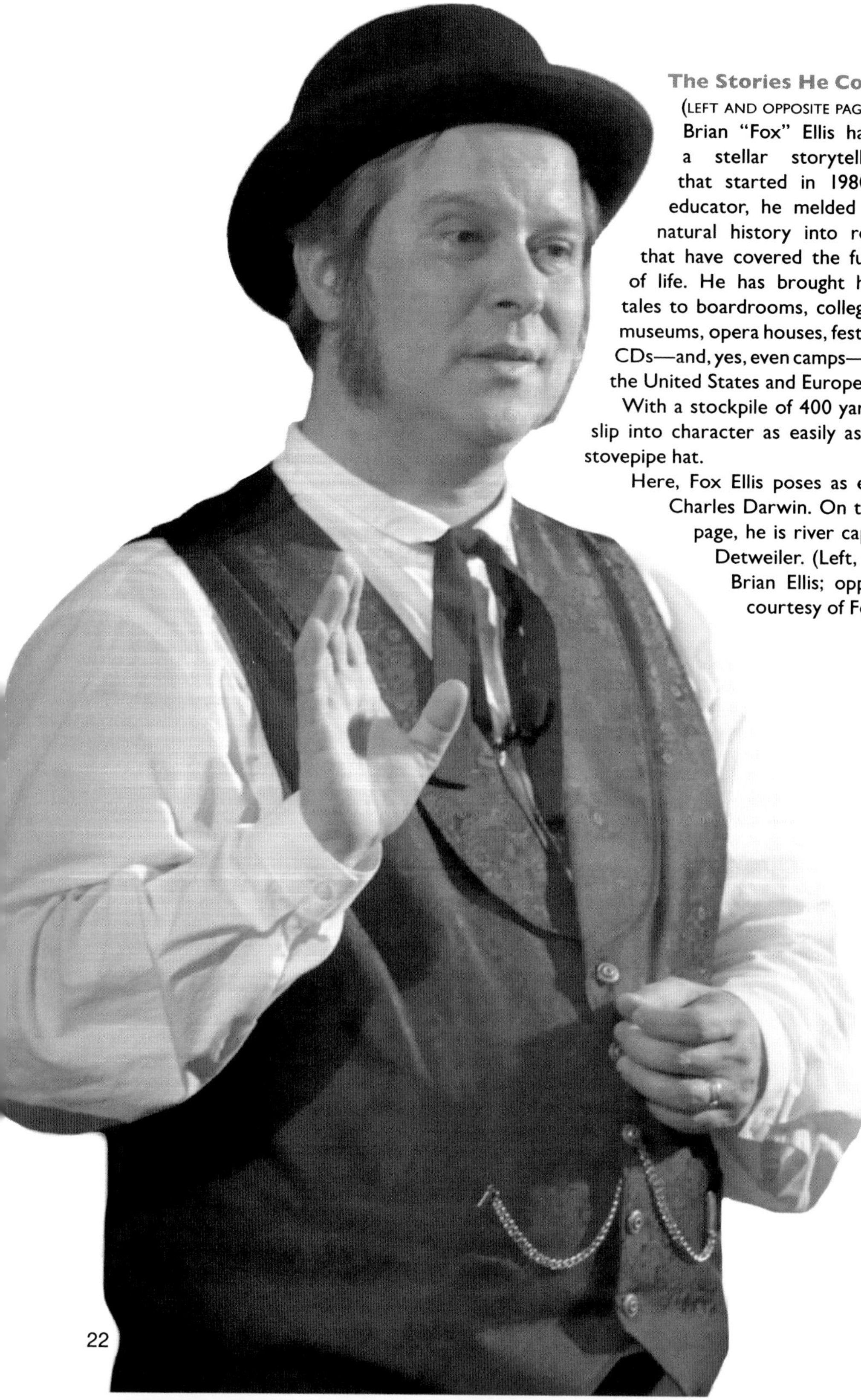

The Stories He Could Tell

(LEFT AND OPPOSITE PAGE)

Brian "Fox" Ellis has fashioned a stellar storytelling career that started in 1980. Ever the educator, he melded human and natural history into rousing tales that have covered the full spectrum of life. He has brought his campfire tales to boardrooms, colleges, schools, museums, opera houses, festivals, books, CDs—and, yes, even camps—throughout the United States and Europe.

With a stockpile of 400 yarns, Fox can slip into character as easily as dropping a stovepipe hat.

Here, Fox Ellis poses as evolutionary Charles Darwin. On the opposite page, he is river captain Henry Detweiler. (Left, courtesy of Brian Ellis; opposite page, courtesy of Fox Ellis.)

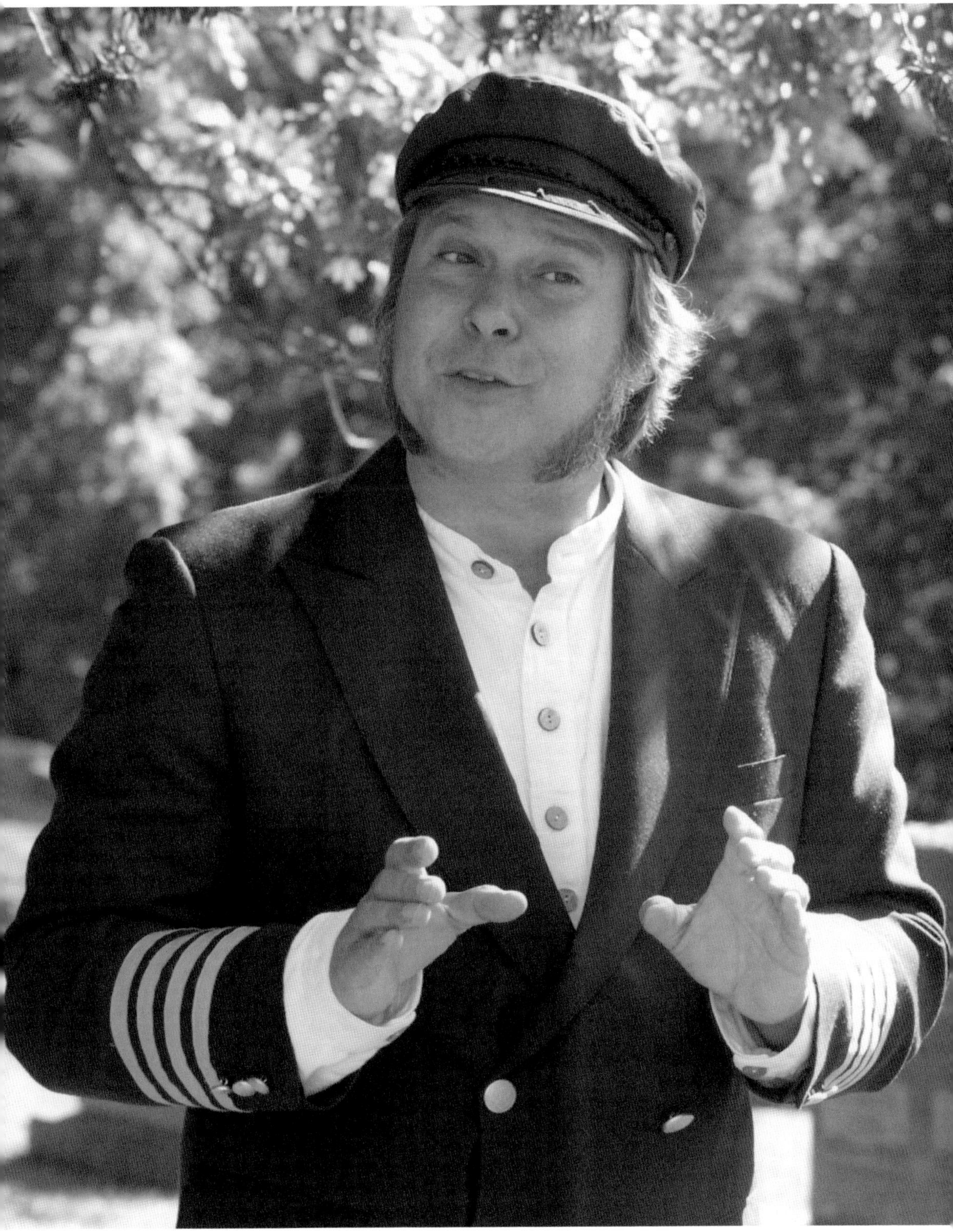

Lifesaver (BELOW AND OPPOSITE PAGE)
Born in Texas in 1906, Allene Jeanes spent 1940–1976 with the USDA Northern Regional Research Laboratory. An expert in complex sugars, she and her team developed dextran, a blood plasma substitute that controlled massive blood loss, in 1950, just in time for the Korean War.

She also invented the process of making the now-ubiquitous xanthan gum, a bulker in many products today, from ice cream to medicines and to cosmetics. In all, Dr. Jeanes's pioneering career has accounted for 10 patents.

Among her many honors, the Agricultural Research Service in 1999 selected her posthumously as the first woman for its Science Hall of Fame; she died in 1995.

She remains a heroine to anyone who has suffered catastrophic blood loss or has applied lipstick.

Pictured below is the USDA Northern Regional Research Laboratory's entrance. (Below, courtesy of Karen Camper; opposite, courtesy of the NCAUR.)

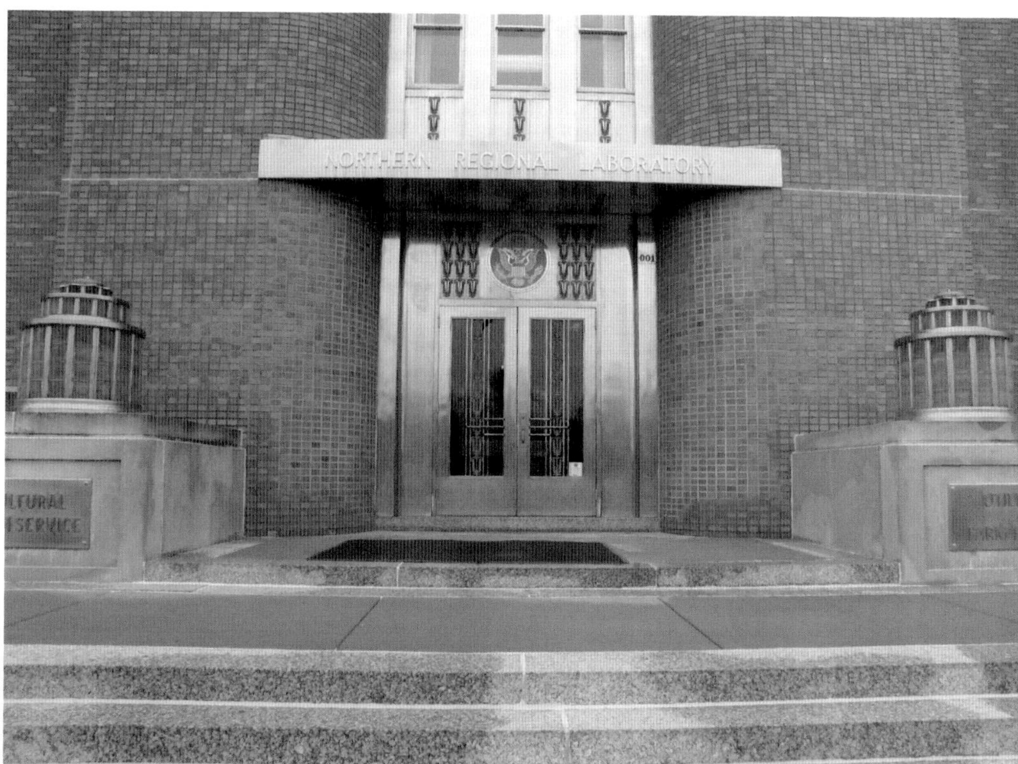

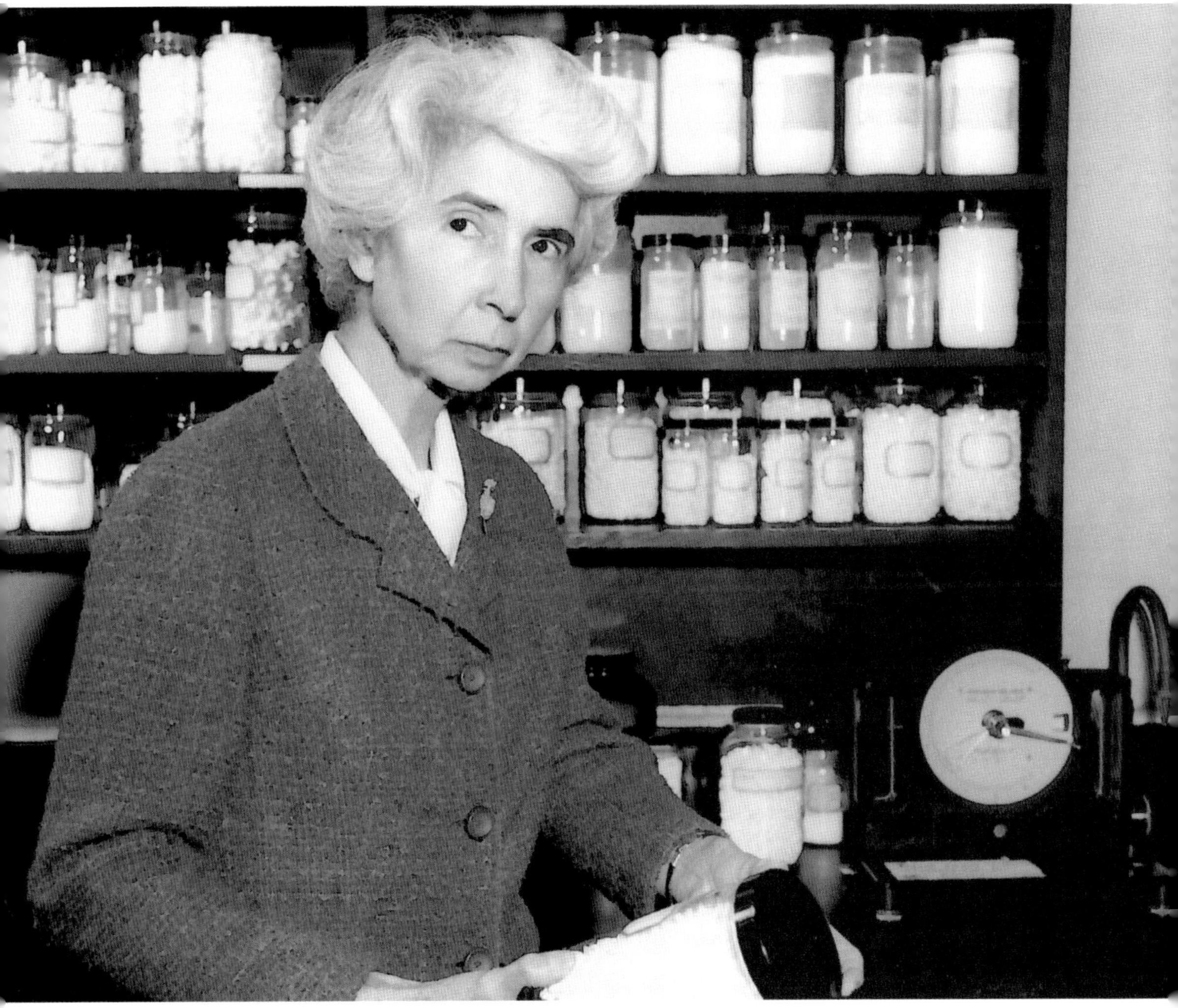

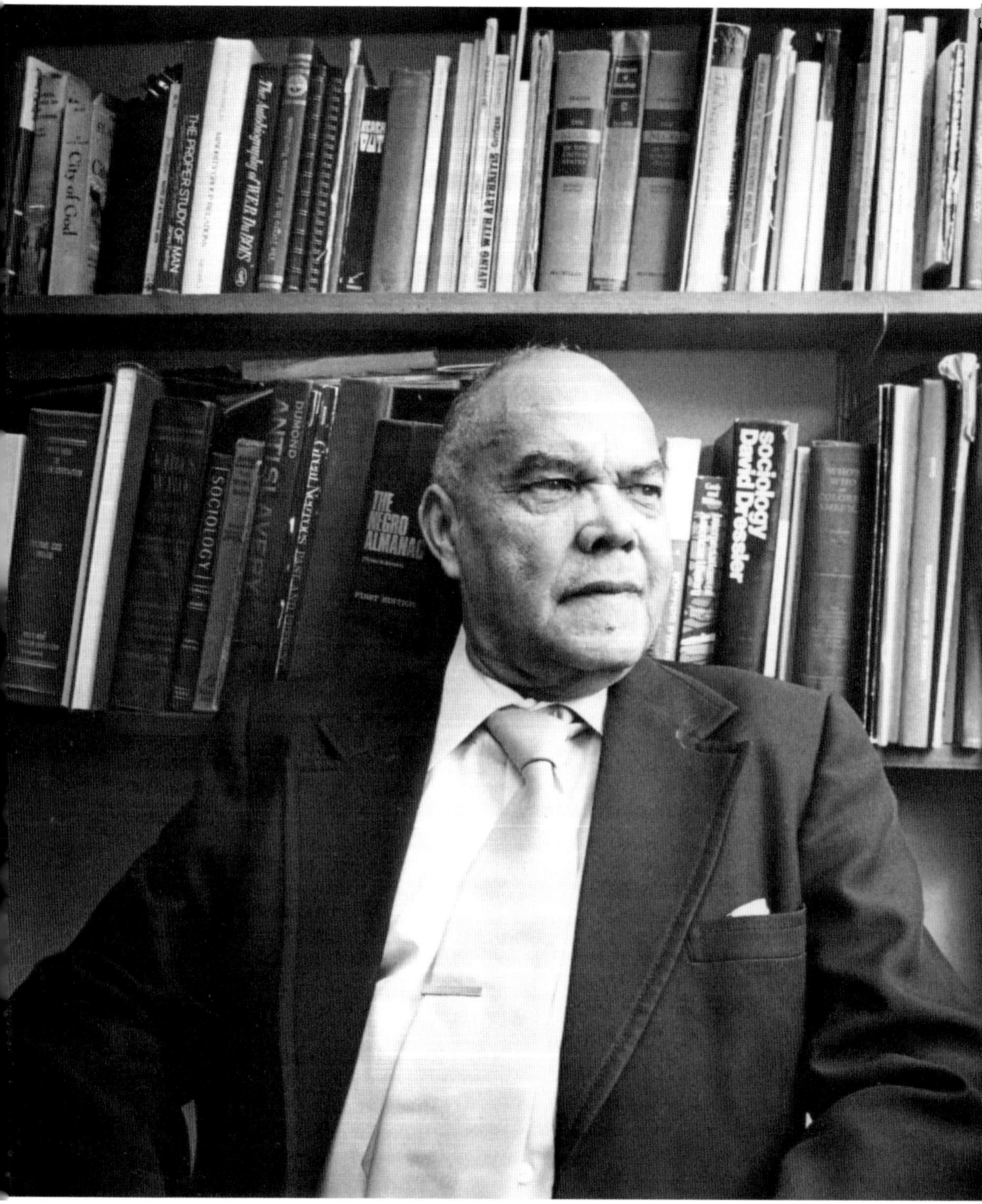

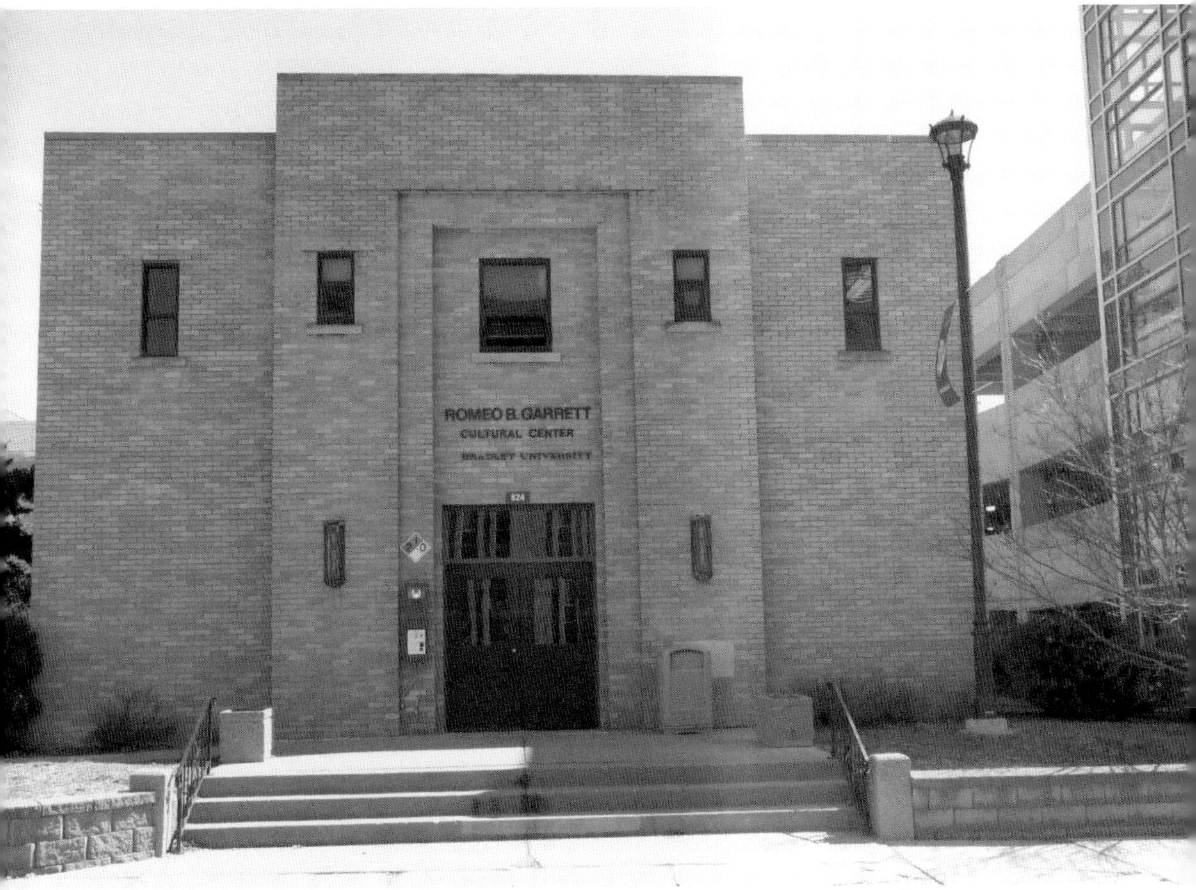

Diversity's Single-Minded Professor (ABOVE AND OPPOSITE PAGE)
Romeo B. Garrett (February 2, 1910–March 2000) from Natchez, Mississippi, grew up with Jim Crow segregation. But he showed pluck by earning a 1932 bachelor's degree in sociology from Straight (now Dillard) University in New Orleans. He taught adult education for the Works Progress Administration in the Big Easy before World War II.

In 1947, Garrett became the first African American to earn his master's from Bradley University; he earned his doctorate at New York University in 1963. He then became the first black professor in Bradley University history, teaching tolerance and black history awareness.

He died in 2000. Today, Peoria and Bradley honor his legacy with the Garrett Cultural Center (shown above), "Garrett Week," and Romeo B. Garrett Avenue. As Garrett once stated, "We must be patient and we must love all people regardless of race." (Opposite, courtesy of the Local History and Genealogy Collection, Peoria Public Library; above, courtesy of Karen Camper.)

The Vow

They met at her 1951 Halloween party.

Spalding sophomore Dick Hammond came as The Extra and stayed forever in Barb Rothan's heart. They married in 1957 while he worked at George J. Rothan Millwork Company, founded in 1873; Dick and Barb raised five children. Barb obtained her bachelor's in education from Illinois State University and her master's from Bradley. She taught first grade at Bartonville's Oak Grove School for 38 years; Dick retired from Barb's family's business in 1998 after 45 years.

Their greatest work, however, extended beyond the reaches of Greater Peoria.

It began in the late 1970s when the Hammonds were on a Caribbean cruise that pulled into Port-au-Prince in Haiti. Distressed by the sight of extreme poverty, but stirred by their faith, the Hammonds returned to Peoria determined to do something.

That something was tackling medical care in the world's poorest country.

With its doctor-to-patient ratio of 1/40,000 (excluding voodoo docs), Haitian health had death and disease double-drumming on it; yet the Peoria couple went against the beat. They rallied their Bartonville St. Anthony's Church to become the first Catholic parish in Illinois (13th in the country) to adopt a Haitian church. They also organized mini-medical missions under their church's aegis, beginning in the early 1980s. Before long, they realized the limitations of episodic church-based care and formed the Friends of the Children of Haiti (FOTCOH), a medical nonprofit dedicated to caring for Haiti's future—its children. FOTCOH has evolved into six two-week clinics a year with its all-volunteer teams (16–26 health care professionals) providing the full spectrum of health care for 15,000 Haitians annually. In 1998, the Hammonds raised enough money to buy land and build a permanent clinic in Cyvadier near Jacmel on Haiti's southern shore; this was a critical step in their dedication to a year-round health center run by a well-trained Haitian staff. To that end, the FOTCOH Sponsorship Program, championed by Barb Hammond, provides education funding to students to keep them in school.

In the late 1960s, while camping in northeast Nevada's Ruby Mountains, Dick Hammond made a vow, "Lord, if you can find me a place where I can enjoy the mountains and the ocean, I'll do anything." He kept that promise made in the Rubies with FOTCOH when God provided Haiti's mountainous southern coast. (Author's collection.)

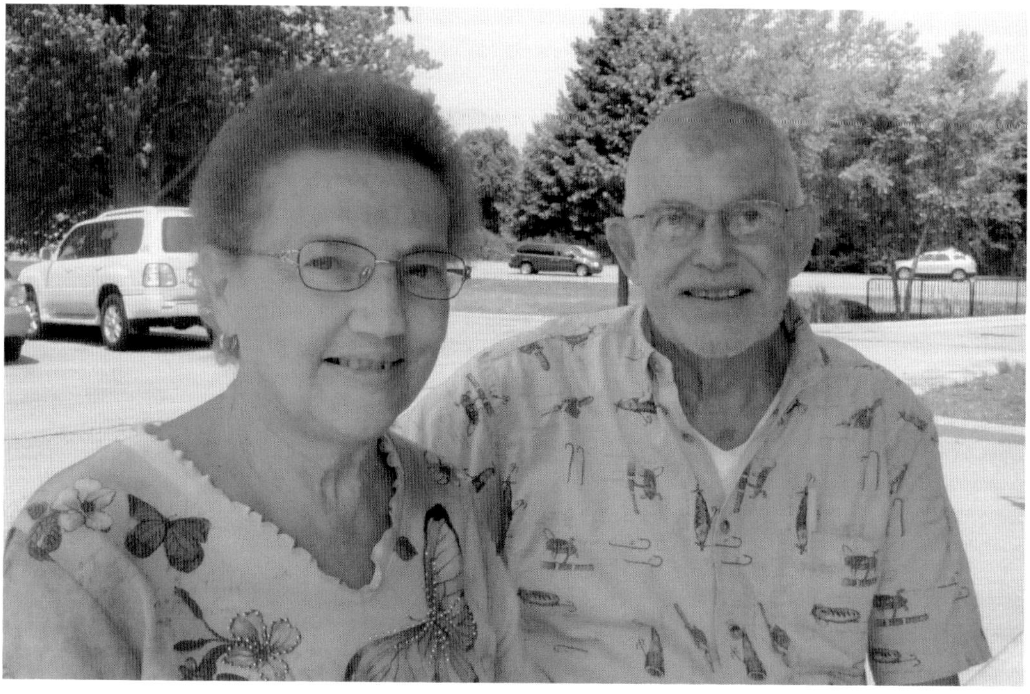

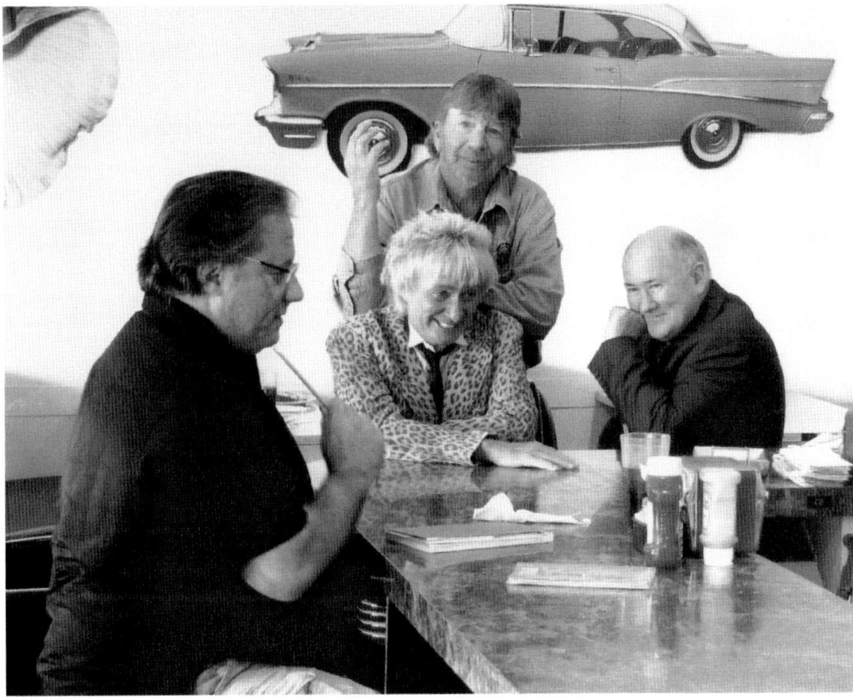

Phil in the Pages

Kudos have piled high on *Peoria Journal Star* columnist Phil Luciano ever since he, wet-eared with a Sangamon State master's degree, joined the downstate Illinois newspaper colossus on July 11, 1988. He had arrived in town already a black-belt muckraker, having helped, as the editor of the Northern Illinois University's *Northern Star* student newspaper in 1986, grease the downfall skids for the university's president Dr. Clyde "The Glide" Wingfield for his misuse of public funds.

The Glide resigned after 10 months in office; "Looch" had his first boss, something Pulitzer-winning Chicago columnist Mike Royko couldn't do with his Moby—Windy City mayor Richard "Boss" Daley. Not bad for a writer who had stepped onto the DeKalb campus as a business major.

Writing four general-interest columns a week would wobble most city journalists, but for spunky Luciano, it is a warm-up. The all-terrain newsroom ranger has written a number of reviews on books, concerts, and food (a guy's got to eat). Additionally, he has run the city desk, penned entertainment features, and edited copy.

While Phil Luciano has belted out some 5,000 stories during his first 25 years, the date July 11, 2013, marked his Silver Anniversary in River City. The *Journal Star*'s "Iron Horse" also has been a host/cohost for three daily radio programs; taught English, philosophy, and algebra among other subjects at Bradley University, Illinois Central, Knox, Midstate, and Robert Morris Colleges; and immersed himself in charities such as Friends of the Children of Haiti (president, 2001), the Dream Center (writing a newsletter for a nonprofit aiding troubled youth and adults), and Riverside Community Church (playwriting).

January 28, 2013, became the "*Ich bin ein* Peorian" moment for the former Chicagolander whose column "Clockin' In as a Genuine Peorian" memorialized his passing more time in River City than anywhere else on the planet. Along the way he has fought city hall, paddling politicians whenever possible. But mostly he has given "Phil Power" to those in need, as he did in 1990 when he helped the University of Illinois see clear to award a degree to a dying former student who had fallen three credits short 35 years earlier so he could provide for his family.

Some days you can't buy a story. Above, a rarely perplexed Phil Luciano sits at the Metro Centre's The '50s Diner amid muse imitators "Rod Stewart" (Steve Bobbitt), "Phil Collins" (Michael Murphy), and "Chuck Norris" (Bob Camper). (Courtesy of Karen Camper.)

Moldy Mary and the "Wife with No Name" (OPPOSITE PAGE)
Gotham City may have had Batman and Robin. And yes, they did save thousands by fighting crime. But the early 1940s action of a River City duo saved hundreds of millions by dogging rot.

In the summer before Pearl Harbor, the push to mass-produce penicillin—a backseat antibiotic since its 1928 discovery by Alexander Fleming—came to heartland America from war-bit Britain. The scientists at the USDA's year-old Northern Regional Research Laboratory (NRRL or "Ag Lab") at Peoria discovered the process that exponentially mushroomed the quantity of the lifesaving fungus.

After December 7, 1941, the need for even-higher yields (the War Department's second-highest priority during World War II) meant searching for better sources of rotting foods and soil mold. Throughout the war theaters, US Army Air Transport Command carted Allied dirt to Peoria with the hope of finding *Penicillium*'s Omega strain.

Meanwhile, back in River City, NRRL's Dr. Kenneth Raper, the penicillin dream team's chief microbiologist assigned to identifying mildew, tasked his lab technician Mary Hunt to find samples of rotten food at the local markets to test.

Knowing the war hung in the balance, it was a job she did with glee. She became a regular at food shops and, combined with her zest, became forevermore "Moldy Mary: The Seer of Spoilage."

Unfortunately, Mary's forays did not produce the magic putrid, but they may have channeled—along with Ag Lab pleas in the local newspaper for garbage—a Peoria housewife. It was the "Wife with No Name" who, in 1943, brought a cantaloupe covered with a golden patina of blight to the lab. (One version has "No Name" leaving the nasty melon on the lab's doorstep like an unwanted baby.)

It was the "Mother Lode of Mold," the fabulously fertile fungus (*Penicillium chrysogenum*) that, at 3,000 times the potency of Fleming's original penicillin strain discovery, helped win World War II and birthed the antibiotic age. (Courtesy of NCAUR.)

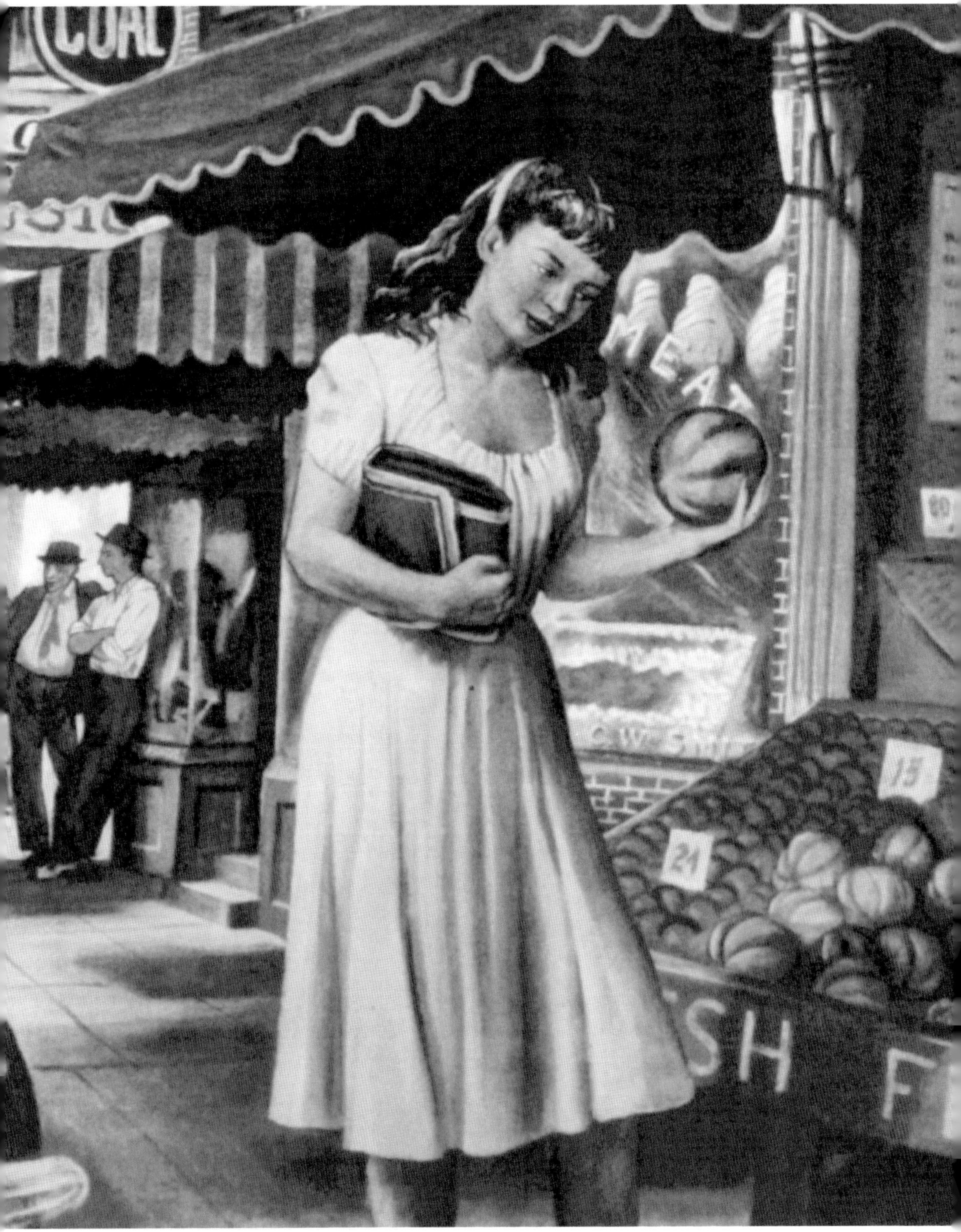
COAL
MEAT
24
15
SH
F

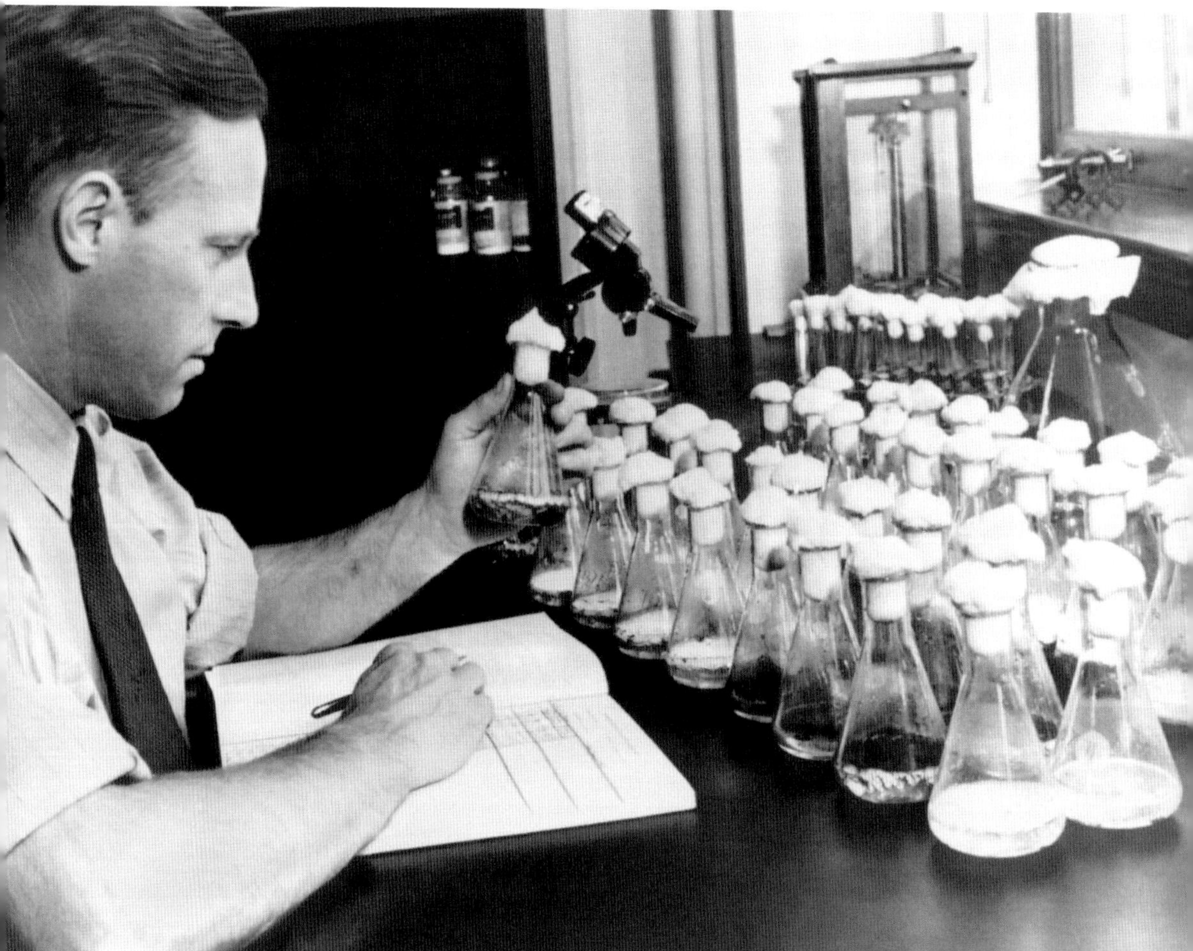

A Star Beyond Star City (OPPOSITE PAGE)
Andrew J. Moyer (1899–1959) was a superstar on the penicillin team that developed the miracle drug's mass production, ushering in medicine's Antibiotic Era. Later, he became a penicillin villain by going beyond the scientific pale.

The son of a Star City, Indiana, farmer, Moyer earned his bachelor's degree from Wabash College (1922), his master's from North Dakota Agricultural College (1925), and his doctorate in plant pathology from the University of Maryland (1929). He joined the USDA, becoming an expert in fungal nutrition. Though important, the topic was a yawner at parties. Luckily, he landed in Peoria in December 1940 at the newly-minted Northern Regional Research Laboratory.

A year later, he was the toast of the medical world.

It began in July 1941, when Drs. Howard Florey and Norman Heatley, Oxford University researchers who had spent years trying to mass-produce penicillin, came to Peoria for help. Inside of four months, Moyer had the solution, which was to add corn-steep liquor (a byproduct of corn milling) plus lactose (milk sugar) to the fungal cultures and deep submerge the mix in vats. The Peoria Ag Lab's results were historic.

Antibiotic yields were 10–20 times that of previous methods; penicillin mass-production had become a reality.

Moyer, whose warty personality and anti-Brit sentiments were well known, chose this moment to foment a storm. He figuratively slapped Heatley by leaving his name off the pioneering paper about the process. He omitted his name not just because it "felt good," but also because as a sole author, Moyer could then apply for British patents and make some cash—something he could not do in the United States as a government employee. However, this action made him a pariah. Though legal in Britain, its science community viewed royalty-taking as ghastly. Under pressure from the USDA, Moyer had to toss back any royalties he had made.

He continued at the lab until retiring in 1957; he died two years later.

He became the first government researcher inducted into the National Inventors Hall of Fame in 1987. His methods of antibiotic production are still used in the 21st century.

His was the key contributor to the mass-production of penicillin that has saved hundreds of millions of lives. (Courtesy of Library of Congress.)

The Raven . . . Evermore (OPPOSITE PAGE)
Celebrated artist Preston Jackson, born March 1, 1944, in Decatur, Illinois, to Shirley and T.J. Jackson, has always kept faith with his true spirit, the Raven, gatekeeper of ethereal memories. Through stories told by his parents and grandparents, the youngster with nine siblings cached a mind-trove of family and African American history that he would express later in all his works.

Growing up in Decatur, he cycled through the usual stages of art-as-storytelling, beginning at age seven, at the blaze of a prodigy. He also burned the cinders at Stephen Decatur High (class of 1962), sprinting a 9.7-second 100-yard dash.

He began his university years at Decatur's Milliken University and then Southern Illinois University, where the self-taught jazz guitarist found success and graduated with a bachelor's degree in 1969. He earned his master's at the University of Illinois in 1971.

He'd continue in academia as a teacher with postings at Milliken (1971–1972), Western Illinois (1972–1989), and, in 1989, at the School of the Art Institute of Chicago, where he became professor emeritus of sculpture in 2008. He taught not only the nuances of sculpting and drawing, but also the critical introspection that must precede and then breathe through each work.

In tandem with his academic calling, Jackson has redefined "prolific" at his Peoria riverfront Checkered Raven Gallery. His cast-bronze and steel masterpieces have found their way to institutions, galleries, parks, and museums throughout the country. And they all express a grit of sociohistory, often an unflinching African American one; they challenge patrons to appreciate life's diversity. His renowned exhibits, Bronzeville to Harlem (1997) and the 2004 paean to his grandmother and Southern ancestry Fresh from Julieann's Garden, have toured the country.

In the Raven tradition of phase-shifting, Jackson tackled the fouling of the earth-nest with his 2012 *Sperm Whale*, a 43-foot-long steel whale skeleton featuring a train of plastic bottles running the length of the creature's gut; it resides at Chicago's shorefront Grant Park.

The State of Illinois honored him in 1998 as a laureate of the Order of Lincoln, the state's highest award.

Outside of the studio, Jackson teaches and practices Tai Chi; plays jazz at the Contemporary Art Center, which he cofounded in 1995, and other venues; and rejoices in love and life with his wife, Melba, daughters, Natalie and Alice, and grandson Blake. (Courtesy of Karen Camper.)

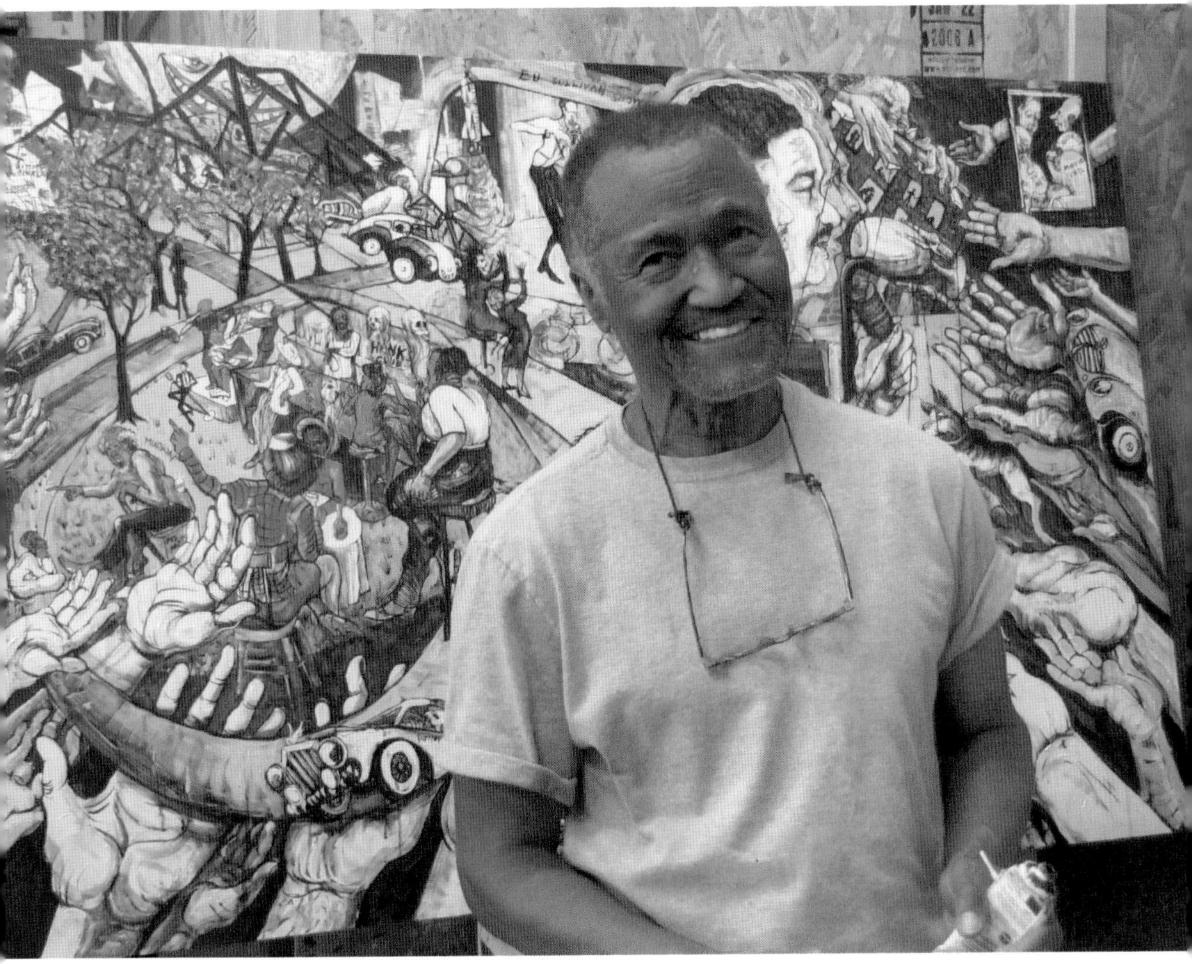

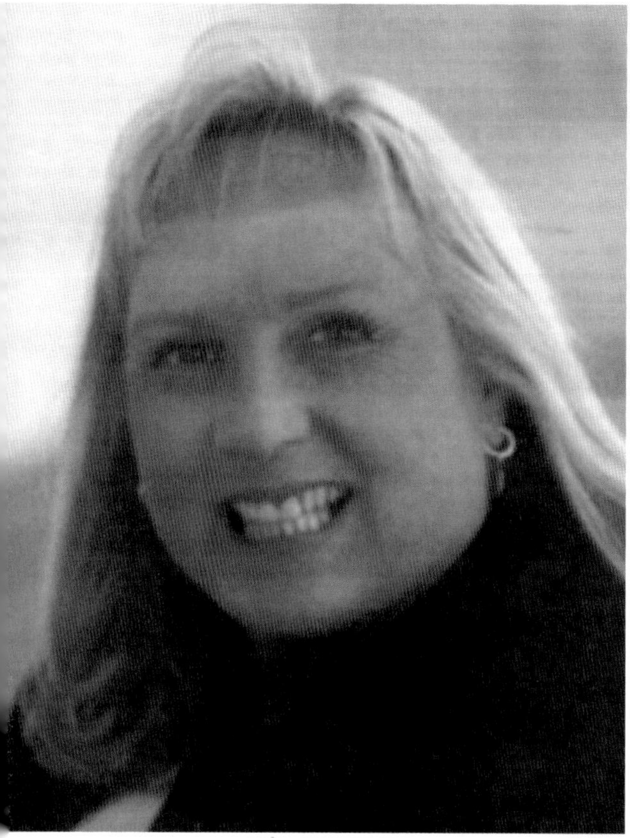

Life Changer (LEFT AND OPPOSITE PAGE) Gail Leiby, after graduating in special education from Vanderbilt University's George Peabody College, began her career at the Community Workshop and Training Center in 1977. Later, she went to DePaul University for rehabilitation administration that led to her long stretch as chief executive officer, retiring from Peoria's hallmark institution in 2011 after almost 35 years of selfless service to helping others help themselves. With her belief that people with disabilities can be self-sufficient and should not be warehoused in bleak dependency, Gail tirelessly, cheerfully enhanced the quality of thousands of lives. (Left and opposite, courtesy of Gail Leiby; below, courtesy of Community Workshop and Training Center.)

CWTC

Where people with disabilities live, work and grow.

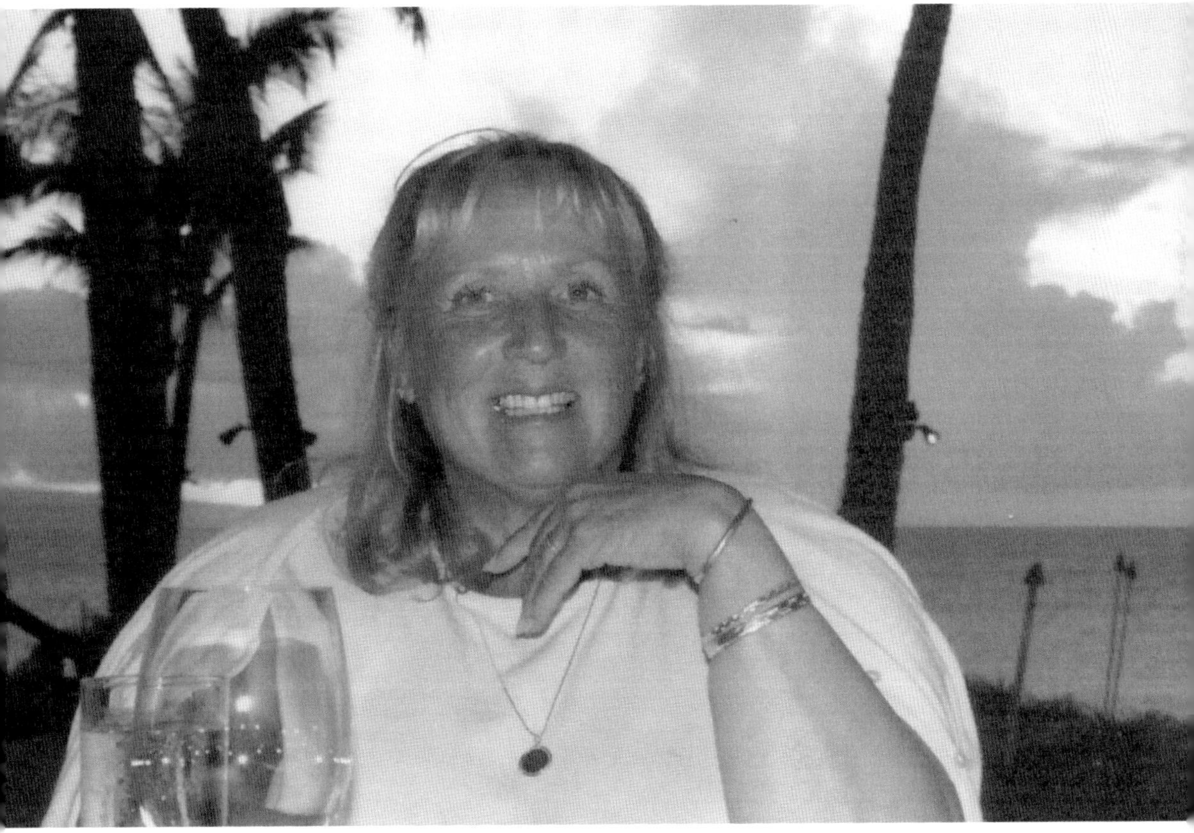

Pep at any price: Mayor's act playing well for P

By Wes Smith

PEORIA—A new clothing store staged a 7 a.m. grand opening here and his honor the mayor of Peoria came in pajamas and slippers.

He served coffee and toasted the 35 new jobs the store brought to town.

Mayor Jim Maloof will sing at your wedding, hug your grandmother and call you "Babe" too. Whatever it takes to put pep back in Peoria.

"I will do anything to make people feel good about this city again," Maloof said.

At age 66, this former high school cheerleader is now leading the cheers for old Peoria in his seventh month as mayor and his first political role.

"I'm all over the place trying to promote Peoria and my "Forward Peoria!" plan. If the business communi- y feels better about this place, then hey will invest more money here," he said.

Peoria needs the pompon treatment. ts metropolitan area of 355,000 has lost about 30,000 jobs—a few thousand of which have been recovered in different ndustries—and at least 10,000 residents n the last five years, according to Bob Schmidt, economist for the Illinois De- artment of Employment Security.

Considering those figures, Maloof's 'Mayor Feelgood" tactics may sound aive and helplessly hopeful to critics. ut most Peorians are in no mood to hrow rocks at any plan for the city's urvival.

"Peoria doesn't have much time to turn it around, and I'm willing to work with anybody to help in any way I can," said Tony Green, president of UAW Local 974, which has lost about 16,000 jobs in the Peoria area in the last five years.

"I think he has the ability to do the job. But it will take more than singing to pull it off," said Green, who did not support Maloof's campaign.

Not even Maloof's sharpest critics doubt his sincerity. He has long been a Peoria booster and, as a businessman, his fortunes are tied closely to those of his native city. In 1968, Maloof sold the dry-cleaning business begun by his immigrant Lebanese father and opened a real estate office.

Riding the city's boom in industrial growth, Maloof Realty's six offices did $50 million in sales in 1979. But by 1983, Maloof Realty nearly failed as business plummeted along with the city's fortunes. Maloof said he broke even last year and will show a modest profit for 1985.

"I nearly lost it all myself, and I saw so many people lose their homes and their jobs, it really bothered me," Maloof said. "I decided to run for mayor because I felt the city was not doing enough to help itself."

Once a slightly smug, seemingly recession-proof bastion of breweries, distilleries and heavy industry, Peoria has lost nearly all of its beer and liquor-related industry—including Pabst and Hiram Walker—and its heavy industry is sorely hurting.

They have serious troubles in this Illinois River city. And many of them can be traced to the weakened giant, Caterpillar Tractor Co. The manufacturer of the trademark yellow heavy-construction equipment is based in Peoria and has four major facilities there.

Caterpillar employed 36,200 in the Peoria area at its peak in 1979 and the UAW-negotiated wages and benefits of blue-collar workers helped to create a community coddled by what local folks then called "The Great Yellow Father."

Boats, Winnebagos and finished basements were the marks of prosperity for many Cat workers, who benefited from low-cost loans provided by the employee's credit union—the second-largest financial institution in the area.

The company's presence was so strongly felt that when Caterpillar closed for two weeks each summer to send its employees on vacations, many area bars, bowling alleys and bait shops shut down,

But the overseas m to compete competition and the re unprepared are still bei

The comp employees now employ in the area 1980.

And thing those worke

Recently, firmed plan gram that attrition an jobs worldw to spend $6 ties worldw measures clear, but can attrac won't lean the future.

In the pas Peoria got

Unemploy running al with slightl state and a try.

Homes p years ago $125,000 pr time, there Peoria. Th more than prosperous

Even the

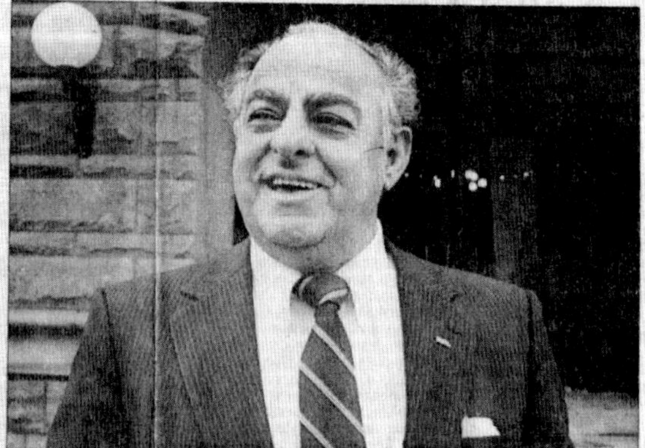

Tribune photo by Jerry Tomaselli

His boisterous style alienates some Peorians, but few question first-term Mayor Jim Maloof's sincerity in working to rejuvenate the city. "I have the guts to bring Peoria back the way Lee Iacocca brought Chrysler back and I'm gonna do it," he said.

Wes Smith is a member of The Tribune's staff.

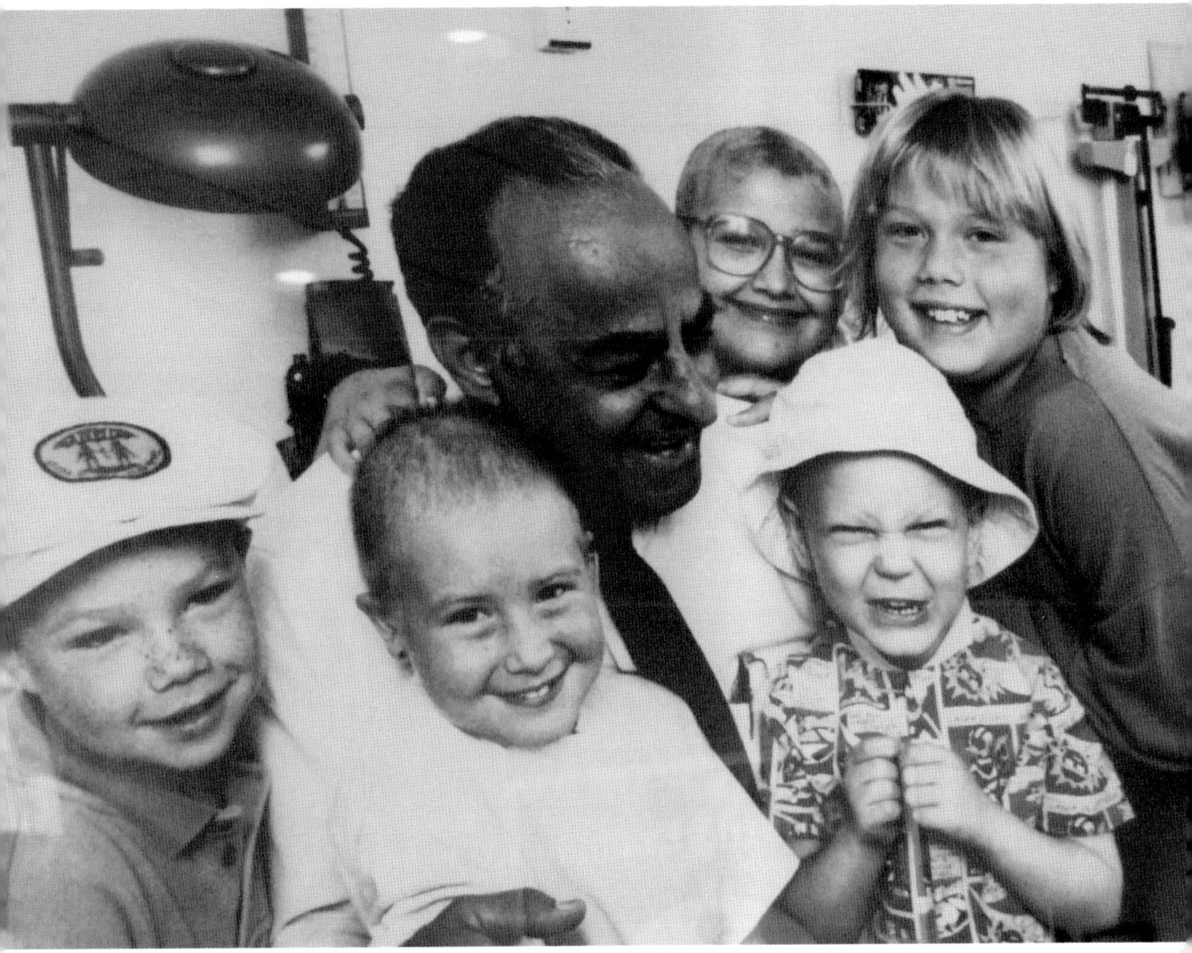

A Fighter against Lost Causes (ABOVE AND OPPOSITE PAGE)
Jim Maloof may have had his reasons to pray to St. Jude, the patron saint of lost causes, but that wasn't in his nature. Instead, the self-described "little pants presser from Peoria" became a real-estate mogul and then tackled the town's tough times, becoming "America's Singing Mayor" from 1985 to 1997, which is the second-longest tenure in Peoria's history. All the while, he championed the cure of childhood cancer and the mission of St. Jude's Children's Hospital in Memphis. On the strength of his hard work, vision, and a friendship with Danny Thomas, Peoria has the state-of-the-art Children's Hospital of Illinois, a St. Jude Midwest Research Affiliate that treats more children than any other hospital outside Chicago. In Jim Maloof, young patients indeed have their believer. Shown above are Jim Maloof and St. Jude children. (Above, courtesy of Karen Camper and Maloof Realty; opposite, courtesy of the Local History and Genealogy Collection, Peoria Public Library.)

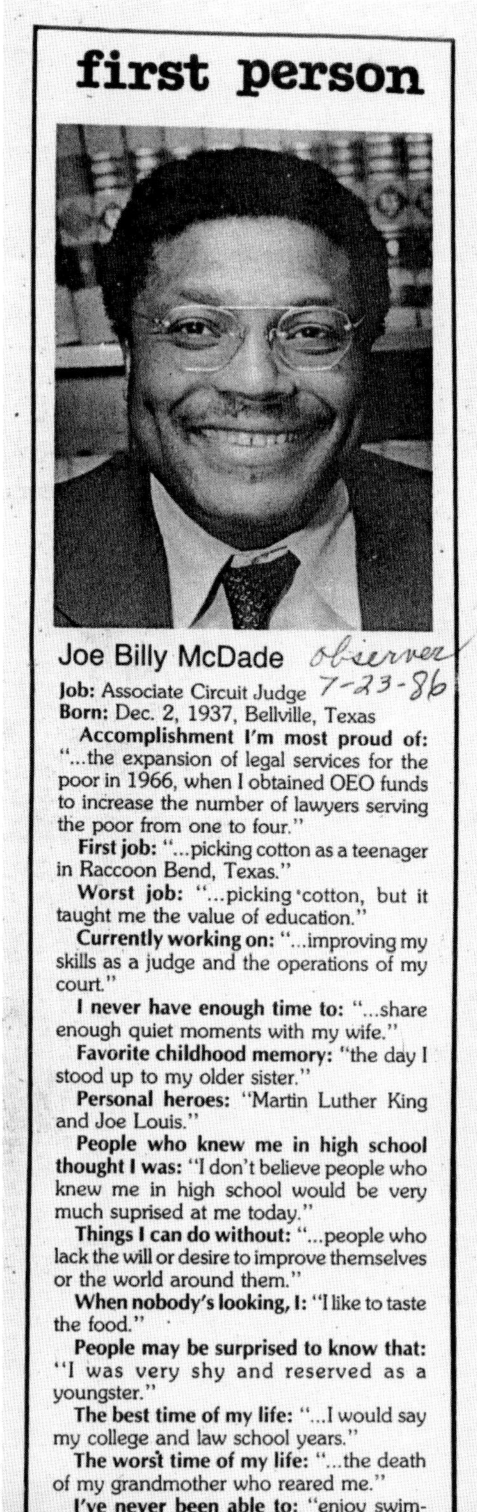

first person

Joe Billy McDade

Observer 7-23-86

Job: Associate Circuit Judge
Born: Dec. 2, 1937, Bellville, Texas

Accomplishment I'm most proud of: "...the expansion of legal services for the poor in 1966, when I obtained OEO funds to increase the number of lawyers serving the poor from one to four."

First job: "...picking cotton as a teenager in Raccoon Bend, Texas."

Worst job: "...picking cotton, but it taught me the value of education."

Currently working on: "...improving my skills as a judge and the operations of my court."

I never have enough time to: "...share enough quiet moments with my wife."

Favorite childhood memory: "the day I stood up to my older sister."

Personal heroes: "Martin Luther King and Joe Louis."

People who knew me in high school thought I was: "I don't believe people who knew me in high school would be very much suprised at me today."

Things I can do without: "...people who lack the will or desire to improve themselves or the world around them."

When nobody's looking, I: "I like to taste the food."

People may be surprised to know that: "I was very shy and reserved as a youngster."

The best time of my life: "...I would say my college and law school years."

The worst time of my life: "...the death of my grandmother who reared me."

I've never been able to: "enjoy swim-

Star on the Bench

The road from Racoon Bend, Texas, to Peoria is the road less traveled, but it was one taken by Joe Billy McDade. He was an orphan at age 10 and raised by his hardworking grandmother in Houston. He won an academic scholarship to Bradley University in 1954 and starred on three powerhouse basketball teams while excelling in class, earning his bachelor's (1959) and master's degrees (1960). He received his juris doctorate from the University of Michigan Law School in 1963.

McDade returned to Peoria in 1965 and practiced law until 1982, when he became a judge, eventually named to the US District Court in 1991; he headed the federal court from 1998 to 2004.

The Hon. Judge McDade has shown society its grandest achievement is fairness for all.

(Left, courtesy of the Local History and Genealogy Collection, Peoria Public Library; below, courtesy of Judge McDade.)

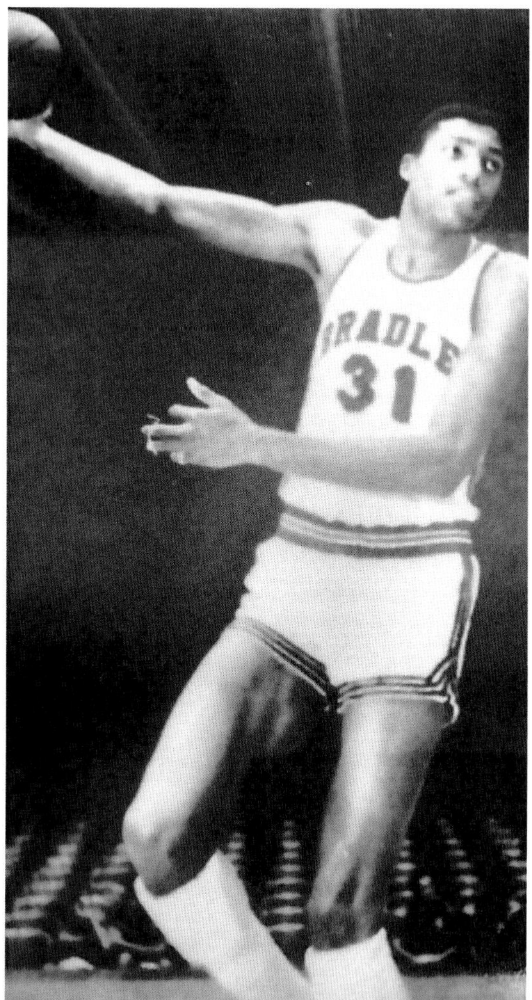

Take Me Home, County Roads

Robert "Dale" Page was the second-born of four sons of Galesburg locomotive engineer Robert L. Page and his wife Violet (Ekstrom), and travel was in Dale's blood.

The onetime six-year-old went from building tracks for his Lionel trains to major road projects in Peoria County for 47 years, first with the Illinois Division of Highways (1956–1981) and then with the Peoria County Highway Department (1981–2003), where he became superintendent of highways/county engineer in 1988, a position he held until his retirement. During his tenure, he oversaw tens of millions of dollars in the modernization of many county thoroughfares, including the replacement of 44 defective bridges, the development of a road reclaimer program, and the arrangement of the area's Adopt-A-Highway plan.

As a result, the county roads are easier, safer, and cleaner for travelers.

A devotee of education, the Galesburg High (1952) and Bradley University (1956) civil engineering graduate continued his learning journey at the University of Chicago, Northwestern, and, without affecting a New England Brahmin accent, Harvard.

He is an even stronger devotee to his childhood Sunday school sweetheart, Betty Swegele, whom he began dating while at Bradley; they married in December of his junior year. Over time, they would have five children: Cindy, Pam, Michele, Bob, and Ed.

While the Pages have followed the wind since retirement, Peoria honored its road meister with the R. Dale Page Park in 2005. It may not compete with Alaska's vast Denali National Park, but it's a grand Midwest-sensible tribute to the affable king of Peoria's county byways. Dale is pictured with his wife, Betty, spending a spring day at the park named after him. (Courtesy of Karen Camper.)

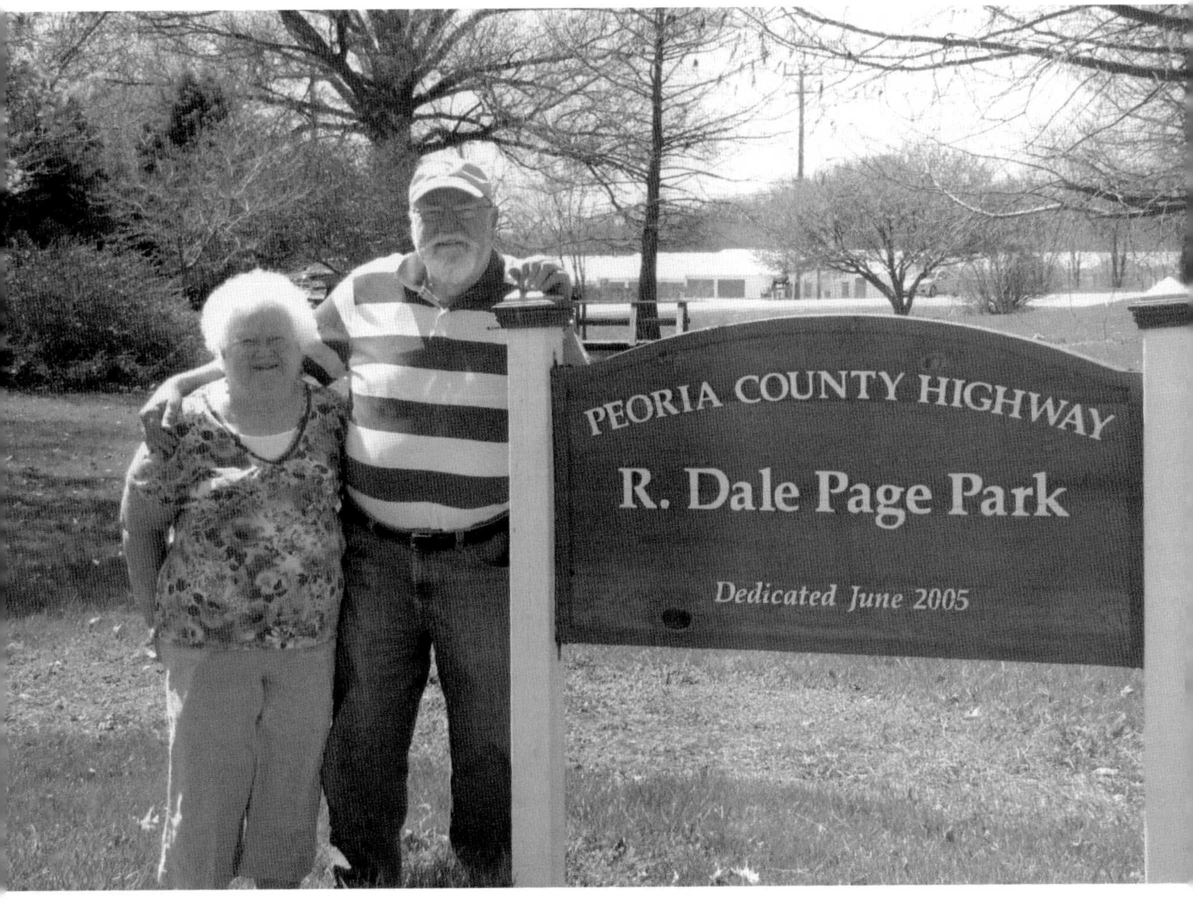

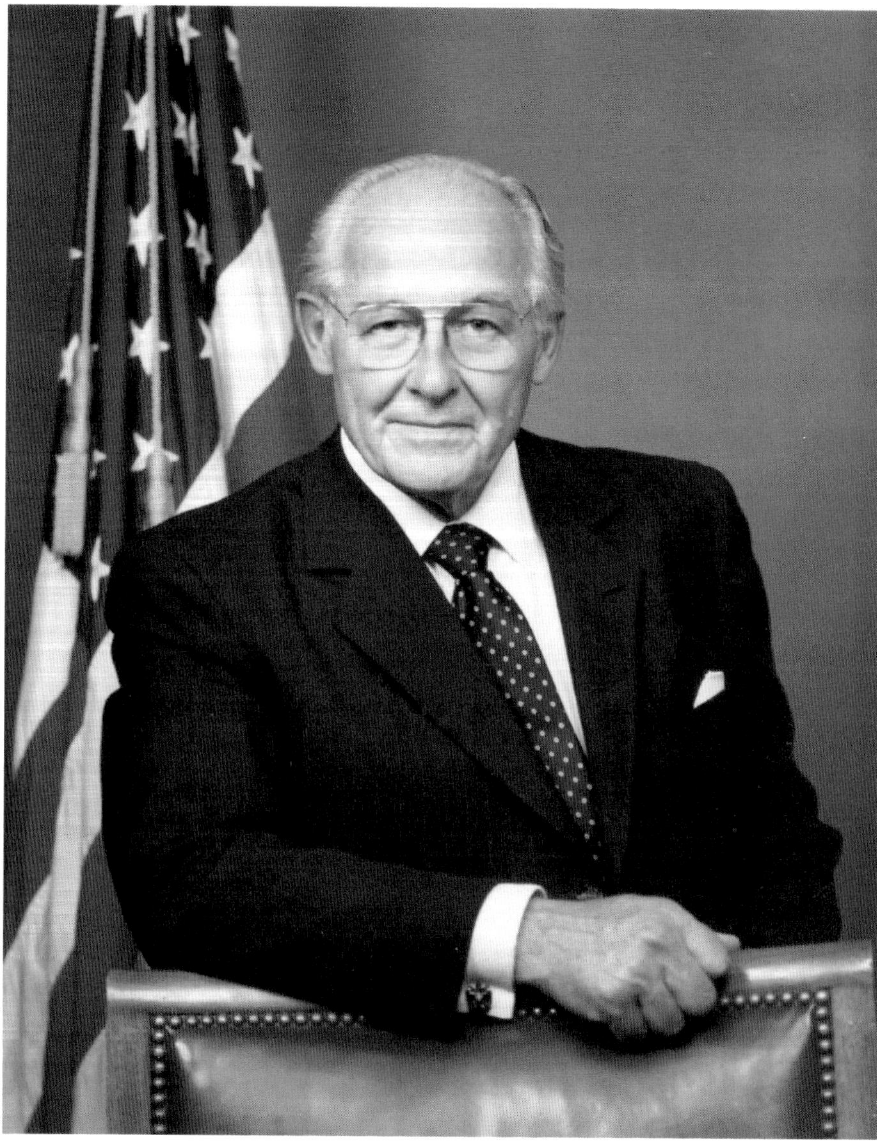

All About Bob (ABOVE AND OPPOSITE PAGE)
Robert Michel served as a highly visible US congressman from the central Illinois 18th District for 38 years (1957–1995). A graduate of Bradley (1948), he joined Congressman Harold Velde's staff in 1949. With Velde's handoff in 1956, Michel would win the next 18 elections, becoming Republican minority whip (1975–1981), and then House minority leader (1981–1995).

Savvy in the art of bipartisanship, he won numerous honors, including the Presidential Citizens Medal—second-highest civilian award—presented by President Reagan in 1989, and the Presidential Medal of Freedom—for the highest achievement by a citizen—conferred by President Clinton in 2000. His name abounds throughout Peoria, including the Bob Michel Community Base Veterans Affairs Outpatient Clinic for his tireless efforts on behalf of veterans.

He married his college sweetheart, Corrine Woodruff, in 1948. They had four children. (Above, courtesy of the Robert H. Michel Papers, the Dirksen Congressional Center, Pekin, Illinois; opposite, photograph by Duane Zehr; courtesy of the Dirksen Congressional Center, Pekin, Illinois.)

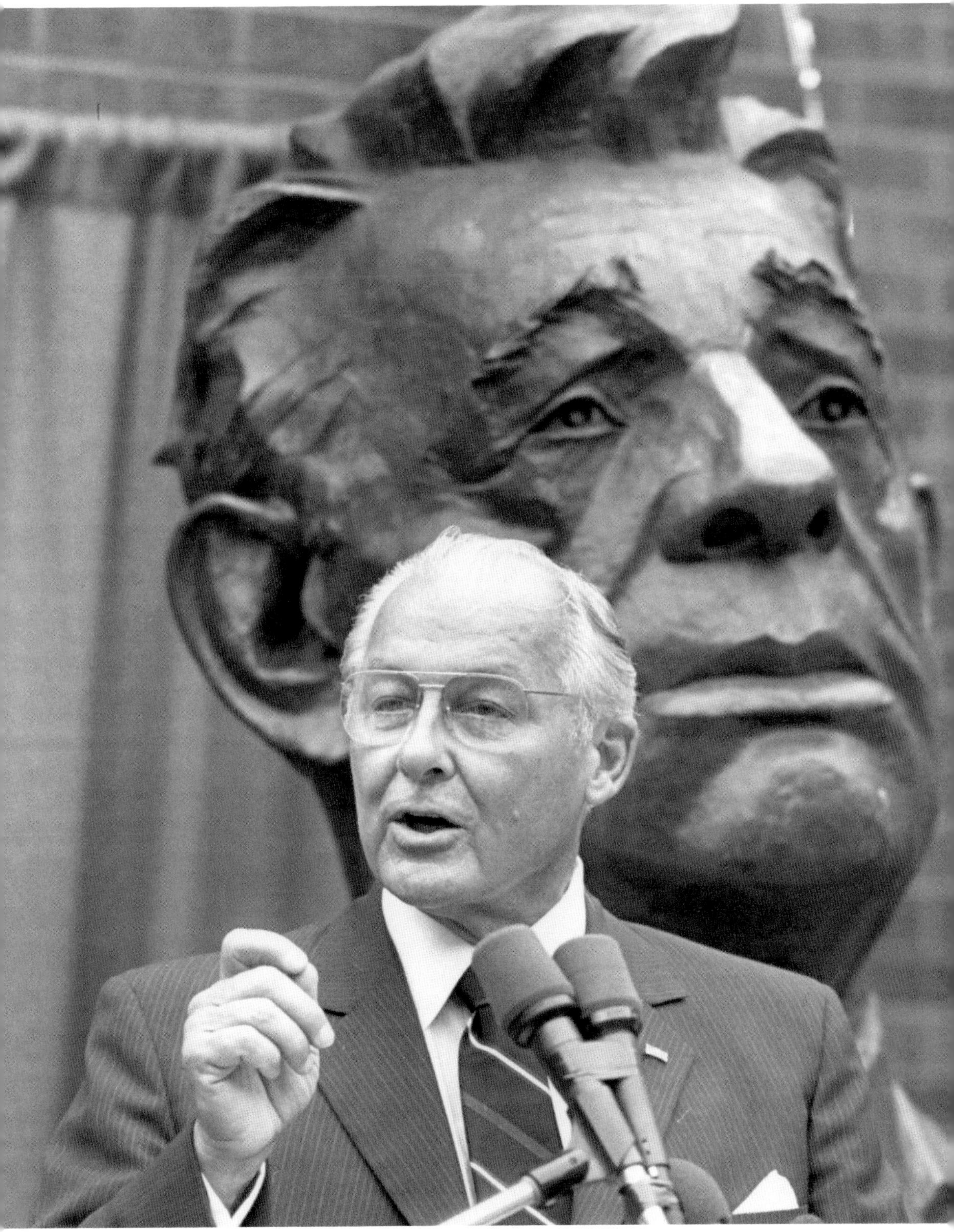

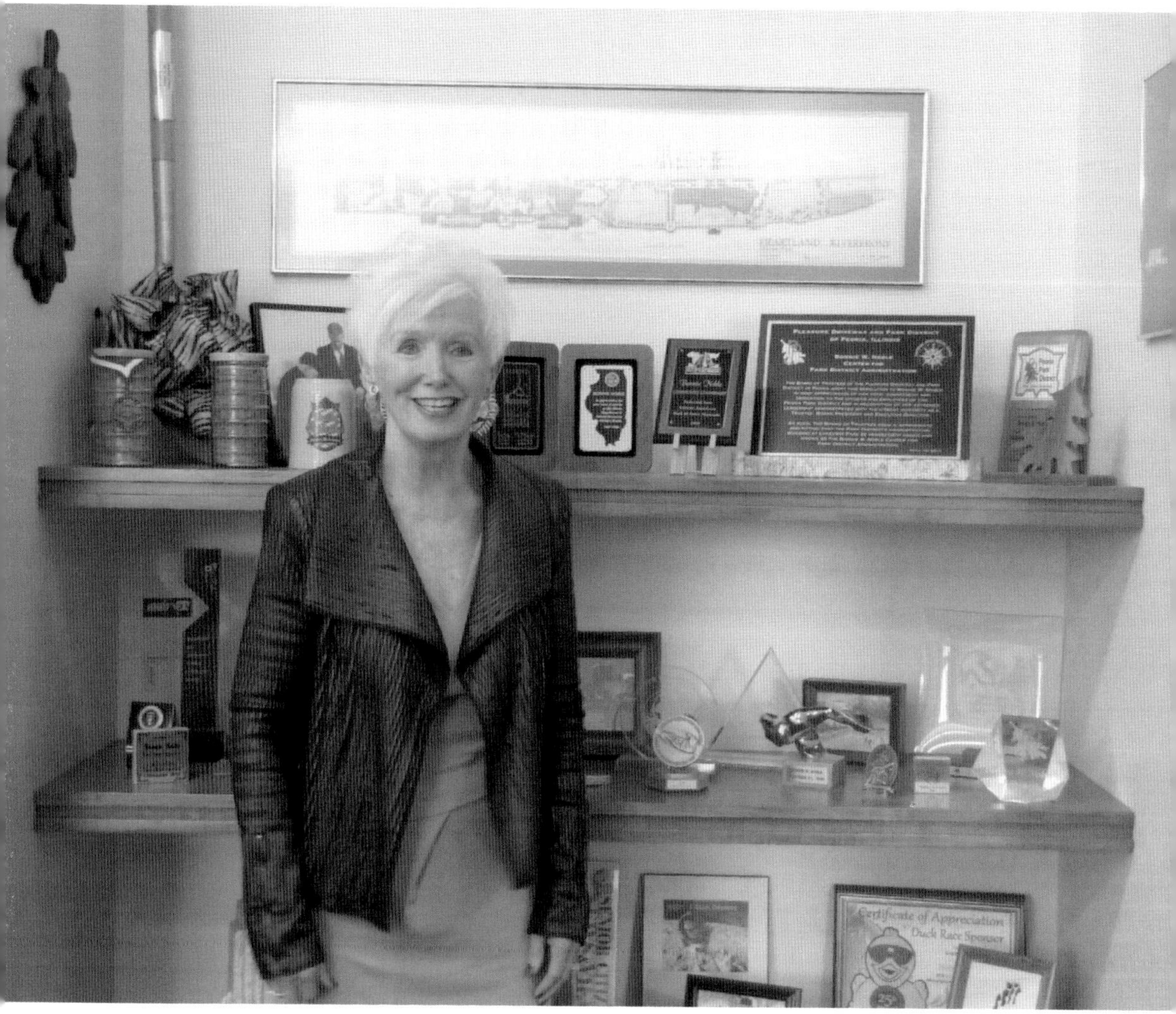

Park Dynasty (ABOVE AND OPPOSITE PAGE)
For the Peoria Park District, the state's oldest park system (1894), and its executive director Bonnie Noble, honors keep on coming.

Ever since her election in 1973 as a park district trustee, the University of Illinois graduate has kept Peoria in the forefront of green urban gems across America. Under her leadership, the district has greatly expanded its park acreage and has won the Gold Medal Award, the highest honor for a park agency, three times (1994, 2001, and 2010) and has been a finalist nine times. The district earned Illinois's first accreditation as a Distinguished Park District; additionally, it was tops in the state for open-space per capita and among the national leaders.

Incredibly, Noble has decreased the district's debt by a third since 2001.

Peoria can thank Bonnie Noble for its great green vistas. On the opposite page, she is pictured outside her namesake park district administrative building. (Both, courtesy of Karen Camper.)

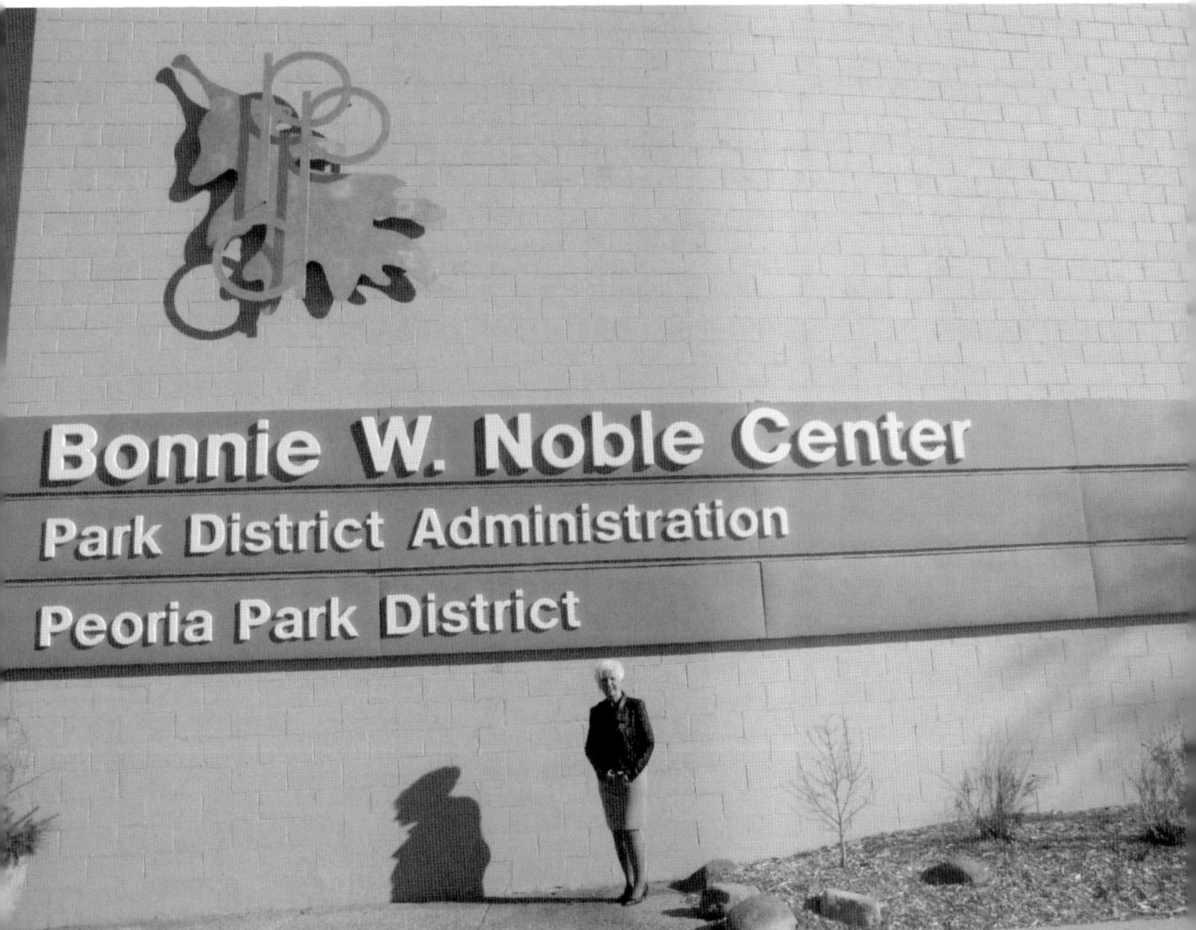
Bonnie W. Noble Center
Park District Administration
Peoria Park District

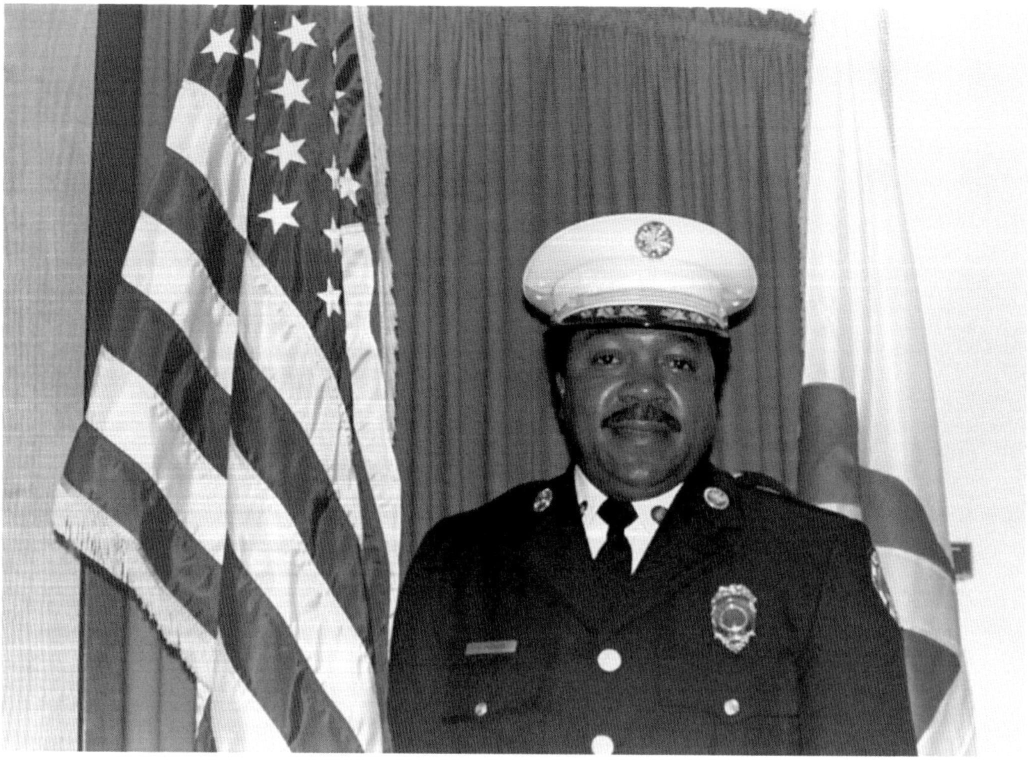

Beyond the "Pail"

His given name is General John Parker, but his friends call him "Dump," short for "Dumpling," an endearment his mother gave him before his birth on December 29, 1941, in Drew, Mississippi. In 1945, after the 1944 birth of his brother Loys Jr., the family of Loys Sr. and Annie Mae (Tyler) Parker moved north to Peoria, seeking a better life and a refuge from odious Jim Crow segregation.

Parker graduated from Manual Training High in 1960, the step-off year to the Seething Sixties. He joined the Marines, and after his 1964 discharge, worked at Caterpillar. With the 1965 city annexation of Richwoods Township and the need for more firefighters, Parker, who growing up had never seen a black fireman, began a livelihood that would lead him to the top, Peoria fire chief, by 1988. Along the way, he earned degrees in political science and fire science technology at Illinois Central College. He also served from 1976 to 1990 in the Illinois Air National Guard (Peoria), topping out as deputy fire chief.

Renowned for his regard of others, he faced bigotry dead-on throughout his career, especially in the areas of recruitment, retention, and promotion of minorities. Sensing a need, Parker helped with the founding of the Afro American Firefighters of Peoria.

He left Peoria in 1990 to become the first black fire chief in Pomona, California. In Pomona, which is 60 percent Hispanic with a mostly white fire department, he began implementing a court-ordered mandate to improve minority hiring and promotion. Soon, he was enemy number one with some in the city council and the union, and his every step was undercut. Though revered outside of those two *pari delecti* factions, his tenure was met mostly with "No." Rather than concede to reality, the city council dissolved the fire department and contracted with Los Angeles County for fire protection—spiting itself with a greater cost and slower response times. Parker continued as a fire battalion chief for Los Angeles County until retiring in 1999.

Chief Parker lives far from the water pail on Georgia's Ogeechee River, 15 miles from Savannah and 40 minutes by boat from the ocean. He's not a languid retiree, as he busies himself with the issues of others, most notably as president of the Savannah chapter of the 100 Black Men of America and commander of the Savannah American Legion Post No. 500. (Courtesy of G. John Parker.)

When Bad Things Happen to Good Cells

Dr. Jasti Rao was already a world-famous neuro-tumor researcher at Houston's high-status University of Texas M.D. Anderson Cancer Center when he became head of the University Of Illinois College of Medicine at Peoria Cancer Research Center in 2001. A farmer's son, Rao used his tireless work ethic and intellect to earn bachelor's and master's degrees from India's University of Andhra. He received his doctorate in biochemistry at the University of Madras.

Rao came to America in 1982 as a research assistant at the University of Kansas Medical Center. From there, he went to the M.D. Anderson Cancer Center's Department of Neurosurgery in 1986 and international superstardom.

While in Peoria, he has secured more National Institutes of Health neuro-oncology grants than anyone else in America.

In 2012, the town voted Dr. Rao its first Peorian of the Year. (Author's collection.)

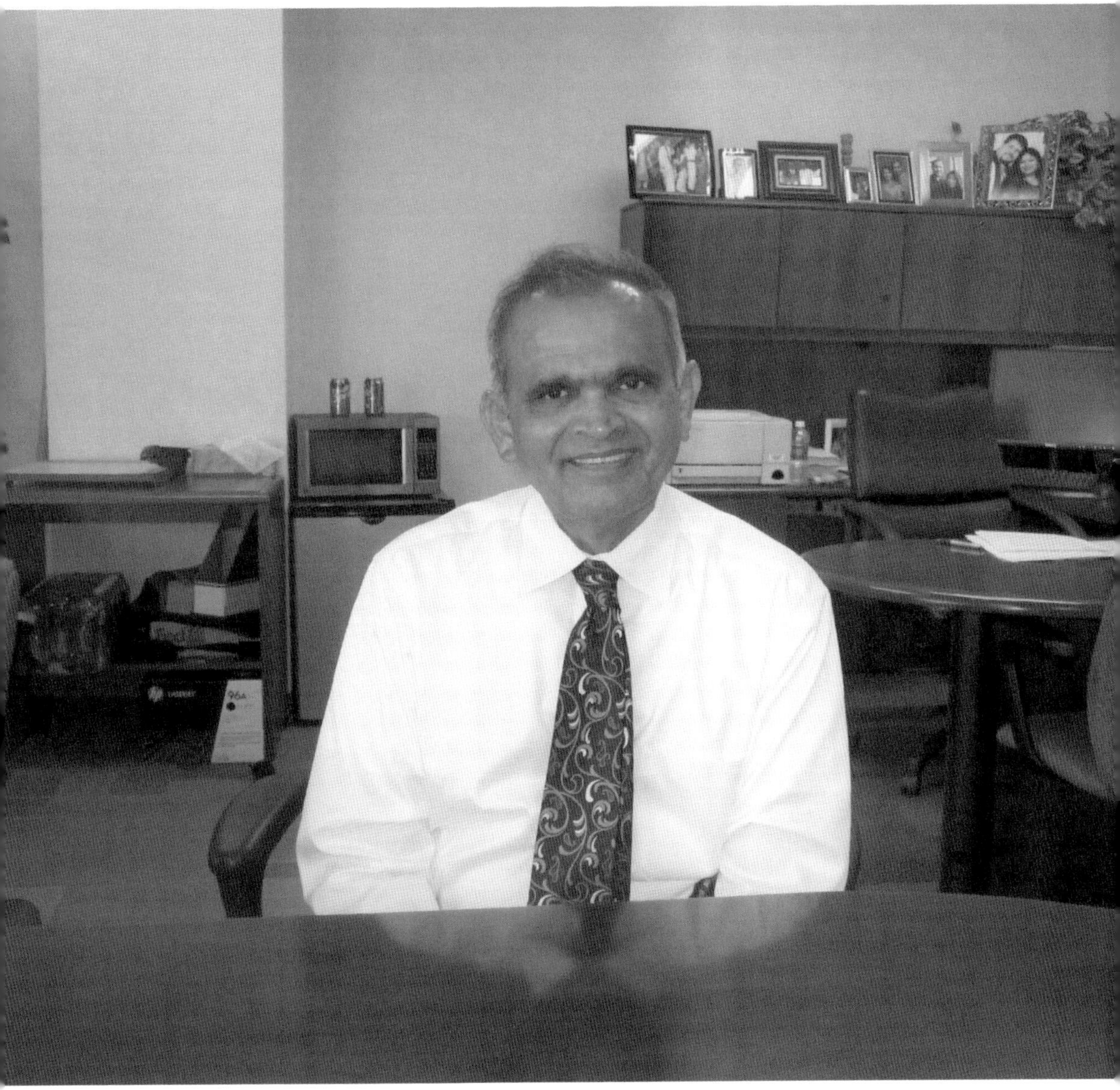

If They Own It, They Will Read It

Maybe it was kismet that drew Janet (Alleman) Roth to an *Oprah* magazine story about a book-giving program that improved student reading at an impoverished school. Then again, it may have been the perceptive uber-volunteer sensing another chance to help; with a lifetime of stepping forward, one glance is all she'd need to see limitless possibilities. Her moxie and vision led to her 2008 founding of Look. It's My Book!, an innovative, all-volunteer nonprofit that gives six new books per year to Peoria Public School District No. 150 kindergarten-through-fourth-grade students; the children make their own choices of reading-level-appropriate material. For many, the books are the first ever in their homes.

By 2015, Look. It's My Book! had distributed over 120,000 books to all 14 District 150 schools, including 33,000 during the 2014–2015 school year. Better yet, kindergarten through fourth grade reading and math scores were up.

Achievement is nothing new to the Anderson, Indiana, native. After she graduated with a political science and journalism degree from Indiana University, she married Indiana University law graduate Peorian Charles Roth. Following his Vietnam-era Army stretch, the couple settled in Peoria, and she began her career with the Peoria Social Security Office, spending her last seven years as district manager in Springfield.

Her illustrious career included a stint as president of the Chicago Regional (eight states) Management Association; Janet was also awarded the prestigious Regional Commissioner's Citation and the Joe Collins Award, the Social Security Management Association's highest accolade. She retired in December 2004. Throughout, she unsparingly gave her time to others in the arts, women's groups, mental-health facilities, business associations, fundraisers, and numerous civic boards. If the cause is just, she will greet it with a smile and rolled-up sleeves.

Yet, Janet Roth always had plenty of time for her husband, daughter, son, and grandchildren. (Courtesy of Karen Camper.)

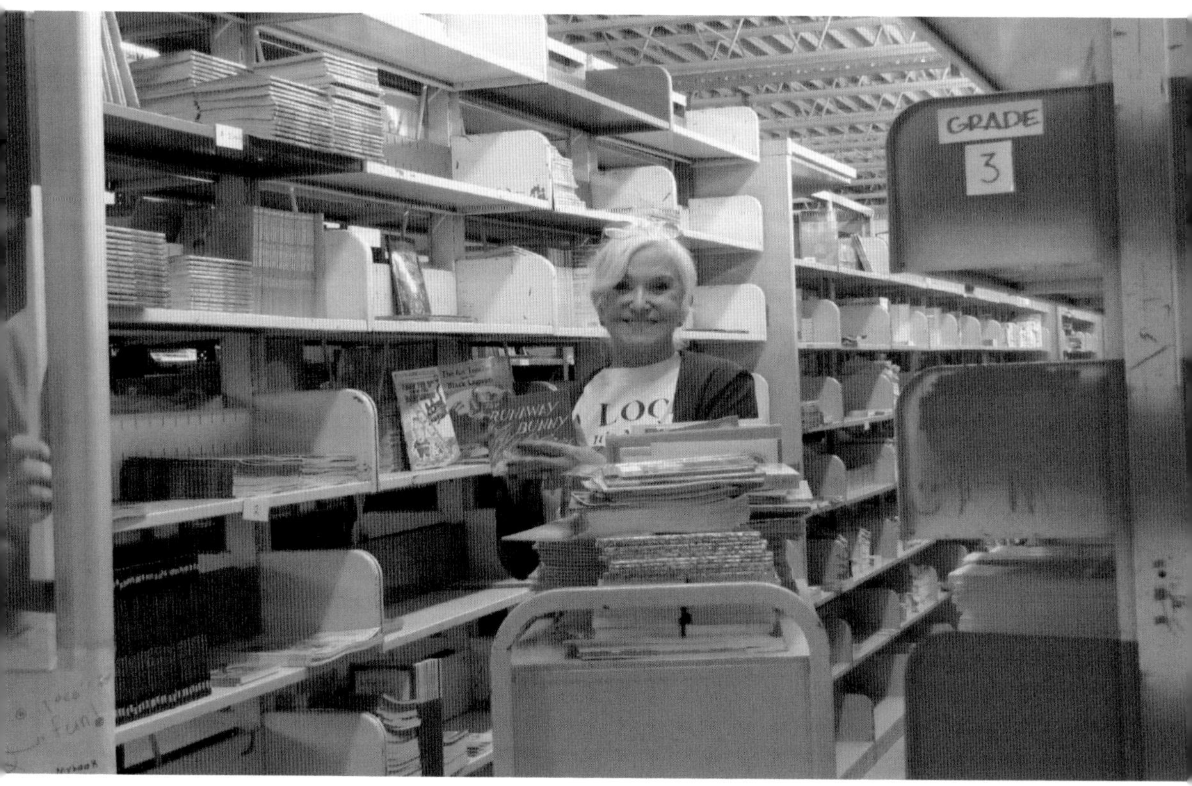

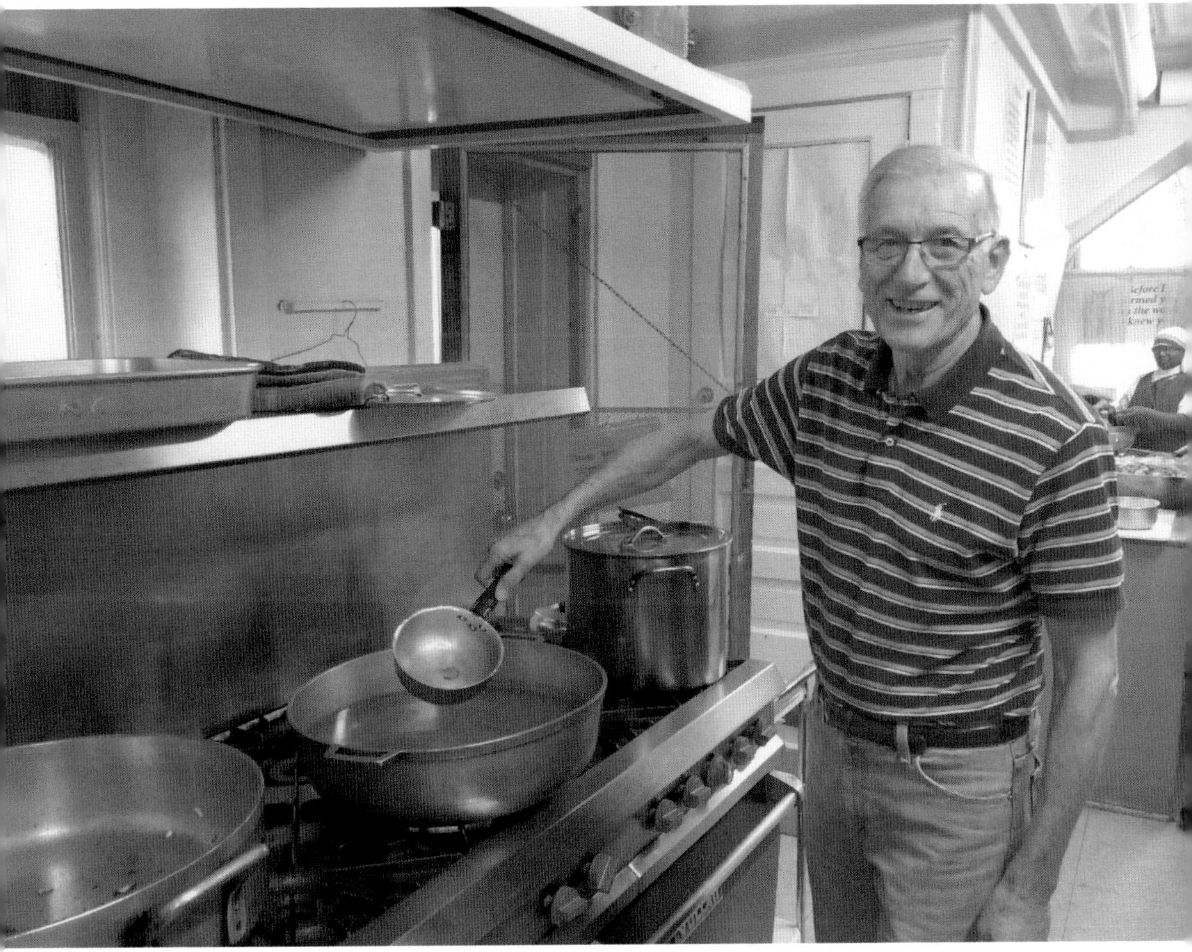

Dr. Iz: The Drill Is Gone
Dr. Isidor "Izzy" Ruscheinski, a Romanian by birth raised in Germany before landing in Chicago after World War II, graduated from Loyola College of Dentistry in 1964. He practiced in the Windy City until 1971, when he joined his fellow classmate Dr. Art Swearinger in Peoria. Grateful for the opportunities America had provided, Izzy served several years in the Air Force and as the base dental surgeon for the Peoria Air National Guard. The mild-mannered dentist may have hung up his drill in 2000, but never his desire to help others.

Without fanfare, Izzy has cheerfully ladled soup into many a bowl at the South Side Mission's Lighthouse Diner ,where the poor receive relief for the body and nourishment for the soul. (Author's collection.)

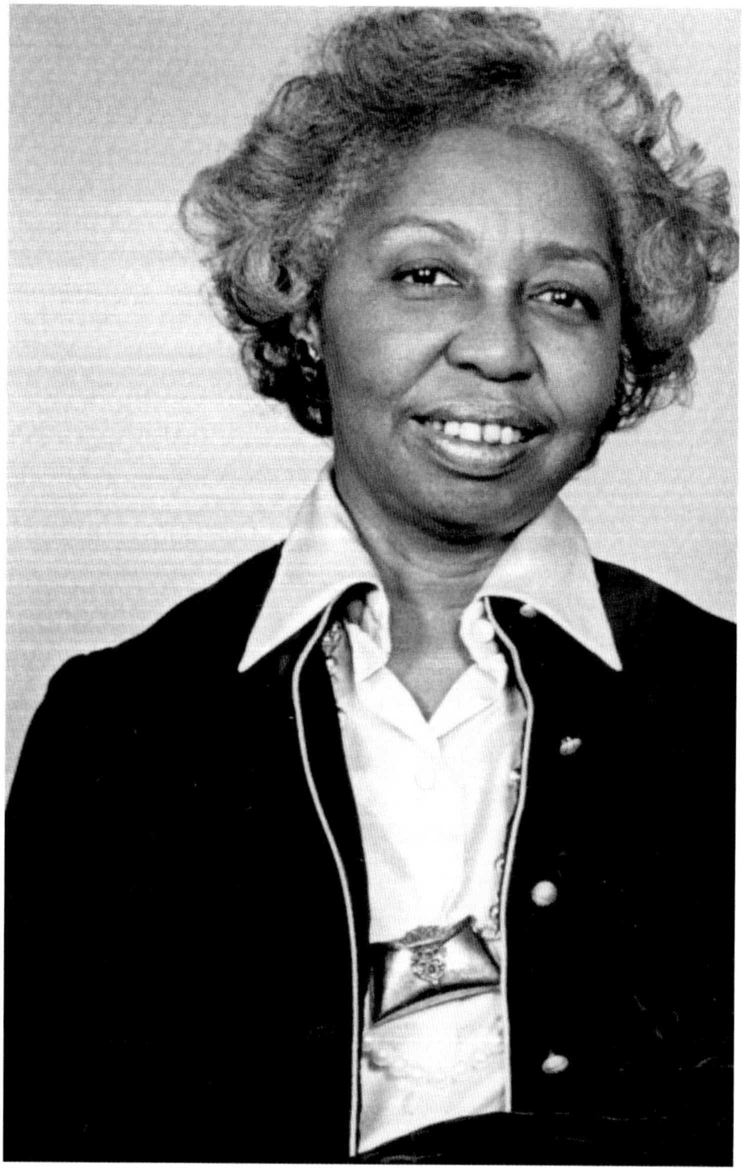

Star Launcher

In 1948, Texas-born Juliette Whittaker (1926–2007) earned her University of Iowa master's degree in drama and took a chance—she came to Peoria.

As founder and principal of the Carver Community Center's School of Arts and Drama, she saw a star in every child who came her way, including one skid-heading youngster who would become one of the world's greatest comedians—Richard Pryor. Over the decades, she nurtured thousands with skill and compassion.

She left Peoria only once, in the mid-1950s, attempting to settle a score with a dream: could she make it on Broadway? Obvious talent aside, it was the cutthroat New York theater scene that brought her home to River City.

She renewed her faith in children and championed all the Peoria arts until her death at age 80. (Courtesy of *Peoria Journal Star*.)

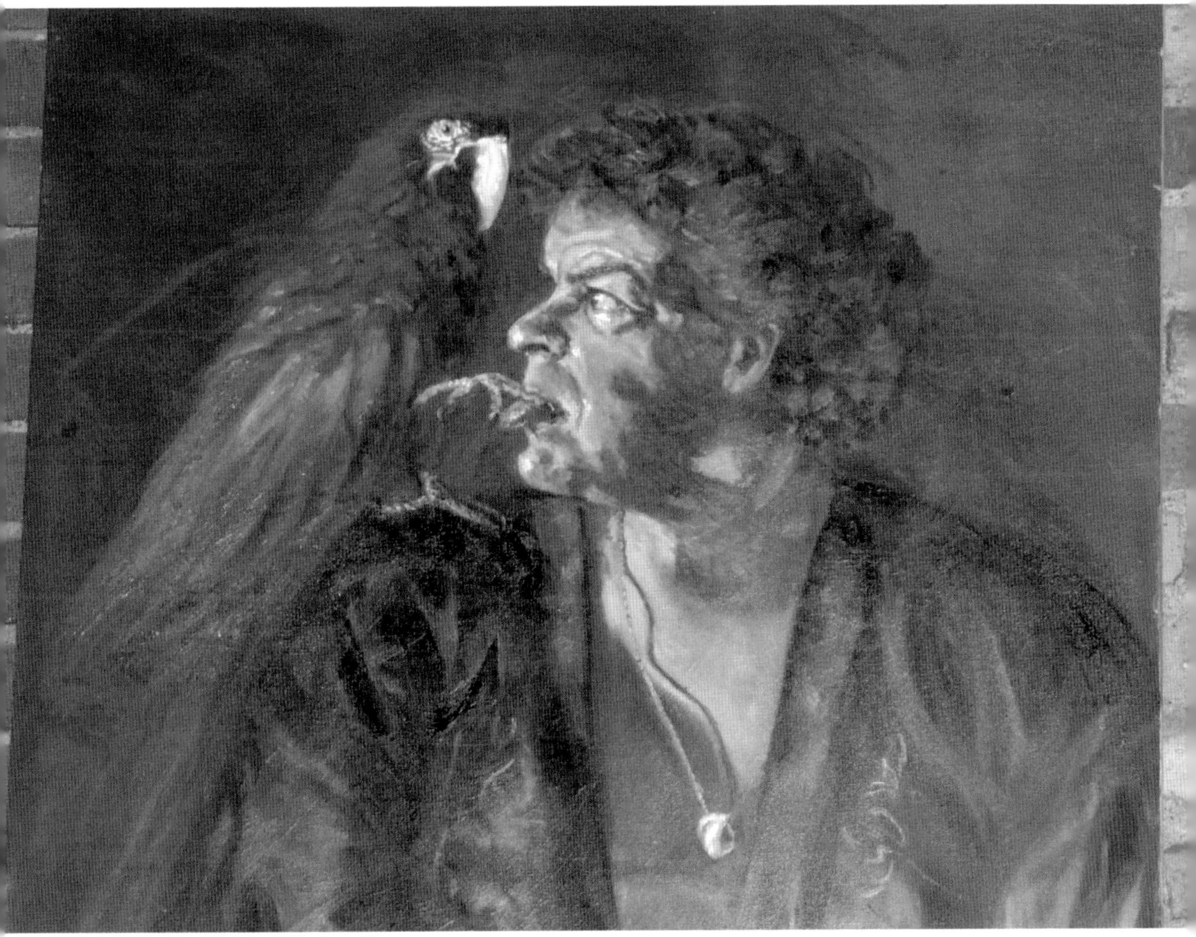

The River City Rowdy

Born in Princeton, Illinois, Gary Sandberg (1948–2013) drove into an unsuspecting Peoria in 1968 after finishing his architectural studies at Southern Illinois University; over the next 45 years, he rattled the town enough that city leaders viewed him as a Bowtie Brando or Dirty Gary.

But Peoria's longest-sitting city council member, of 24 consecutive years, defied easy tags.

He was a maverick who believed in preserving the town's historic landmarks, reviving the downtown, and fighting against civic money squandering, also known as town pork. And, perhaps concerned that the city chambered-horseshoe might be mistaken for a Stalinist Politburo, he would usually smack a contrary lone vote just to prevent council unanimity.

No one in the horseshoe felt his hot gust—the Sandberg sirocco—more than the outspoken Mayor Jim Maloof. Their Franken-spats in the 1990s turned town meetings into verbal cage fights. (Had these tiffs occurred after the advent of reality television, *Real Pols of Peoria* would have been a ratings smash.)

Yet, most in town admired his zest and compassion on all matters Peoria. All he asked of his colleagues and himself was honest, informed debates followed by beer and pizza for all.

The big throttle-up that started in 1989 ended on July 19, 2013, when Sandberg died of heart disease. Besides his children Cari and Colt, Peoria's wild one left behind his adored macaw, as well as muse, Jelly Bean; a mint-green Harley-Davidson; and a quieter horseshoe. (Courtesy of Pat Sullivan, photograph by Karen Camper.)

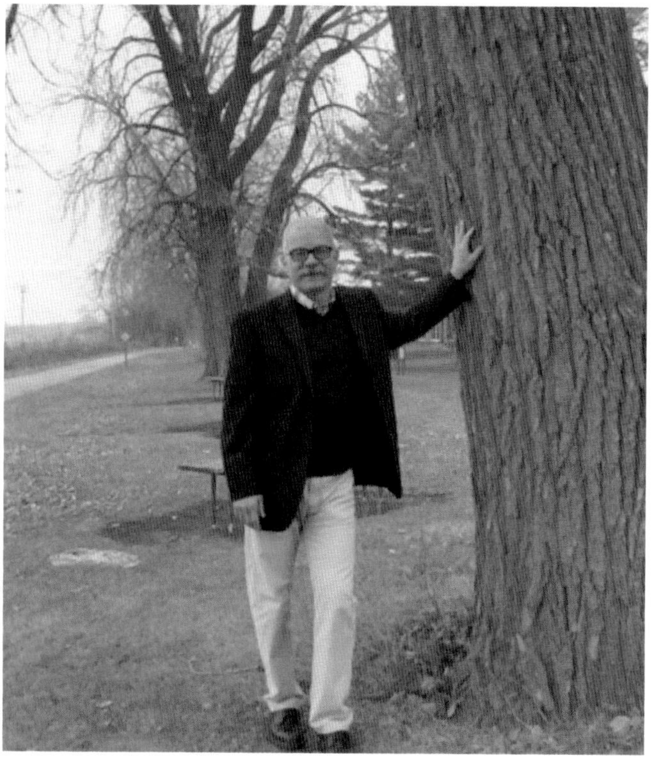

The Lyricist of Lincolnland

In 1984, Dr. Kevin Stein, the then newly hooded doctoral graduate of Indiana University, drove into Peoria for the first time. The poet's new city had the aura of his home in Anderson, Indiana; both were Midwest one-iron-horse towns—Caterpillar (Peoria) and GM (Anderson). With his change of scenery being so similar, this also meant the Bradley University English professor did not have to change his loafers for wingtips.

The fit couldn't have been better.

For a former teen lyricist whose garage band barely made it out of the driveway, he has penned plenty of atmospheric works that have rubbed shoulders with America's literati. Likewise, his day job as a teacher has been an appealing one, encouraging his students to explore their own creative yonder reaches. And he has done it with easy wit, expertise, and verve. His skills have earned him numerous honors including the 1989 Bradley Professor of the Year, and, since 2000, the Caterpillar Professor of English.

Illinois governor Rod Blagojevich in 2003 tapped Stein as the Illinois Poet Laureate, succeeding the iconic Gwendolyn Brooks who had died in 2000; Howard Austin and the world-renowned Carl Sandburg also had held the post. So far, Dr. Kevin Stein's tenure as the state's fourth poetry guru has been sonnets away! He has proved that poetry is a performance art by giving over 170 events throughout the state in his first decade in a range of venues including free verse in factories and slam on Chicago rock stations. As befits a 21st-century laureate, he runs two websites dedicated to Illinoisans and has produced a CD of readings by 24 Illinois poets—a long haul from the 1350s parchment days of the World's First Poet Laureate Petrarch.

He has welcomed all into rhyme's big top, even those groundling limericks.

With works such as *Wrestling Li Po for the Remote* (2013) and his personal dynamism in public places, Dr. Stein is proof that poetry lives. And it is no longer a uni-verse.

He reminds us, too, that Midwest cornpone died years ago after driving an Edsel into a crick. (Courtesy of Karen Camper.)

CHAPTER THREE

Everyday Legends

Since a city's goodness comes from its people, Peoria is a great city. Environmentalist Bill Rutherford has donated 20,000 acres for green use in Peorialand and 600,000 acres around the globe. Former Caterpillar chief executive officer Glen Barton has applied his retirement energies to educational and civic initiatives in the city. Medal of Honor recipient Hal Fritz, who has served two terms as Medal of Honor Society president, fights for better lives for veterans throughout the country. On the tube from the 1950s until the 1970s, Captain Jinks and Salty Sam sailed the SS *Albatross* into childhood homes every afternoon. On the front lines on April 9, 2004—Good Friday—the 724th Army Reserve Transportation Company held its own against the worst ambush of the Iraqi occupation. After 9/11, Peoria police officer Greg Metz busted up an al-Qaeda money-laundering scheme during a car stop.

Fighting against national food chains with creative local fare, the owner of Spotted Cow, Frank Abdnour, is the River City (national chain) Rattler. Retaining historic apartments and homes is a labor of love for LaDonna and Charles Bobbitt. Meanwhile, Steve Bobbitt (no relation to Charles) is the raspy River City Rooster of Rock, the mirror image of superstar Rod Stewart, who will cut a lawn or a rug. Robin Hunt has kept Peorians fit with Jazzercise and entertained them with her acting on local stages. Kevin Harmon, who became a quadriplegic after a waterslide fall, showed fortitude to write a book. George Manias, whose humbleness has become a national news item, has shined over a million pairs of shoes, including several presidents' and every other celebrity who has been in Peoria; all of his customers are given the very-important-person treatment. Unheralded Bill Noel's vast network of friends, family, and even clergy has leaned on him for well over a decade for weekly funerals and more. He is Peoria's Rock.

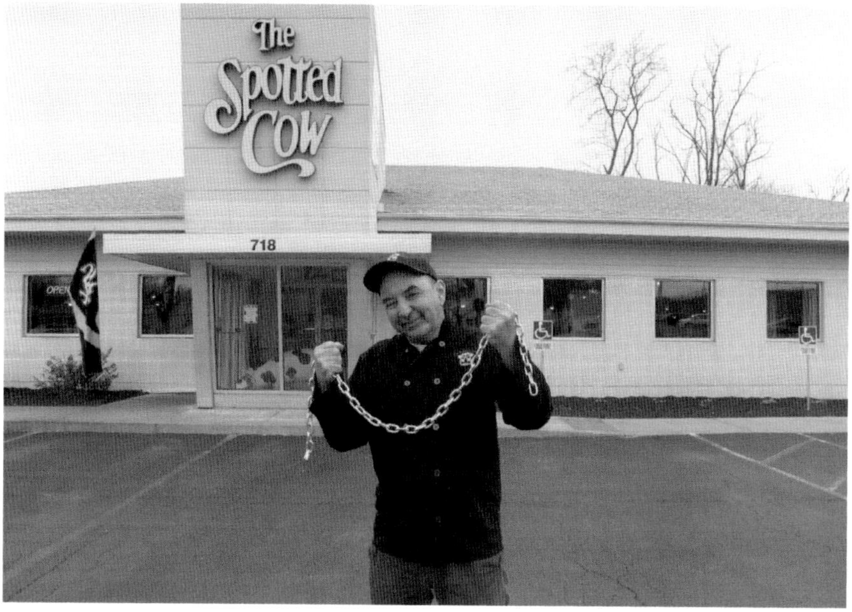

The Scoop on Peoria's Big Dipper

Streator-born Frank Abdnour lost his dad when he was seven years old. But his father's love of baseball, the Chicago White Sox, Johnny Unitas, and the Baltimore (now Indianapolis) Colts would live on. So too would a fancy for ice cream—the packed kind that worked the teeth, not the airy soft-serve variety.

After his father's passing, Frank's mother, Frieda, had no time for grief; she had six children who depended on her, including her youngest, Frank. The family moved to Peoria, where she worked in her brother's Haddad's Grocery Store. Frank's first job at age 13 was sorting soda bottles at his uncle's store.

He went to St. Bernard's Grade School and Spalding Institute, class of 1976, where he was the second-sacker on the baseball team for three years. Upon graduation, he worked eight years as a landscaper, including his "wilderness years" in Austin, Texas, from 1979 to 1980, and Denver from 1983 to 1984. He returned to Peoria forever in 1984 and waved goodbye to Don Winkler, his last-ever boss.

He went cold and accepted his ice cream destiny.

His ice cream cart outside of Bradley Hall, The Spotted Cow, became a campus hit. The dynamo helmsman was so successful that the university food service in 1986 booted its rival after four semesters. Unfazed, Abdnour moved The Spotted Cow to a root beer stand at War Memorial Drive and University Street before herding his operation indoors at Main and University Streets for a year, making his own creations for the first time.

The Spotted Cow took off for Peoria Heights in 1987 and stayed for 19 years as Abdnour's fame as a flavorista rocketed, concocting over 250 gems. In 1998, two years after St. Francis Medical Center surgeons repaired his daughter's heart condition, Abdnour opened a satellite Cow in the Order of St. Francis Medical Center's vending machine room. When he left in 2008, it had become the hospital's highest gross profit area per square foot.

More importantly, the grateful, family-centered Abdnour redoubled his already-herculean charity efforts, deciding he would help all.

The Spotted Cow's last relocation, to Glen Avenue, came in 2006, and with it came an expansion into family dining—another intuitive move that has proved Frank Abdnour's adage that the harder he works, the luckier he becomes.

Somewhere in the cosmos, "Entrepreneur-Supreme" Sox owner Bill Veeck is chuckling.

The "River City Rattler," Frank Abdnour, rattles the national chain eateries. (Courtesy of Karen Camper.)

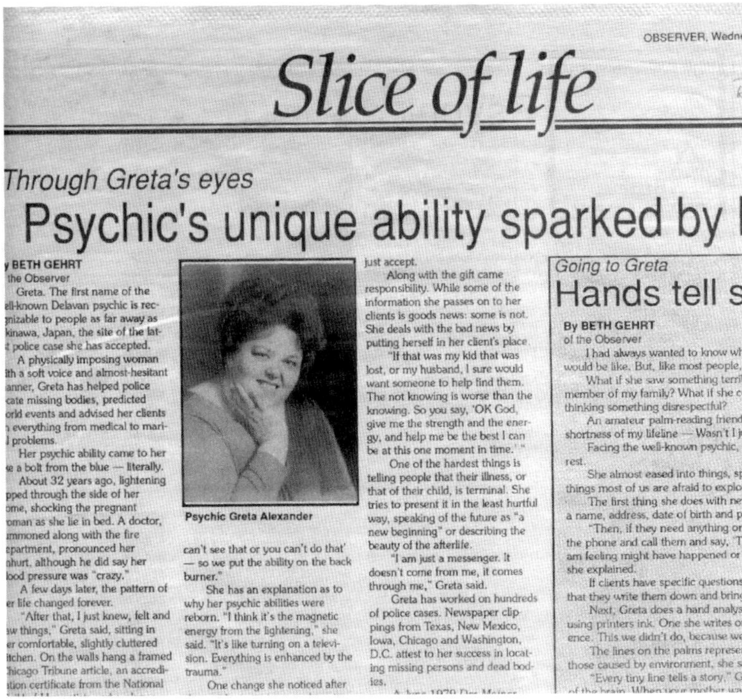

OBSERVER, Wedne

Slice of life

Through Greta's eyes

Psychic's unique ability sparked by l

y BETH GEHRT
the Observer

Greta. The first name of the ell-known Delavan psychic is recgnizable to people as far away as kinawa, Japan, the site of the latt police case she has accepted.

A physically imposing woman ith a soft voice and almost-hesitant anner, Greta has helped police cate missing bodies, predicted orld events and advised her clients everything from medical to maril problems.

Her psychic ability came to her e a bolt from the blue — literally.

About 32 years ago, lightening pped through the side of her ome, shocking the pregnant oman as she lie in bed. A doctor, ummoned along with the fire epartment, pronounced her nhurt, although he did say her lood pressure was "crazy."

A few days later, the pattern of er life changed forever.

"After that, I just knew, felt and aw things," Greta said, sitting in er comfortable, slightly cluttered itchen. On the walls hang a framed hicago Tribune article, an accreditation certificate from the National

Psychic Greta Alexander

can't see that or you can't do that' — so we put the ability on the back burner."

She has an explanation as to why her psychic abilities were reborn. "I think it's the magnetic energy from the lightening," she said. "It's like turning on a television. Everything is enhanced by the trauma."

One change she noticed after

just accept.

Along with the gift came responsibility. While some of the information she passes on to her clients is goods news: some is not. She deals with the bad news by putting herself in her client's place.

"If that was my kid that was lost, or my husband, I sure would want someone to help find them. The not knowing is worse than the knowing. So you say, 'OK God, give me the strength and the energy, and help me be the best I can be at this one moment in time.' "

One of the hardest things is telling people that their illness, or that of their child, is terminal. She tries to present it in the least hurtful way, speaking of the future as "a new beginning" or describing the beauty of the afterlife.

"I am just a messenger. It doesn't come from me, it comes through me," Greta said.

Greta has worked on hundreds of police cases. Newspaper clippings from Texas, New Mexico, Iowa, Chicago and Washington, D.C. attest to her success in locating missing persons and dead bodies.

Going to Greta

Hands tell st

By BETH GEHRT
of the Observer

I had always wanted to know wha would be like. But, like most people, I

What if she saw something terribl member of my family? What if she co thinking something disrespectful?

An amateur palm-reading friend h shortness of my lifeline — Wasn't I jus

Facing the well-known psychic, m rest.

She almost eased into things, spe things most of us are afraid to explore

The first thing she does with new a name, address, date of birth and ph

"Then, if they need anything or if the phone and call them and say, 'Thi am feeling might have happened or th she explained.

If clients have specific questions t that they write them down and bring t

Next, Greta does a hand analysis, using printers ink. One she writes on; ence. This we didn't do, because we v

The lines on the palms represent those caused by environment, she sai

"Every tiny line tells a story," Gre

The Diviner

In 1960, Delavan resident Greta Alexander survived a lighting strike and, soon after, discovered a blue-sensory gift (the uncommon "cop hunch") for solving crime cases across the country and becoming a nationally renowned medium. In fact, she has been rated as one of America's top-five psychics of all time, thanks to heavy media coverage—being the hair-domed guest on the bombastic TV show *Geraldo* in 1991 guaranteed her pop status.

Greta kept herself grounded, though, with her outreach programs to the poor such as the Stuff Store, Star of Hope Center, and Peoria's House of Hope. Unpredictably, she died in 1998 at age 66. (Above, courtesy of the Local History and Genealogy Collection, Peoria Public Library; below, courtesy of *Peoria Journal Star*.)

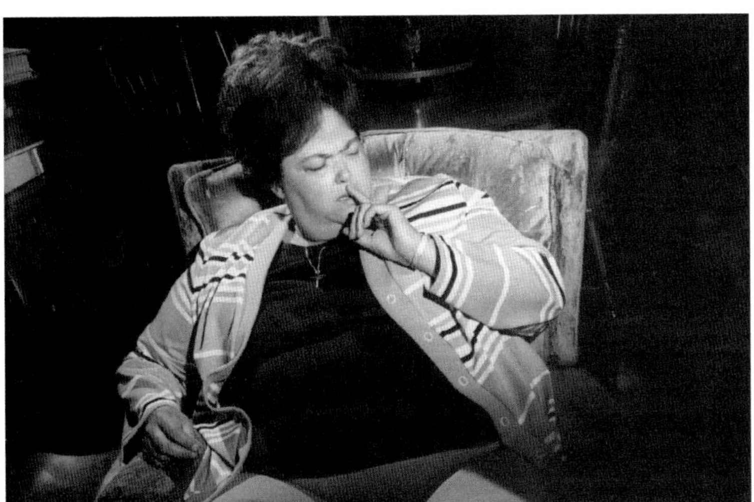

Of Cows, Cat, and a Quest

Glen Barton (born 1939) grew up on a farm in Alton, Missouri, a Grant Wood–esque *American Gothic* town, with a population of 576.

Growing up, he helped his grandfather, two older brothers, and older sister around the farm while his father worked at the post office. During the "o-dark-thirty" daily cow milkings, he daydreamed of owning a dairy with automatic milkers.

He graduated valedictorian of his high school class in 1942, which was something of a Barton birthright because his brothers and sister were also top of their classes. When he walked onto the University of Missouri campus, he saw a world of possibilities, including an introduction to Caterpillar tractors. Armed with a 1961 civil engineering degree, Barton joined Caterpillar in marketing and went on to a 43-year zipline to the top.

Geneva, Switzerland, in 1964 was the first of 14 career postings and a joyful one with the birth of his daughter; on a later assignment there, his son was born. While he would have ports-of-call throughout the world, he always brought Alton geniality along, which he coupled with a 1977 Stanford University executive management degree. He became a Cat vice president in 1987 and the first president of the newly acquired Solar Turbines, his most satisfying appointment outside of his last one as Caterpillar chief executive officer.

In 1991, he was part of a study group that led to a major company refit and stronger viability.

Barton became Caterpillar chairman and chief executive officer in 1999, a time of weakened product demand. He stanched company losses to become the first chairman without a losing quarter.

As the first chief executive officer of the 21st century, he was a visionary. He championed Six Sigma in 2001, which brought frontline employees into the operational quality assessment/improvement process. Cat now saves $400–600 million yearly.

Glen Barton retired in 2004 after five years at the helm. But his would be an activist, philanthropic retirement. He remains on a number of boards, and is one of the founders of PeoriaNext. He and his wife, Polly, helped expand the Peoria Zoo and are a heartfelt presence in Peoria, especially for children through education. Distressed by educational trends, Barton championed the Quest Academy, a charter school that doubles-down on math, science, and reading for its students.

It worked well for an Alton farm boy. Glen Barton is pictured on a rare rest. (Author's collection.)

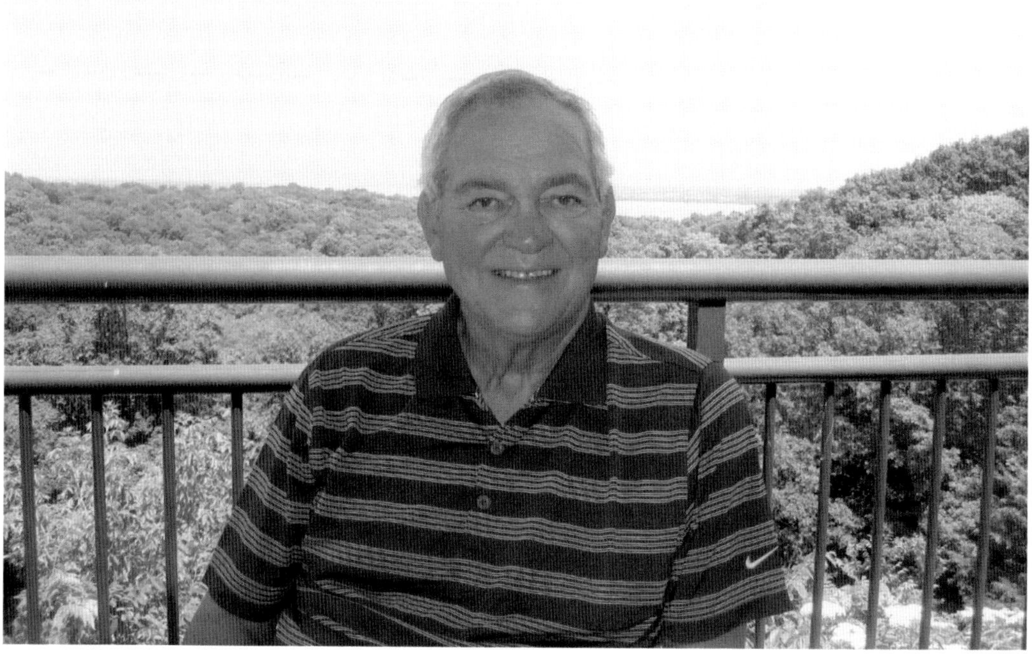

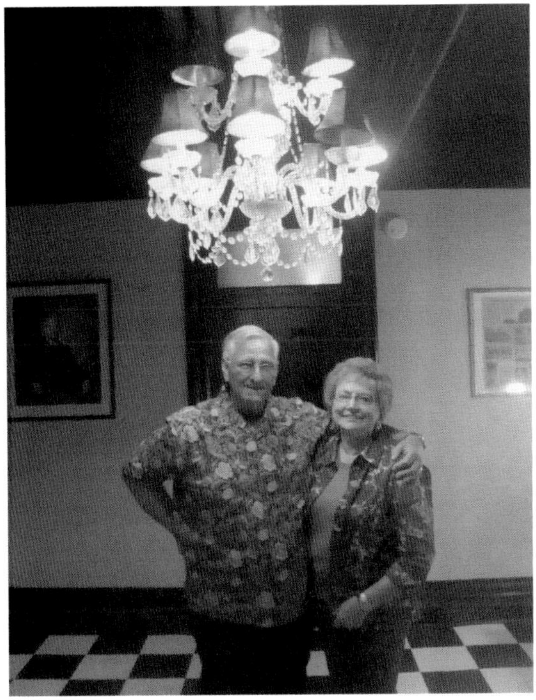

Preserving Historic Peoria

LaDonna and Charles Bobbitt came north from Memphis in 1981 to a Peoria on the edge with a town-stopping Caterpillar strike that would spiral the heretofore "recession-proof" city directly to depression and spur sayings such as "The last one out of Peoria, please turn off the lights." It was here that Kraft's Dairy Group, also known as Sealtest, opened a regional account office with Charles as its credit manager. Where Memphis native Charles saw Peoria as a mini-Memphis, Pryorsburg, Kentucky, native LaDonna felt it was a bit cold for a Southern girl.

Blessed with plenty of curiosity, a keen eye, Memphis State University sheepskins (with a 1967 bachelor's and a 1981 master's degree), and 10 years as president of the West Tennessee Historical Society, Charles dove into the history of—in his view—the world's most famous city of 100,000.

Peoria didn't disappoint.

After he met homegrown historians, and following his father's diktat not to bring home anything that eats, he devoured all the local writings and moved onto collecting Peoria postcards in 1985 as the fastest way to learn about the town. In time, his postcard collection led to two Arcadia Publishing books that he cowrote with LaDonna: *Peoria: A Postcard History* (1998) and *Peoria, Illinois Revisited: In Vintage Postcards* (2000).

Charles didn't leave town when Kraft closed its Peoria office; instead, he became the manager of nearby Credit Bureau of Bloomington Inc., and continued his journey into Peoria history, along with a 1987 move into the historic West Bluff. In 1988, he became chairman of the Peoria Historical Society Preservation Board, which was a position he held until 1996. He then became a member of the Peoria Zoning Board of Appeals from 1997 to 2001.

The Bobbitts in 1991 bought their first historic apartments to protect West Bluff history. Over the years, the couple would own 40 historic dwellings (collectively, the Bobbitt Historic Quarters), including, in 1994, the one-time palace of J.B. Greenhut, the king of Peoria's whisky barons.

In kinship with Peoria's storied past, LaDonna and Charles Bobbitt seek to preserve its physical history brick by brick.

LaDonna and Charles Bobbitt are shown in the foyer of the Presidential Suite of the Greenhut Mansion, where President McKinley once stayed in 1899. (Author's collection.)

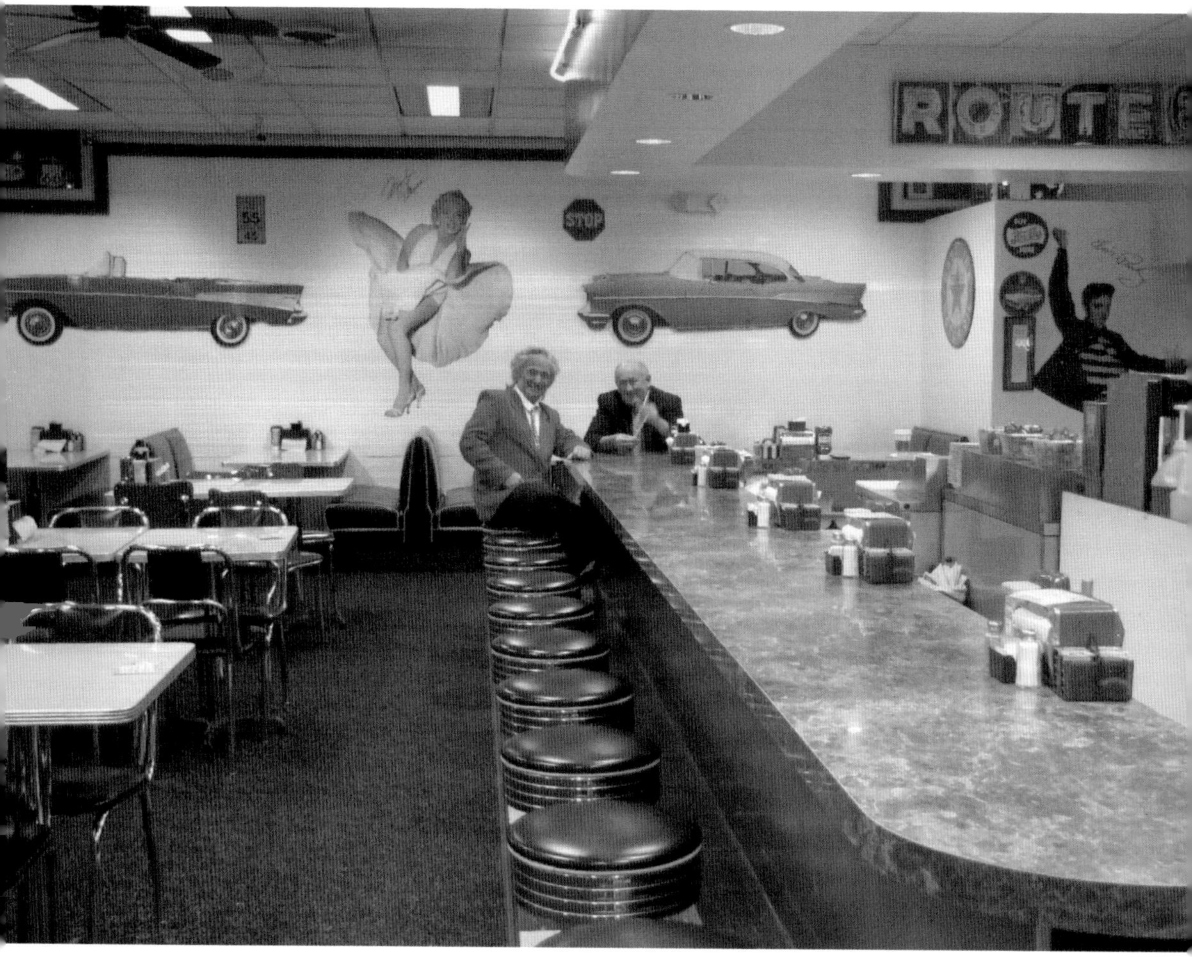

River City's Rooster of Rock (ABOVE AND OPPOSITE PAGE)
As Steve Bobbitt labored toward the end of his 30 years at Caterpillar, a hair stylist suggested a mane change and, using bleach and mousse, she fashioned him into a flaxen-haired, rooster-combed ringer for rock superstar Rod Stewart. Now, he's had gigs throughout the country.

Bobbitt may have served as Stewart's muse, albeit an uncredited one, when in 2001 the superstar faced the greatest crisis of his career—throat cancer. In his 2012 *Rod: The Autobiography*, Stewart said he would get into lawn care if he could not sing again, something Bobbitt has done for years.

Stewart paid the uber-compliment to Bobbitt when the two met, saying, "It's as if I'm looking at myself in the mirror." And the mirror looked back.

"Do ya think I'm raspy?" Steve Bobbitt is the Hoarse Rasperer. Above, at the end of the counter at the Illinois Valley Diner of Dreams are "Rod Stewart," also known as Steve Bobbitt, and "Phil Collins," also known as Michael Murphy. (Above, courtesy of Karen Carpenter; opposite, photograph by Jeff McSweeney.)

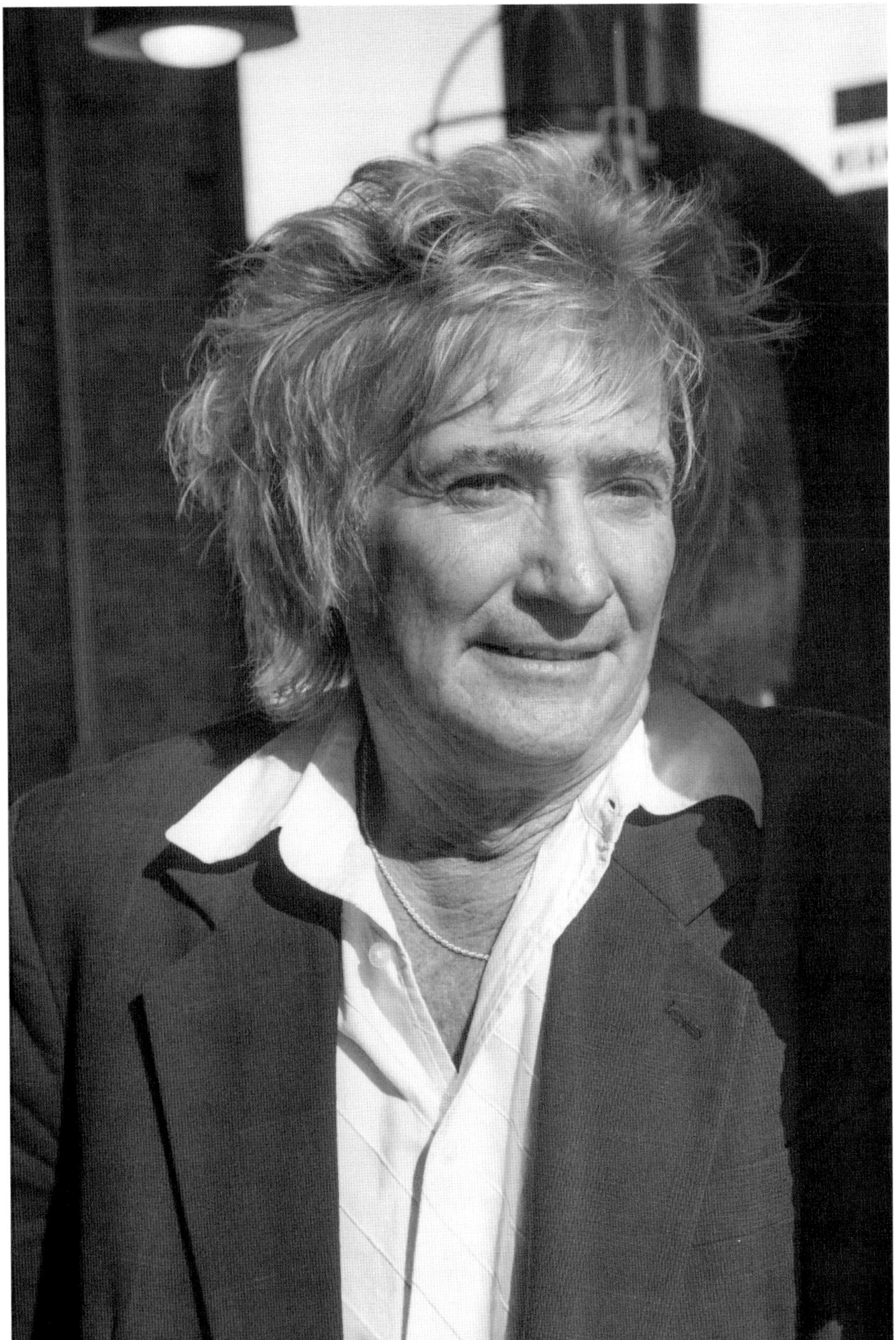

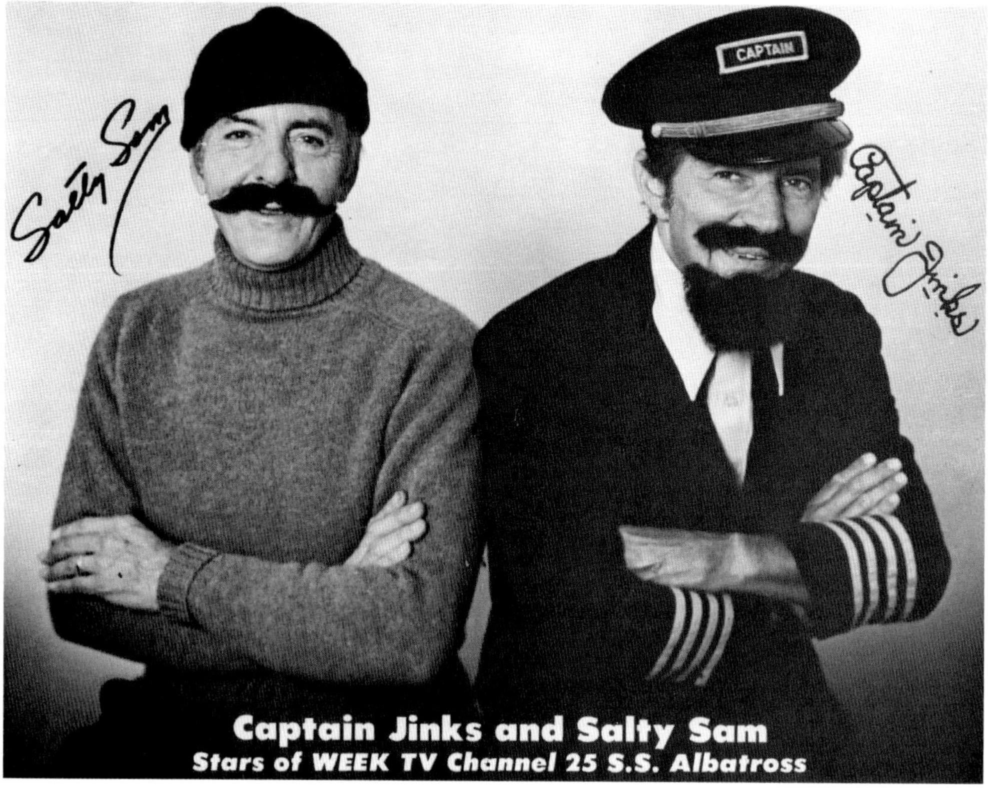

Captain Jinks and Salty Sam: TV Masters of Children's High Sees

One came from Chicago, and the other came from Peoria. They met in the middle—on Upper Peoria Lake aboard the S.S. *Albatross*. They plundered childish laughs throughout central Illinois in the afternoons from 1956 to 1972, and after a six-year beaching of the *Albatross*, from 1978 to 1981. Stan "Captain Jinks" Lonergan was a veteran of Chicago radio (including a 1940s stint at WGN—the same time as Peorian Jack Brickhouse) when he moved on to Peoria's WEEK in 1955. In 1957, a year after the *Captain Jinks* show's debut, Lonergan replaced Hal Searles as the captain and made it the role of his lifetime. Though the born wit ably steered the show, it took adding Peorian George "Salty Sam" Baseleon in 1960 to add Category 5 puff to the sails of the *Albatross*. Baseleon, WEEK's weekend weatherman, had been with the station since its 1947 kickoff. The pair worked without a script, relying on Lonergan's campy improv and Baseleon's catchy chuckles. Soon, college students joined their grade-school brethren in front of the tube.

At the show's 1966 peak—when the *Albatross* jumped the carp—*Captain Jinks* commanded a Ruthian 76-percent viewer share in its time slot.

After the show ended, the stars would continue personal appearances at local hospitals and other children events. "Jinks" Lonergan also kept busy with voice-overs and working as a security guard at Jumer's Castle Lodge, while "Salty Sam" Baseleon became an assistant manager at the downtown Heritage House restaurant.

Neither one ever shooed away an autograph-seeker.

Salty was the first to die, the day after Christmas 1985. Buried without a marker at Springdale Cemetery, Baseleon's grave seemed destined for anonymity until fans, in 2009, placed an icon-befitting headstone.

The memorial also honored Lonergan, who had died in October 1989. Flying his plane, TV weatherman Bill Houlihan had previously scattered the captain's ashes over Upper Peoria Lake's short-fetched waves. (Courtesy of WEEK.)

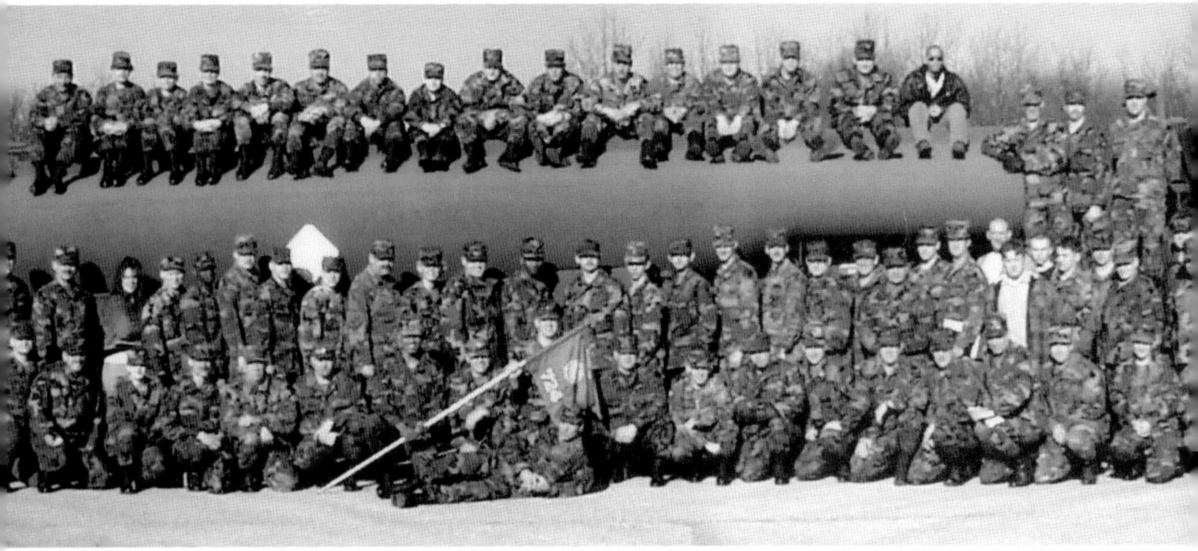

The Mother of All Milk Runs—The 724th Transportation Company
On April 9, 2004, a trinity of trouble was in the Iraqi air: it was Good Friday, the Fall of Baghdad's one-year anniversary, and a Muslim holy day. For insurgents, it meant itchy gnashing of teeth. For Peoria's 724th Transportation Company, it meant running security for a fuel haul from its Balad base to Baghdad, typically a nerve-grinding 90-minute trip along "Route Sword."

This would not be a typical mission.

Near Abu Ghraib, five miles from the finish, the landscape resembled a Middle East ghost town. Then hell in full monty erupted—the largest ambush of Operation Iraqi Freedom. Only personal bravery and skill prevented the overrun of the convoy. Still, three soldiers of the 724th and six civilian drivers died. (Above, courtesy of the 724th, below, courtesy of the Department of Defense.)

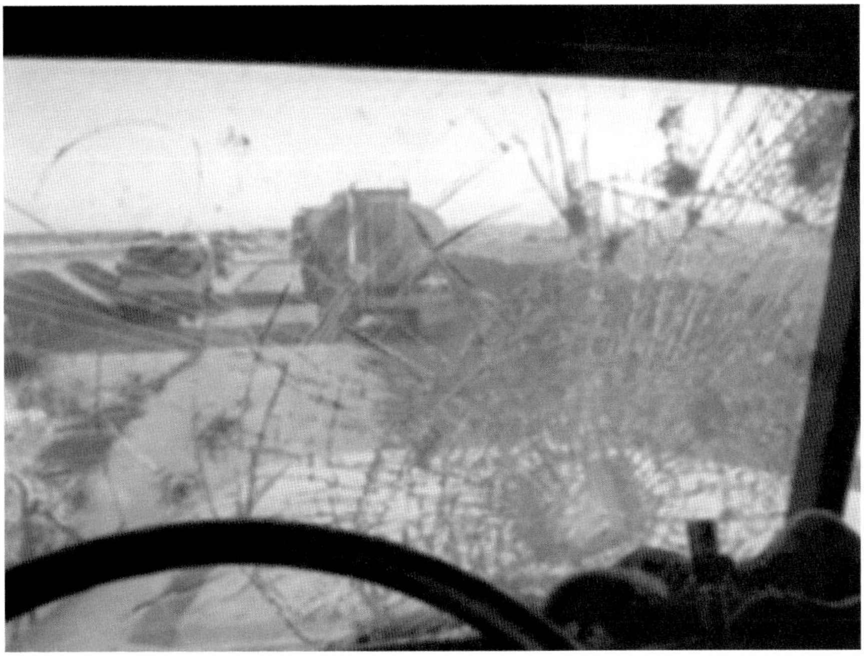

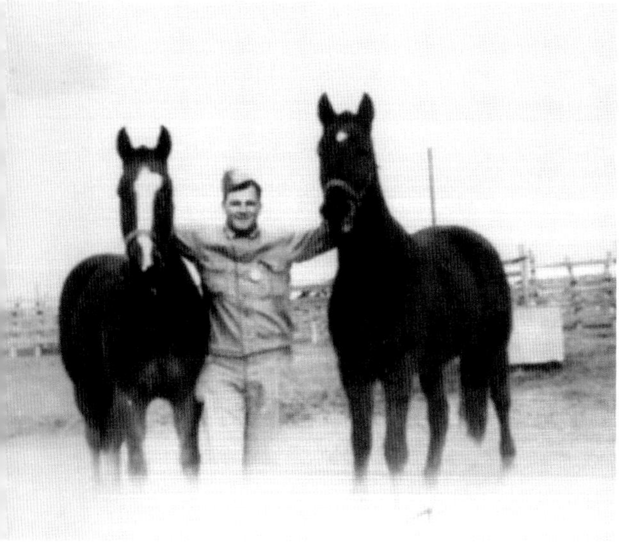

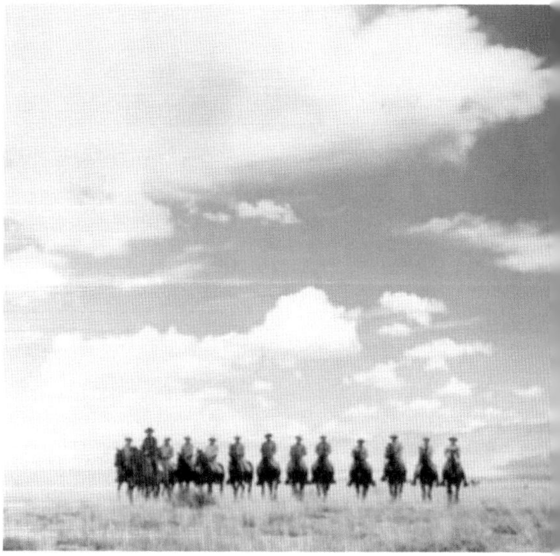

Marvin and the Mushroom

Marvin R. Davis Sr. (1922–2009) grew up in Chestnut, Illinois. In 1942, he joined the Army's Military Police. When there was a call for a special mounted police unit, Davis, who had never been on a horse, thought "it sounded good."

He rode to Los Alamos with the first MP Detachment Mounted (the Army's last horse cavalry), and there, in the predawn of July 16, 1945, he, ten miles away and wearing a cardboard facemask held on by welding glasses, was one of the first 260 to see the future: a fire-crazed atomic mushroom cloud.

Davis instantly became a charter member of a new military breed, the atomic soldier, along with the rest of the "Horsemen of the Atomic Mesa."

He died in October 2009 with the planet still spinning. (Both above, courtesy of the Atomic Heritage Foundation; below, courtesy of Gutenberg organization.)

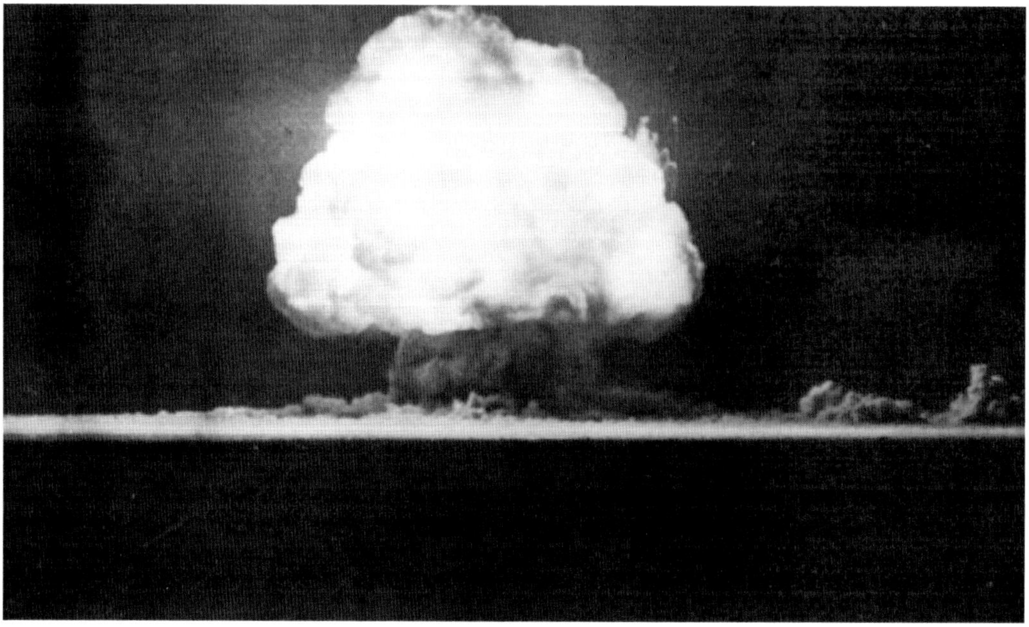

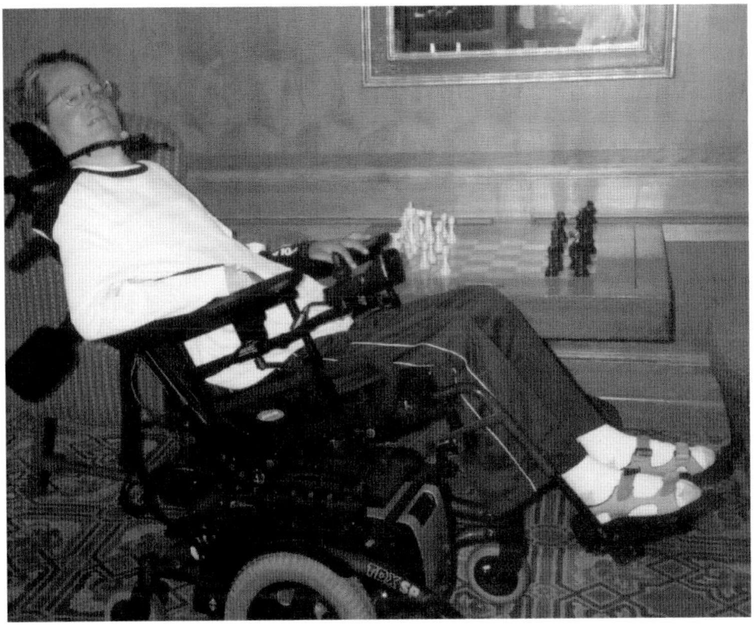

A Free Fall to Forever

Late at night on June 9, 1986, recent Bergan High graduate Kevin Harmon and five buddies went to Lakeview Park's Rainbow Bend water slide. With his turn, Kevin's free fall of a few seconds would paralyze him from the neck down. Life after the fall features his father's love. Kevin's father, attorney Ed Harmon, retired and immediately became Kevin's nurturer.

By 2015, with his father's warm and continuous care of 29 years (except for a couple of days), Kevin readied his second novel for publication. His first, *The Archangel Response*, published in 2012, was an epic achievement in determination, considering his use of a poky voice-activated program to write the 500-page book, with help from his guardian angel named Dad. (Both, courtesy of Kevin Harmon.)

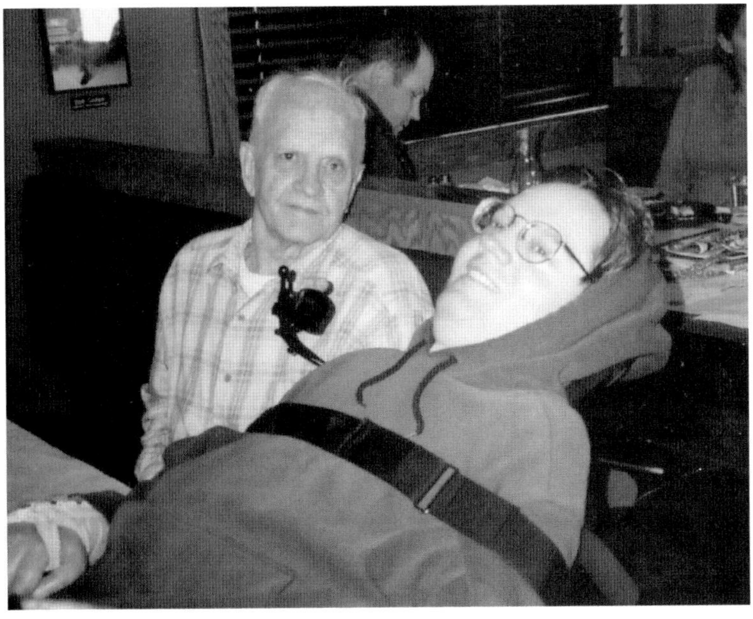

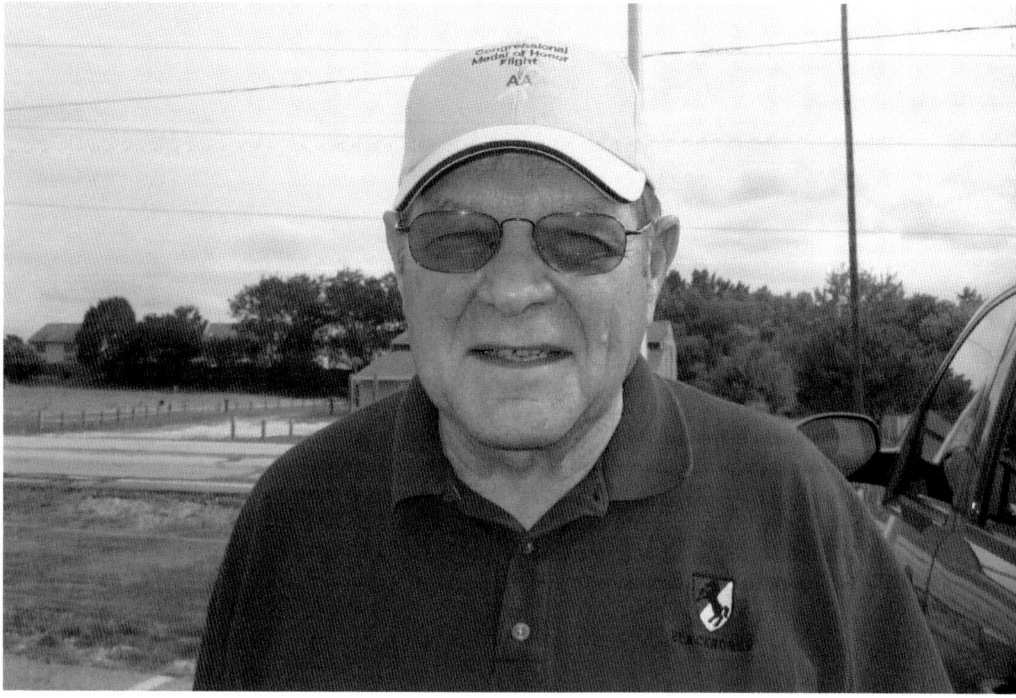

The Tao of a Peoria Brave (ABOVE AND OPPOSITE PAGE)
The parents of Harold A. "Hal" Fritz (born February 1944) met in pre–World War II Chicago, riding their own way—she on an Indian motorcycle, while he favored a Harley. From them, Hal inherited an independent, freedom-loving streak that would crack the throttle in Vietnam.

It was in February 1968 when Second Lieutenant Fritz deplaned at South Vietnam to coiling black smoke in the distance: Welcome to the Nam.

Assigned to the Army's frontline 11th Armored Cavalry Regiment (The Blackhorse), tank platoon commander Fritz showed breathtaking pluck in combat, especially on May 18, 1968, and January 11, 1969. He received, for those two firefights alone, two Purple Hearts; the Silver Star, the Army's third-highest medal for valor; and the Medal of Honor.

In the May 1968 Silver Star action, Fritz led his tank platoon in bunker-busting assaults against an entrenched North Vietnamese Army (NVA) battalion. He fought in full view of enemy crosshairs until wounded.

By 1969, First Lieutenant Fritz had seen it all until January 11. He commanded a seven-vehicle recon column on a sweep of Highway 13, "Thunder Road," the main US supply route on the western edge of South Vietnam. Ambushes were commonplace since the enemy could scurry back to Cambodia, which was off limits to the United States. An overwhelming, heavily armed NVA company jumped the patrol in a hellish crossfire, setting the entire convoy ablaze. Wounded, Fritz directed the column's defenses and helped his injured men while fully exposed to NVA raking gunfire. With only five of his men still standing, he led a startling charge against the enemy that prevented an overrun, proving what Harper Lee wrote in *To Kill a Mockingbird*—that real courage comes from knowing you're licked before you begin but you begin anyway.

He received the nation's highest honor in March 1971.

Lieutenant Colonel Fritz retired in 1993 after 27 years of service and moved with his wife, Mary, to Peoria. He has worked selflessly on behalf of all military veterans, and has served as president of the Congressional Medal of Honor Society, whose members are living messengers about the price of freedom.

He keeps nearby a bullet-bashed, lifesaving cigarette lighter that was in his uniform pocket that January day in 1969—a reminder to fully live each day. (Author's collection.)

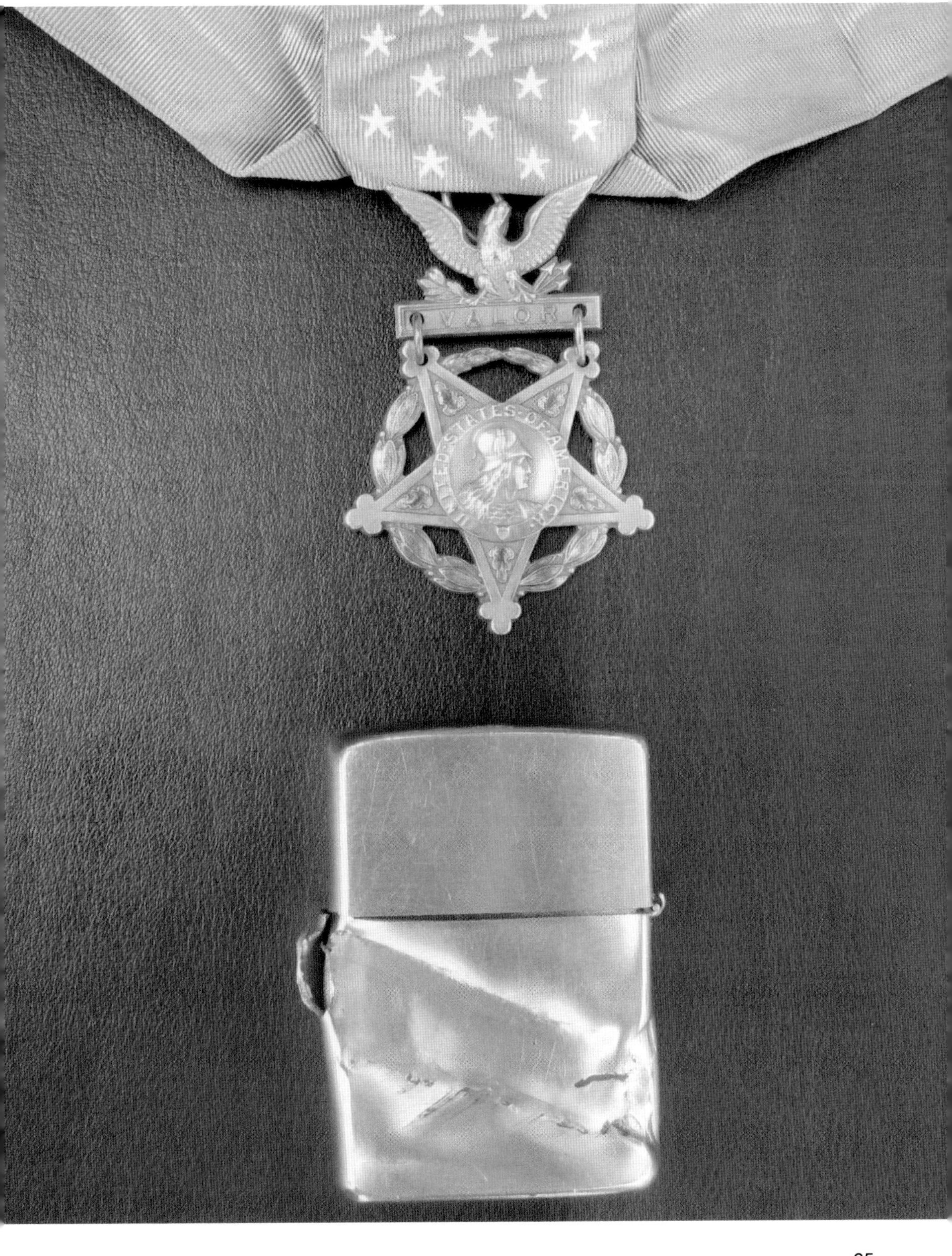
VALOR
UNITED STATES OF AMERICA

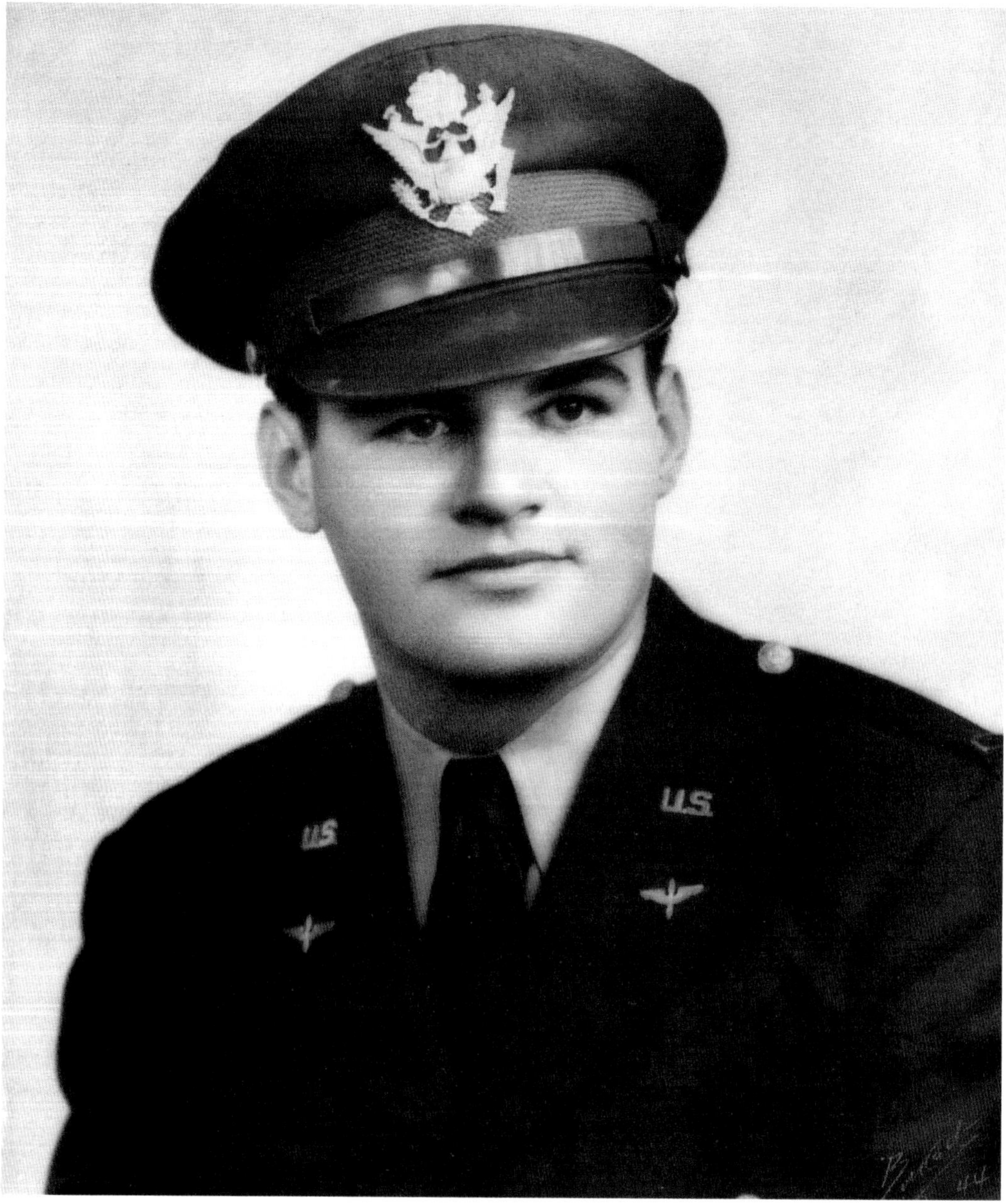

Shakey's Steady Hand

Eugene Herwig had one last bucket-list item left, which was to make it to age 100. In January 2015, he fell four days short. Yet, the 1932 Peoria High graduate achieved a lot, including working as a supply officer, with a "Sergeant Bilko" horse-trading flair, in World War II; becoming National Cash Register's youngest branch manager; designing the prototype pizza parlor layout for the international Shakey's chain; displaying his corporate acumen by being Shakey's top consultant and selling one third of the chain's 300 franchises while owning 15 himself, including Peoria's; and, at 95 years old, proving the young have something to say by writing *Sleeping in the Park*, a book of vignettes of people who had lost it all during the Depression but had the whip to come back. Lt. Gene Herweg is pictured around 1943. (Courtesy of Gene Herweg.)

The Music Ma'am

Robin (Firth) Hunt, the youngest of four children of Robert and Joyce Firth, grew up a tapper (age six) and an actor (high school) in her native Moline, Illinois, and the combo would lead to a curtain-raising life in Peoria.

First though, she turned Blue and Orange, earning both her bachelor's (1987) and master's (1989) degrees in elementary education from the University of Illinois at Champagne-Urbana; she kept up her acting chops with several college roles. In 1987, she married fellow Illini David Hunt, a law student. Two years later, kitted with their graduate degrees, they headed to Peoria, where he would practice law and she would forge her dream career in the performing arts.

The midsized-town was perfect: a quick skip to either hometown Moline or the Big U (Oskee-Wow-Wow!) and a downstate marquee with three community theaters.

She began by teaching math at Pekin's Broadmoor Junior High while staying close to StageWorld as a theatergoer.

Her watershed year was 1991, when a Jazzercise franchise came to town and she joined as a peppy-footed student, then as an instructor, and later as an owner of five franchises. The kick of helping others reach their fitness goals stirred feelings she had with acting, drawing the audience into the play. It led to Hunt's return to the stage after the birth of her two sons Wesley (1994) and Alexander (1995).

The year 2002 marked her River City stage debut. Soon, she became a lively one-person ensemble as an actor (favorite role—"Val" in *A Chorus Line*), a director, and a choreographer. Her ability to inspire hundreds of actors has also extended homeward: her husband and sons have all shared the footlights with her.

In addition to juggling up to three plays at a time, Robin keeps her feet a-tapping, teaching seven Jazzercise classes a week.

When she is not keeping play in Peoria, she devotes her spare time to family, church, and friends. And that is no act. (Courtesy of Robin Hunt.)

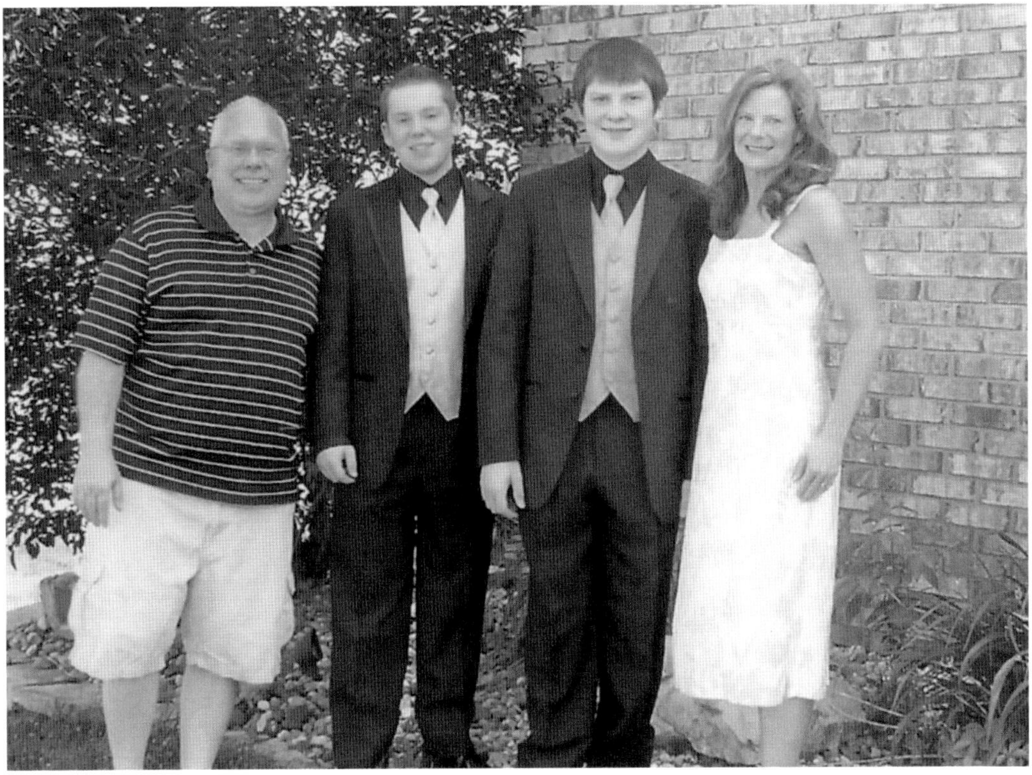

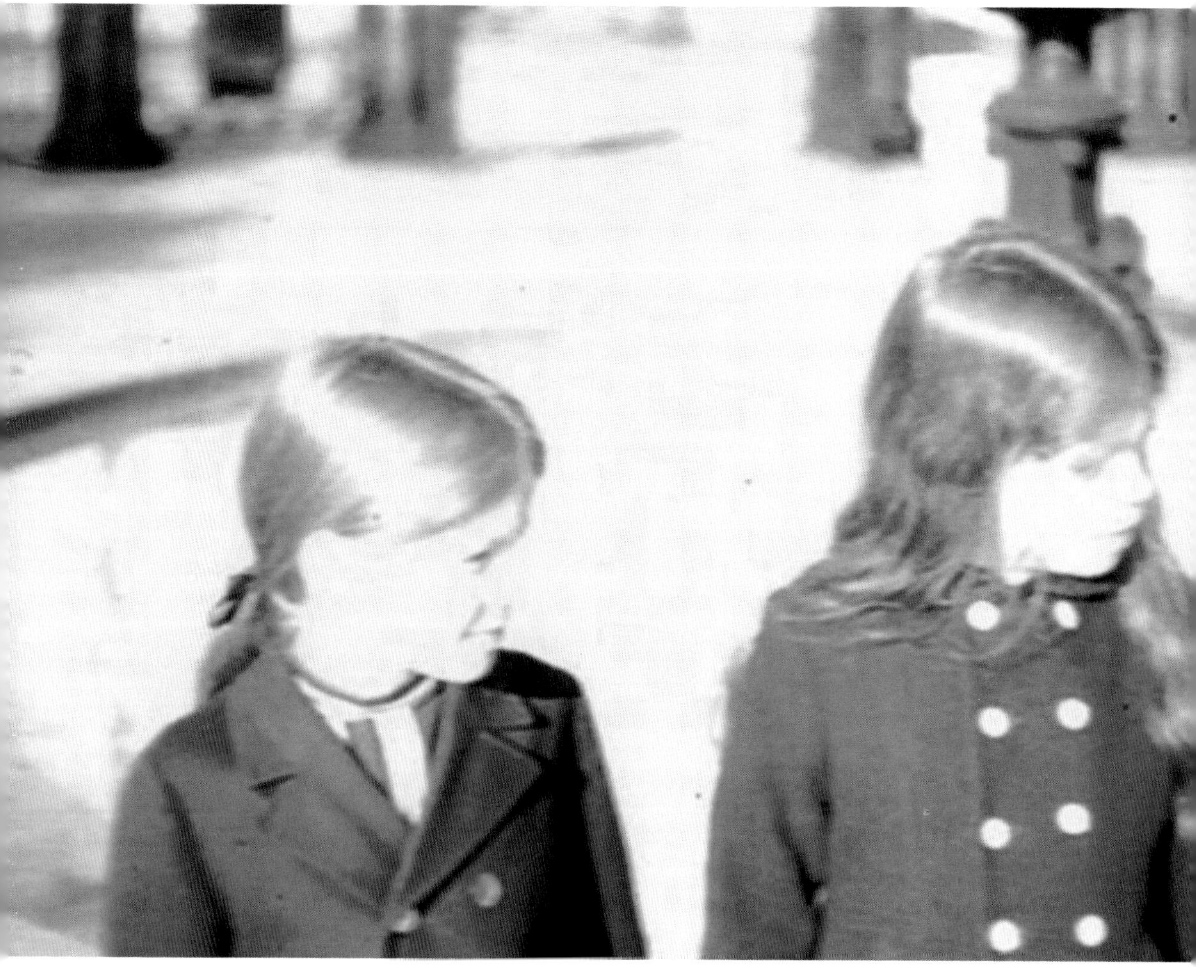

Moonlit Moss
Sometimes, sisters can be more than best friends—they can be collaborators. For writer Kate and artist Sarah Klise, their talents have led to an award-winning run of children's books, beginning with *Regarding the Fountain* in 1998. Within their house on Moss Avenue, their parents, Marjorie and Thomas, championed creativity. After Kate, an English major, and Sarah, a history major, graduated from Marquette University, their paths diverged. Or so they thought. Sarah found her place as an art teacher in Berkeley, California, while Kate wrote for *People* magazine from 1993 to 2008, enjoying the quiet wilds of home in the Missouri Ozarks.

Yet, a pull of memories drew them back to a time in River City when children could play carefree in the moonlight. And imaginings loomed in the shadows. Kate (left) and Sara are pictured here around 1973. (Photograph by Thomas Klise; courtesy of Kate Klise.)

Ragtime

The Old World of Greek immigrants Emanuel and Katina Manias became New World with the birth of their son George in 1931 Peoria. And despite the cultural differences—language, for one—George's parents believed that their steeped traditions of hard work, discipline, modesty, and thrift would give their newborn a fighting chance in America.

In 1935, to aid his ailing grandfather, the family returned to ancestral Crete. The Nazis invaded the island in May 1941 and dragged Emanuel Manias off to a concentration camp, where he remained a prisoner of war until 1945. After 10 years, the near-penniless Manias family came back to Peoria for another go. Helping with the family effort, the 14-year-old, without much of a lick of English, apprenticed as a downtown shoeshiner. The dint of sweat paid off—on December 6, 1946, at age 15, he opened his own one-chair shop on Jefferson Street.

He's been solo ever since, plying polish (kneaded by hand into the leather to ensure a deep rub) to over a million pairs of shoes in 67 years. And it never mattered whose feet were in those shoes: presidents, senators, tycoons, entertainers, sport legends, or ordinary folks. They all received pleasant patter and a sharp shine industriously applied without the haughty, bug zapper–sounding rag snap sendoff.

For Manias, one must be humble.

Yet, fanfare has dogged him precisely for his virtues. National, state, and local governments have proclaimed him their poster child for the American dream. So has the national media. One tribute, though, touched home on June 12, 2012, when His Grace Bishop Demetrios of Mokissos, the head of the Greek Orthodox Metropolis of Chicago, bestowed the rarified Medal of St. Paul, the highest honor for a layperson, on Manias. Bishop Demetrios praised Manias for a lifelong heeding to St. Paul's call for humility in the service of the public.

After the cameras and hubbub had cleared, Manias, in the bootblack's traditional white shirt and bow tie, bent over his chair to put another "best-shine ever" on a pair of scruffies, making sure his medal didn't get in the way.

It is ragtime in Peoria. (Courtesy of Karen Camper.)

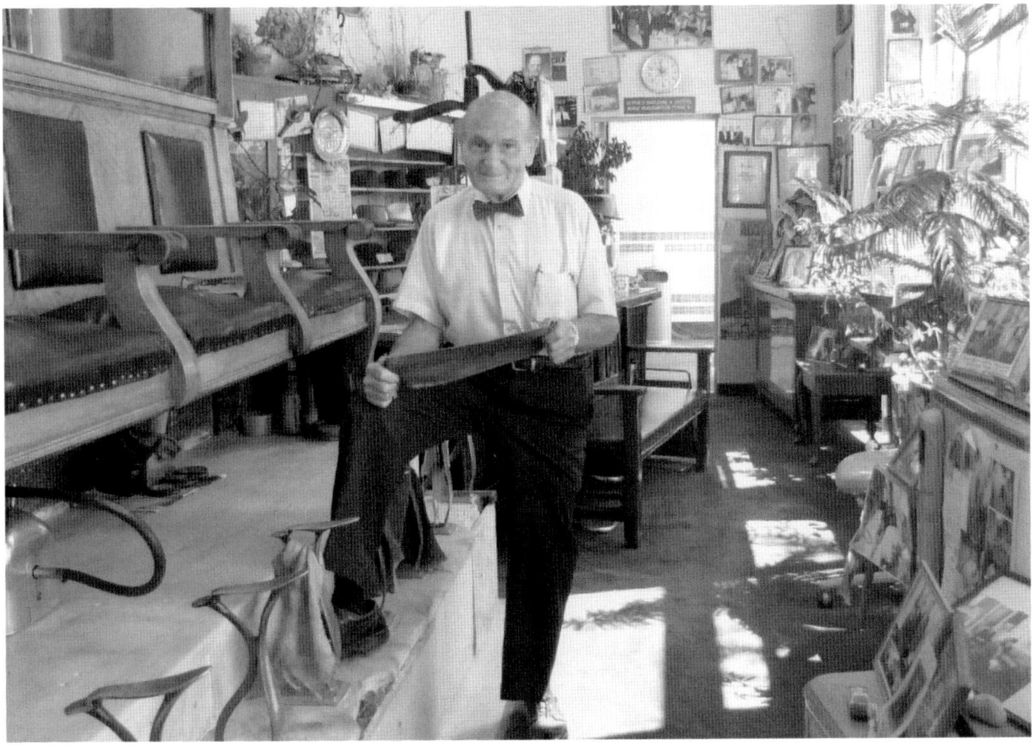

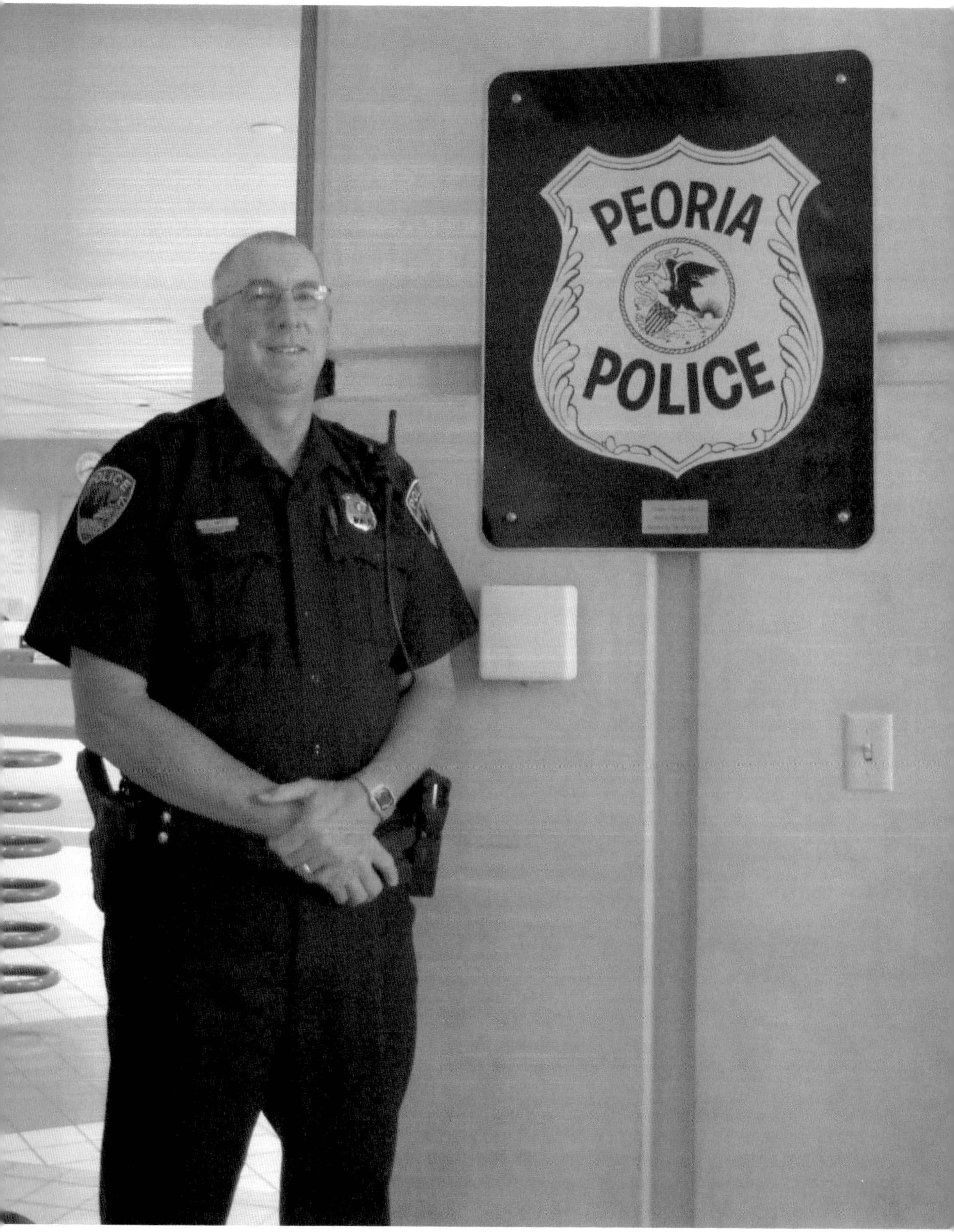
PEORIA
POLICE

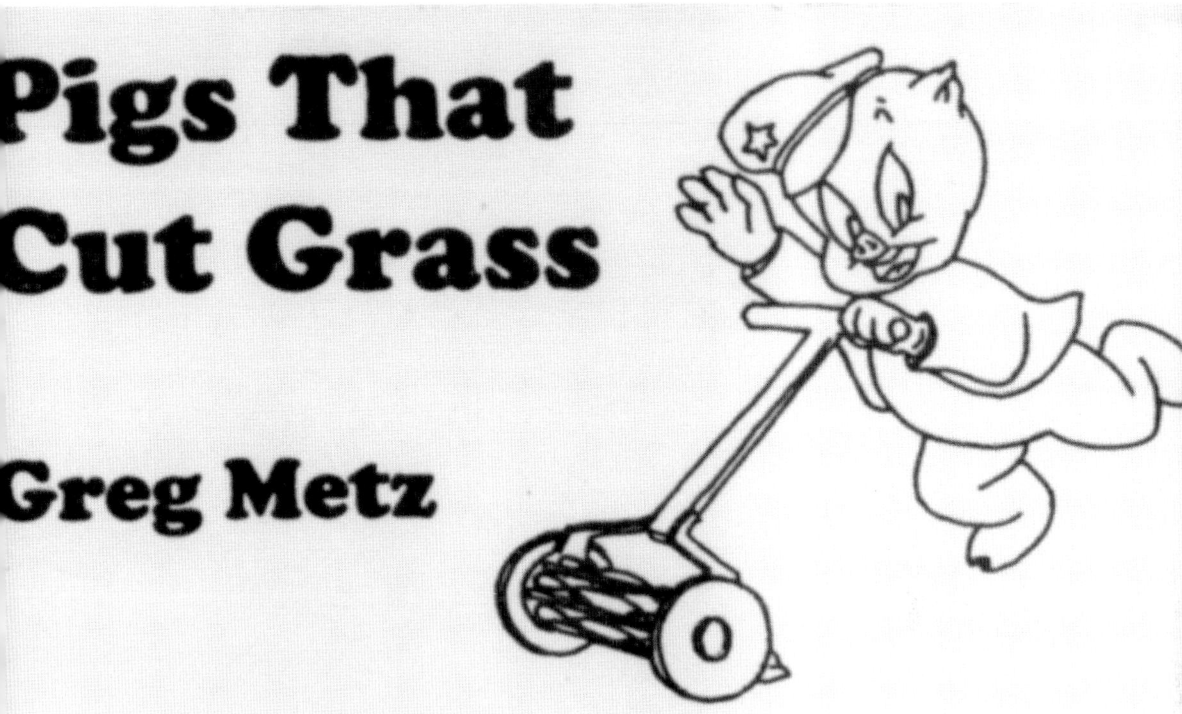

Bagging a Bagman (ABOVE AND OPPOSITE PAGE)
Two days after September 11, 2001, Peoria police officer Greg Metz was on patrol on Sterling Avenue south of the mall when he saw a car with a youngster standing up in the backseat. After a 10-mile-per-hour chase, the child-safety issue would become a national alarm. The driver, Ali Saleh Kahlah al-Marri volunteered he was a Bradley graduate student from Qatar. A background check revealed a 10-year-old outstanding warrant for driving under the influence; to post the $300 bond, they went to the East Peoria Super-8 motel where, in a scene out of *The Godfather*, al-Marri unzipped a suitcase bursting with hundred-dollar bills and paid the bond.

That night, Metz, uneasy about al-Marri, called the FBI, which took over. The officer had uncovered a Midwest al-Qaeda money-trafficking cell.

On April 30, 2009, al-Marri copped to the Heartland fence job.

On the opposite page, he is pictured retiring from the Peoria Police Department in 2015; above is the business card for his retirement career, as he "rides a mower into the sunset." (Opposite, courtesy of Karen Camper; above, courtesy of Greg Metz.)

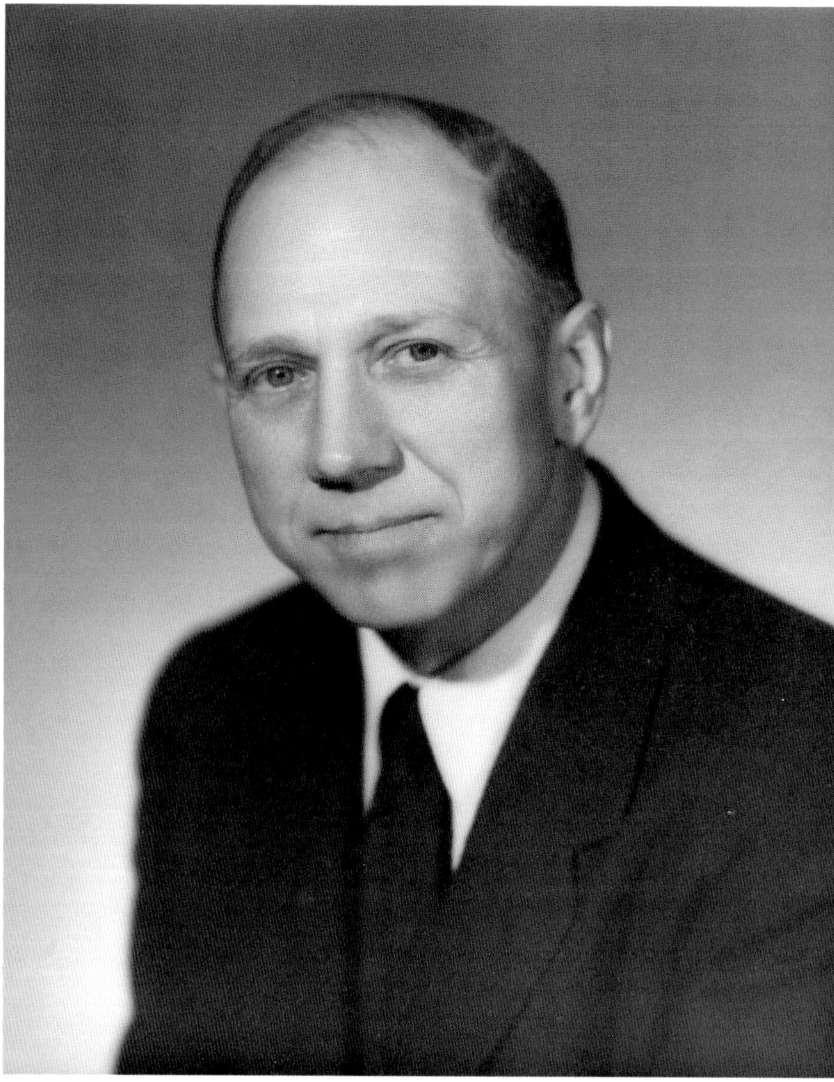

The Master of WEEK Air

WEEK-TV was the House that Fred Built.

Frederick C. Mueller Jr. (1908–1984), whose investment group had purchased WEEK radio in 1947 with him at the tiller, convinced the parent company, West Central Broadcasting, that Peoria needed an air change—from radio to the television airwaves. His pioneering vision gave birth to NBC-affiliate WEEK-TV channel 43 on February 1, 1953, the first station in west central Illinois, an NBC affiliate that also broadcast CBS and DuMont network programs. In 1964, WEEK became channel 25.

The St. Louis native and 1930 graduate of the famed University of Missouri School of Journalism led WEEK-TV in its first 20 years (1953–1973) to unequaled Yankee-esque supremacy in regional ratings and revenues, thanks to his hallmark business savvy and an eye for spotting talent. He discovered, among many others, Chick Hearn, the future hall of fame sportscaster of the Los Angeles Lakers.

When Mueller retired, WEEK reigned as the Hulk of central Illinois TV.

A vibrant hearth was the heart of his success, where his spirited wife, Sara (Love), held forth with their two sons, David (a future Peoria attorney) and Rob (a video production professional).

Peoria TV pioneer Fred Mueller is pictured here around 1960. (Courtesy of Rob Mueller.)

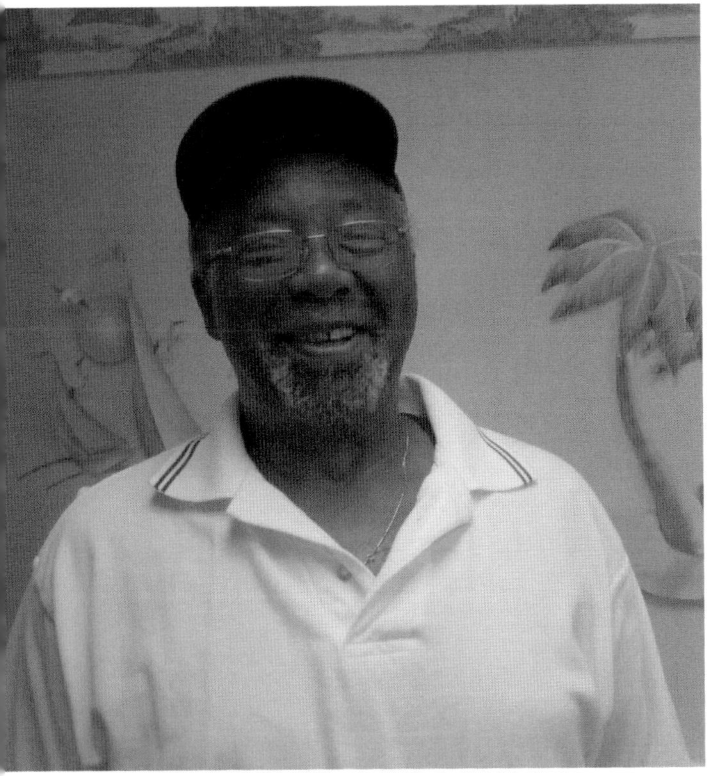

Lean on Me

Bill Noel may not be a household name, but he embodies the resiliency of the human spirit. Since the dawn of the 21st century, he has shouldered the burdens of his many friends and large family. He can count on one hand the number of weeks when he has not had to trek to a hospital or a funeral home. Sustained by unflinching faith and the love of his wife, Shirley, Noel has been the go-to for many in River City, including the clergy who rely on the comfort of his soft-spoken bearing. Long retired from Caterpillar, he is a veteran himself of severe aches that he puts on the back burner so he can help others.

Except for the occasional refuge of an after-hours dental office where he goes for the quieting of his soul, he is Peoria's "Rock." (Both, author's collection.)

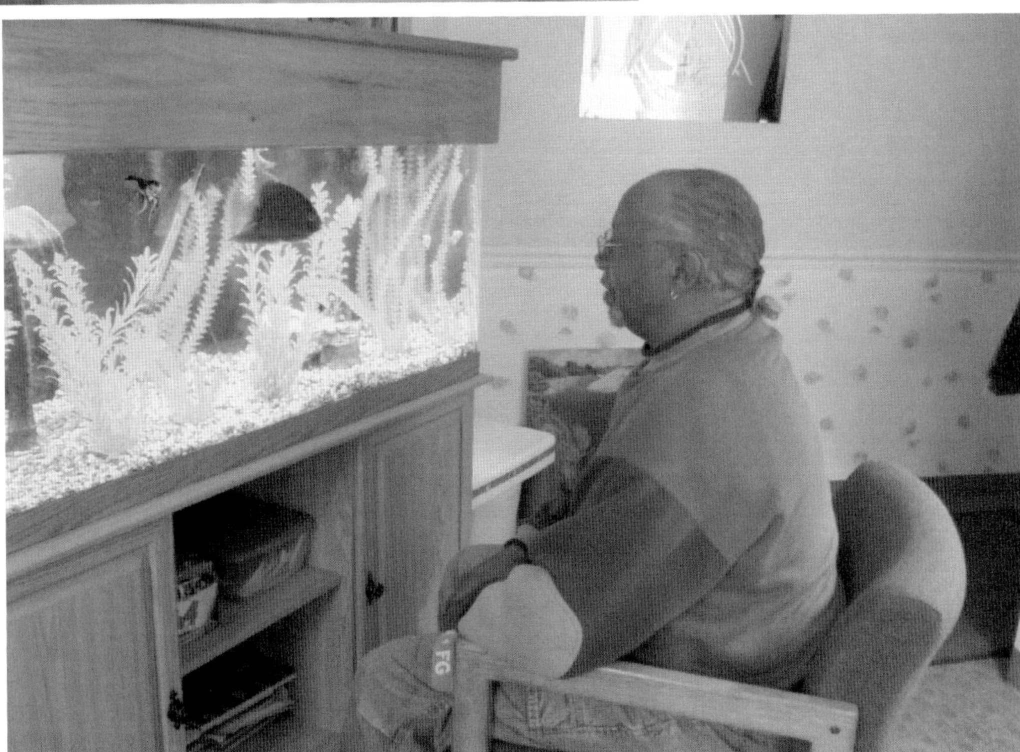

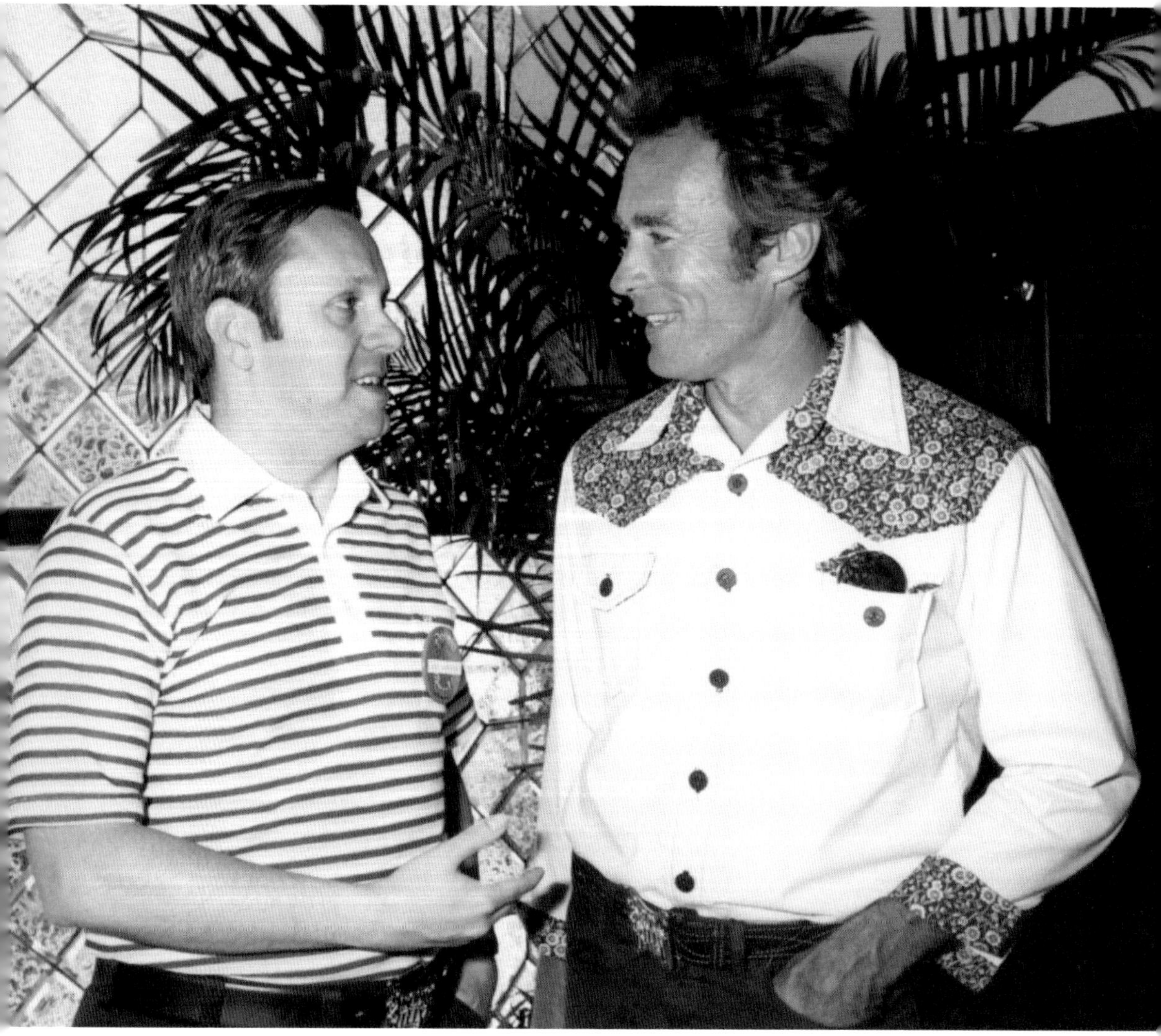

Weather's Iron Horse (ABOVE AND OPPOSITE PAGE)

For the last 40 out of his 51 years in Peoria broadcasting, Lee Ranson was the easy warm front in television weather; his "Uncle Lee" persona was a hit. But in his first gig with WIRL-AM radio in 1960, he was "Leapin' Lee," who put the needle to Top 40 records with the best market share in Illinois. In 1965, Leapin' jumped to country WXCL, where he would become program/music director. He ventured into television in 1971 as Channel 19's weekend weatherman. His radio days were in the rearview mirror by 1981, when he became a full-time weatherman. Following the 1994 death of forecaster Bill Houlihan, Lee moved to WEEK TV-25, and hung up his maps in November 2011. With his forecast of sunny days and fair winds, he continues his lifelong commitment to community causes. Pictured above are Leapin' and Clint "No-Name" Eastwood. On the opposite page, Conrad Twitty makes a house call to be interviewed by Ranson in 1963. (Both, courtesy of Lee Ranson.)

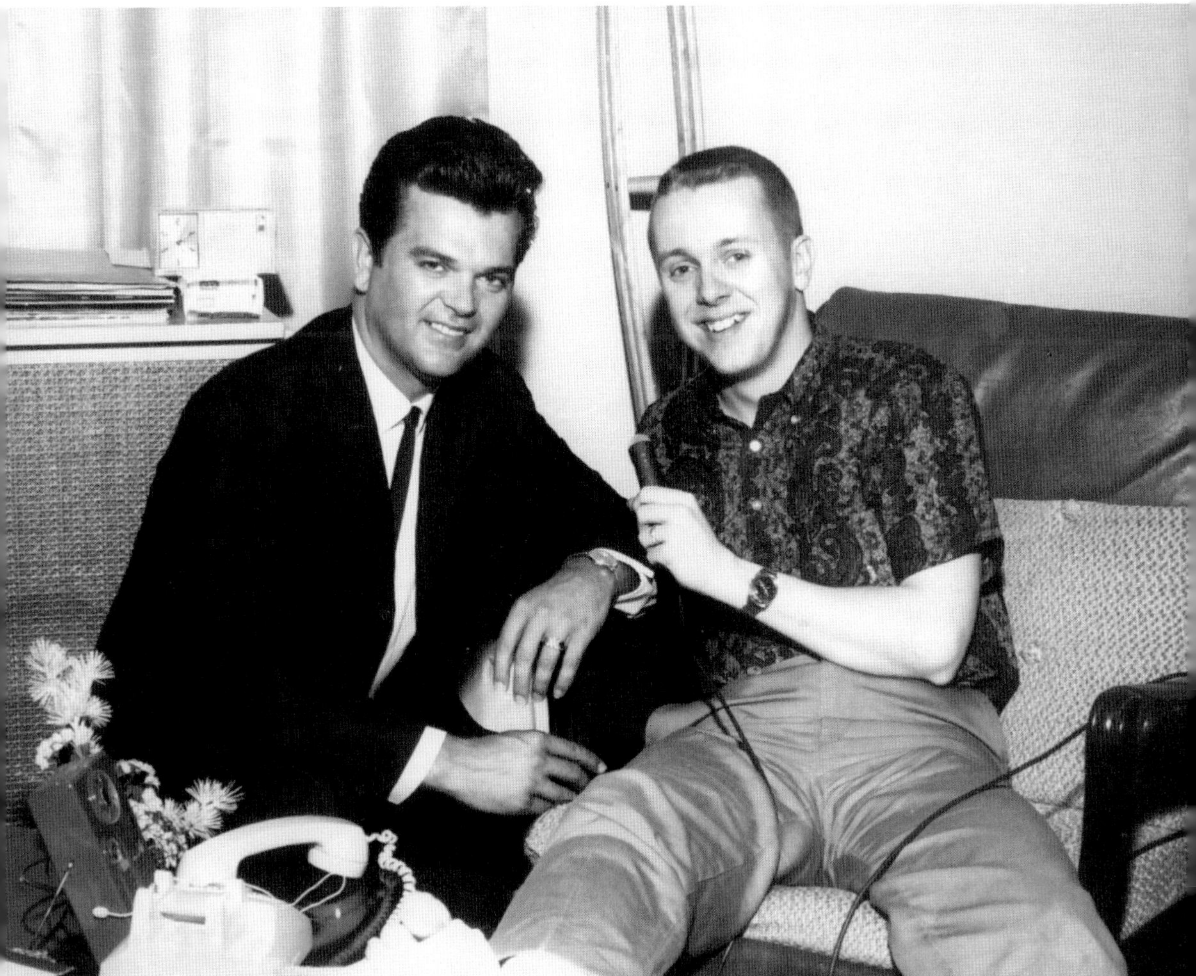

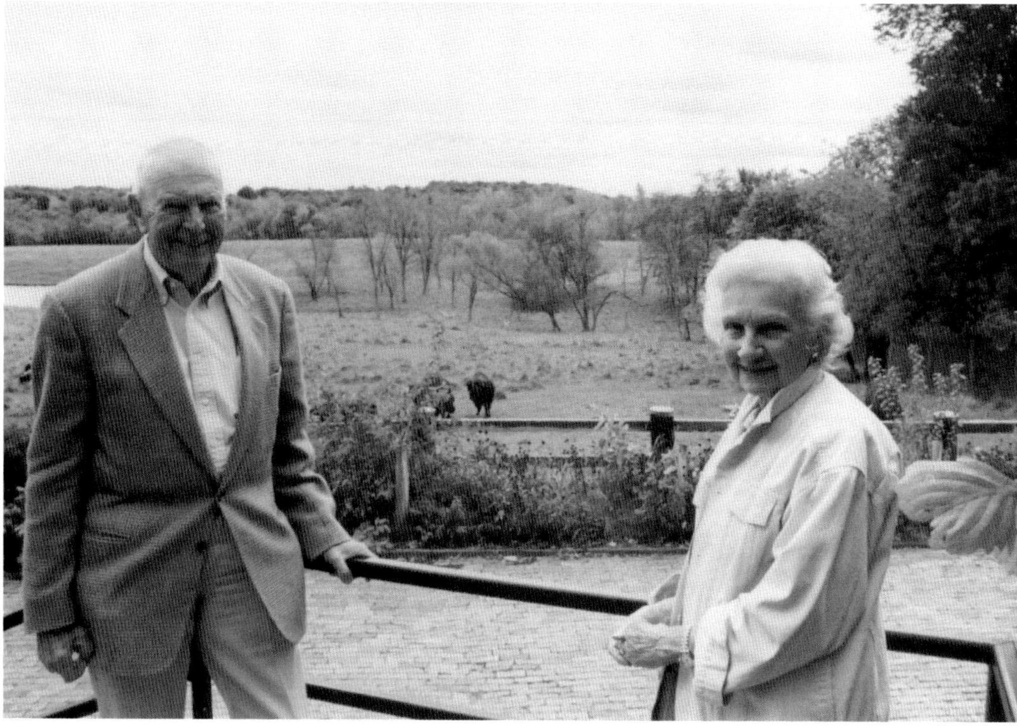

Peoria's Land Donor

Bill Rutherford (1914–2006) was a Peorian with vista vision—land and sky. Educated in town at Peoria High and Bradley, he graduated from the University of Chicago Law School in 1937 before continuing with postgraduate studies in taxation at Columbia University. In September 1937, he married his soul mate, Hazel Sommer, who would also roll up her sleeves next to him throughout their marriage.

During World War II, he served as a consultant to the secretary of war's Army-Navy Munitions Board in 1942 before he became a Navy flight instructor in 1943. He finished the war as a pilot for United Airlines, 1944–1946.

Landing back home, he established a law practice and dedicated his life to the twin tenets of his core: service to mankind and enviro-vigilance. He plied his energies into a number of conservation projects, including those of the Forest Park Foundation that his physician father had the prescience to form back in 1939. They include the Forest Park Nature Center, Rock Island Trail, Heart of Illinois Sierra Club, the Heights Observation Tower, and Wildlife Prairie Park, as a 2,000-acre habitat for some 150 native Illinoisan animals. In all, he has helped secure over 20,000 acres in the Peoria region for public use.

Worldwide, that total went beyond 600,000 acres, with much of it to save the central Australian hairy wombat.

Additionally, the lawyer-pilot lent his services for the creation of the Greater Peoria Airport Authority; later, he pushed for the launch of Mount Hawley Airport.

The philanthropic activist founded, again via the Forest Park Foundation in 1950, the Institute of Physical Medicine and Rehabilitation. His charitable help expanded area medical facilities, especially for the elderly.

For the young, he developed the nation's first Bicycle Safety Town in the 1950s.

Throughout his life, Bill Rutherford worked wonders to save the planet for people now and in the future.

For 91 years, he had his eyes on the ball called Earth. Hazel and Bill Rutherford are pictured at the Peoria area Wildlife Prairie Park they developed. (Courtesy of Sam Shafer and Wildlife Prairie Park.)

Win One for the Kip

Peoria County deputy sheriff John Mullen Sack recognized the name on the warrant, Steven Thomas. In a couple of years with the warrants division, Officer Sack had already served him three times. On October 1, 1987, the 20-year veteran went to the 2102 North University address and tendered the warrant, allowing Thomas to retrieve his ATM card. Moments later, Thomas shot Officer Sack in the back, killing him. Then, in a demonic frenzy, he repeatedly stabbed his wife, Loretta, to death. After an hours-long standoff, the police charged the house and killed him.

John Sack was the fourth Peoria County sheriff in history to die in the line of duty. While he served with the highest of distinctions, many remembered him as their sports-loving pal "Kip." Shown here is the Peoria County Sheriff's Memorial. (Courtesy of Karen Camper.)

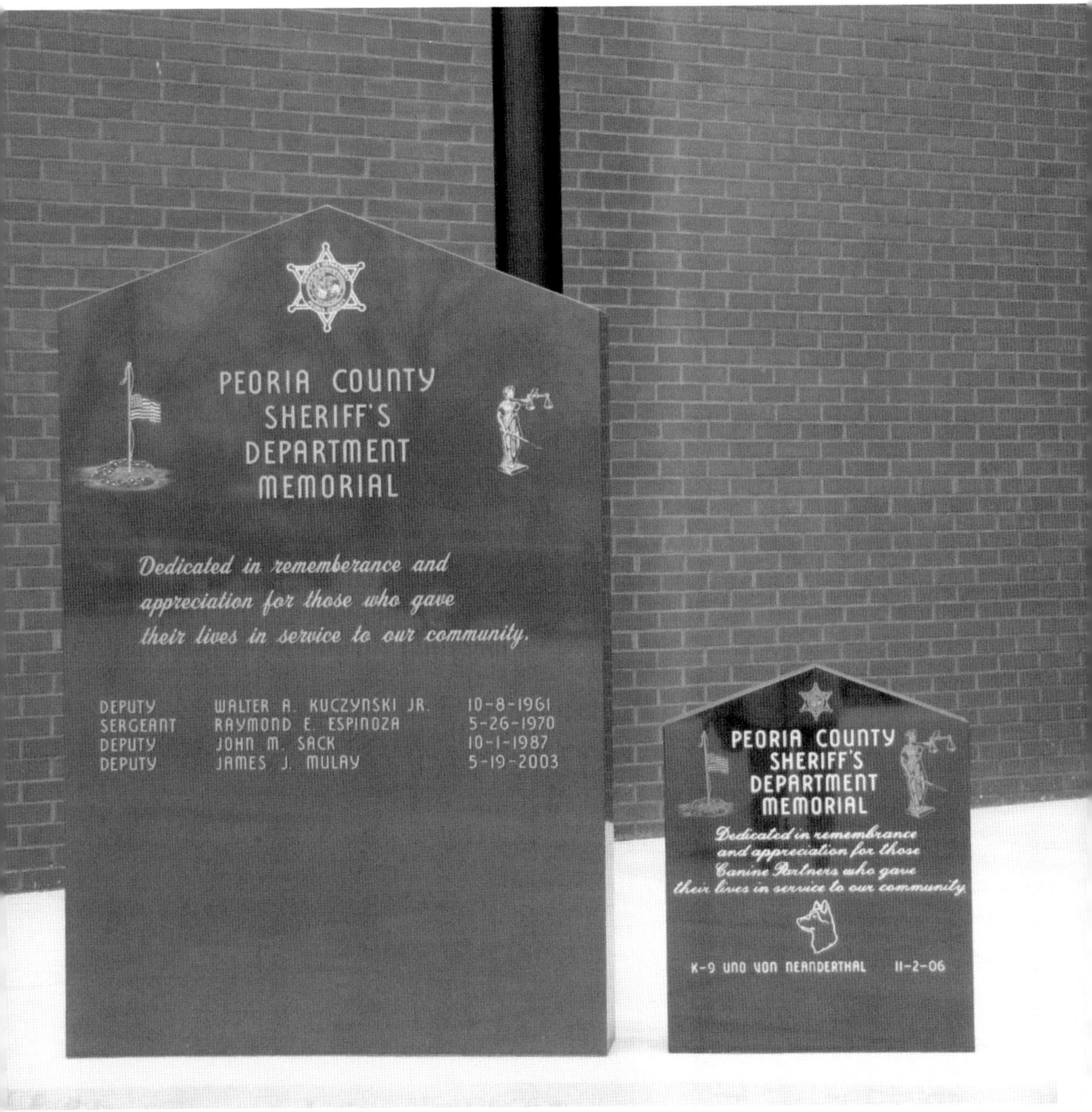

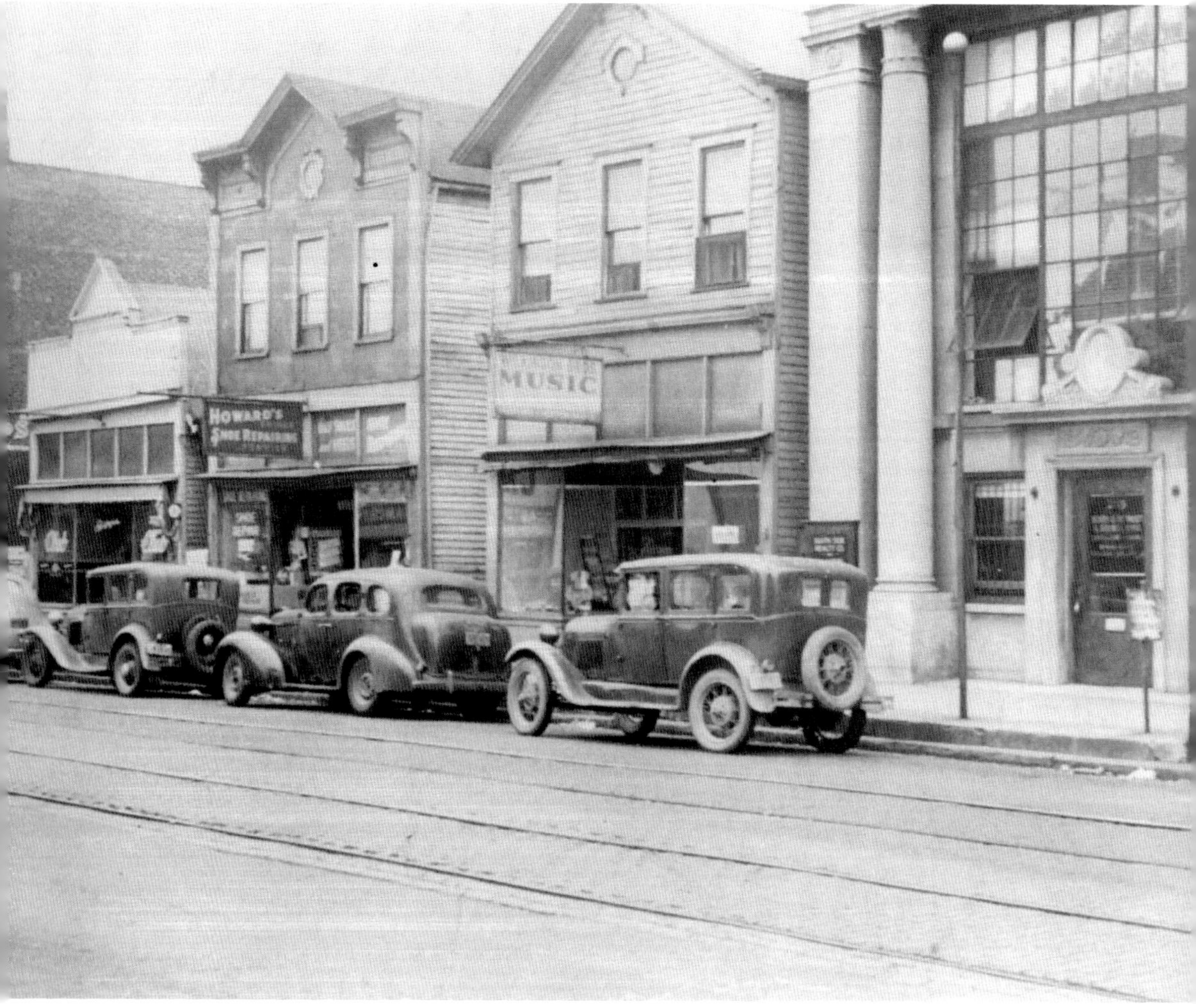

Banking on Local Roots

Before Prohibition, Peoria's downtown district had all the banks, with River City calling the shots in the world's whiskey trade.

But changes were ahead.

The biggest came on January 19, 1920, with Prohibition tripping the town to its distilling knees. Though no longer America's top treasury-filler, Peoria still had entrepreneurs. One group of south Peoria merchants foresaw the advantage of a neighborhood bank and, on January 4, 1922, opened the South Side Bank on Southwest Adams.

Over 90 years later, the South Side Trust and Savings Bank continues its local independence and loyalty of its founding 12 investing families, including the ongoing role of four generations of the Ward family.

Proving that convenience still matters, South Side Bank has 13 full-service locations rooted exclusively in the Tri-County area. The rightmost building pictured here is South Side Bank in 1949. (Courtesy of South Side Bank.)

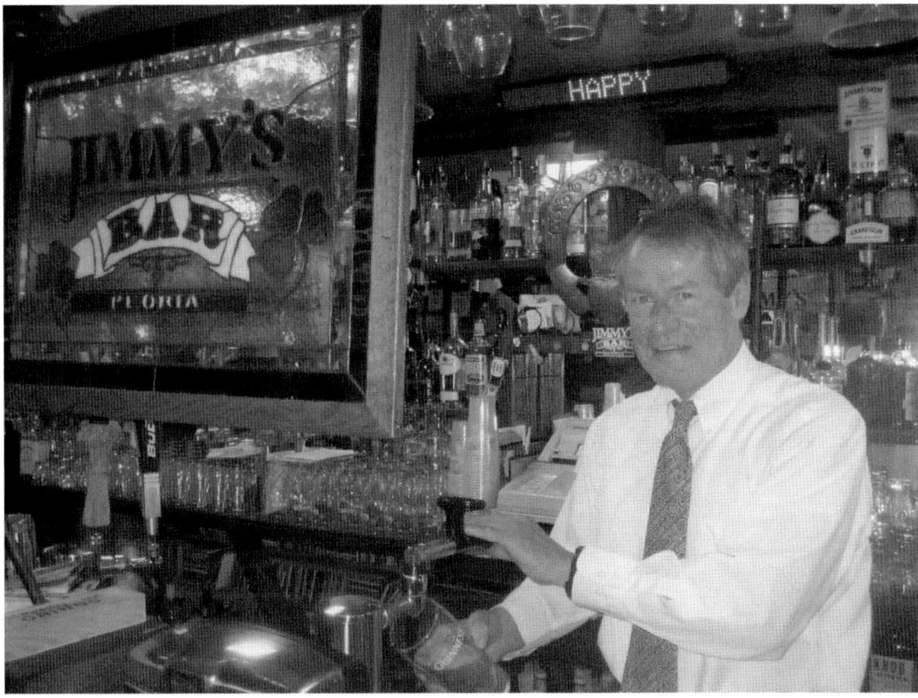

The Fun-Raiser

When they met in Chicago, Theresa Fitzpatrick thought of Joseph W. Spears as Liverpool, England's "Fab One." They started their family soon after moving to Peoria in 1952 with each of their seven babies named Mary Therese until the very moment of birth, when "MT" became Joey, Jimmy, Billy, Bobby, Mike, Pat, and Tommy.

It was a story the mother of seven boys told with delight.

While half of the brothers, Bill, Mike, and Tom, followed their father into the plumbing business, the other three, Joe, Bob, and Pat, went into law enforcement/government. Bill has career-traveled between plumbing and the city council; Jim, after graduating from Spalding Institute in 1972 and Bradley University in 1977, was in business management administration but then tacked to a different course as pub owner.

It was not so much his Irish wiring creating the call as it was a bar's aura of a "loud home," such as is found growing up with six brothers.

Jimmy started as a bartender, grunting it as an undergrad at Fonzi's and the Lariat Club. After college, he began his lifelong day-job in sales at Melton Electric and pulled draughts by night.

Hope met destiny when he, with Lariat Club owner Lou Kouri, bought Lori's Loading Dock in West Peoria and opened Jimmy's on July 28, 1982; with seamless ease, the one-time 1800s Peoria-to-Macomb stagecoach station became the place to plop for Peorians of all stripes and Bradley students. With an amusing decor of local and Chicago (Go Hawks!) sports keepsakes nailed to the walls and ceiling, there is as much to see as there is to sip.

Spears became Jimmy's sole owner in 1999.

And besides his pub with its cheery karma, he gives to many Peoria causes, including fundraisers for Friends of Fatherless Boys. In 2014, he cofounded Peoria Area Prostate Awareness Society.

He also fulfilled his parents' dream by having three daughters: Alice, Grace, and Maeve. (Mary Therese, alas, will have to wait.)

Guided by his mother's eternal smile, there is no better friend to a stranger than fun-raising Jimmy Spears. Here, Jimmy, under his Zodiac sign Happy, throttles up another draught for the Prairie Parrotheads who thrive at his pub. (Author's collection.)

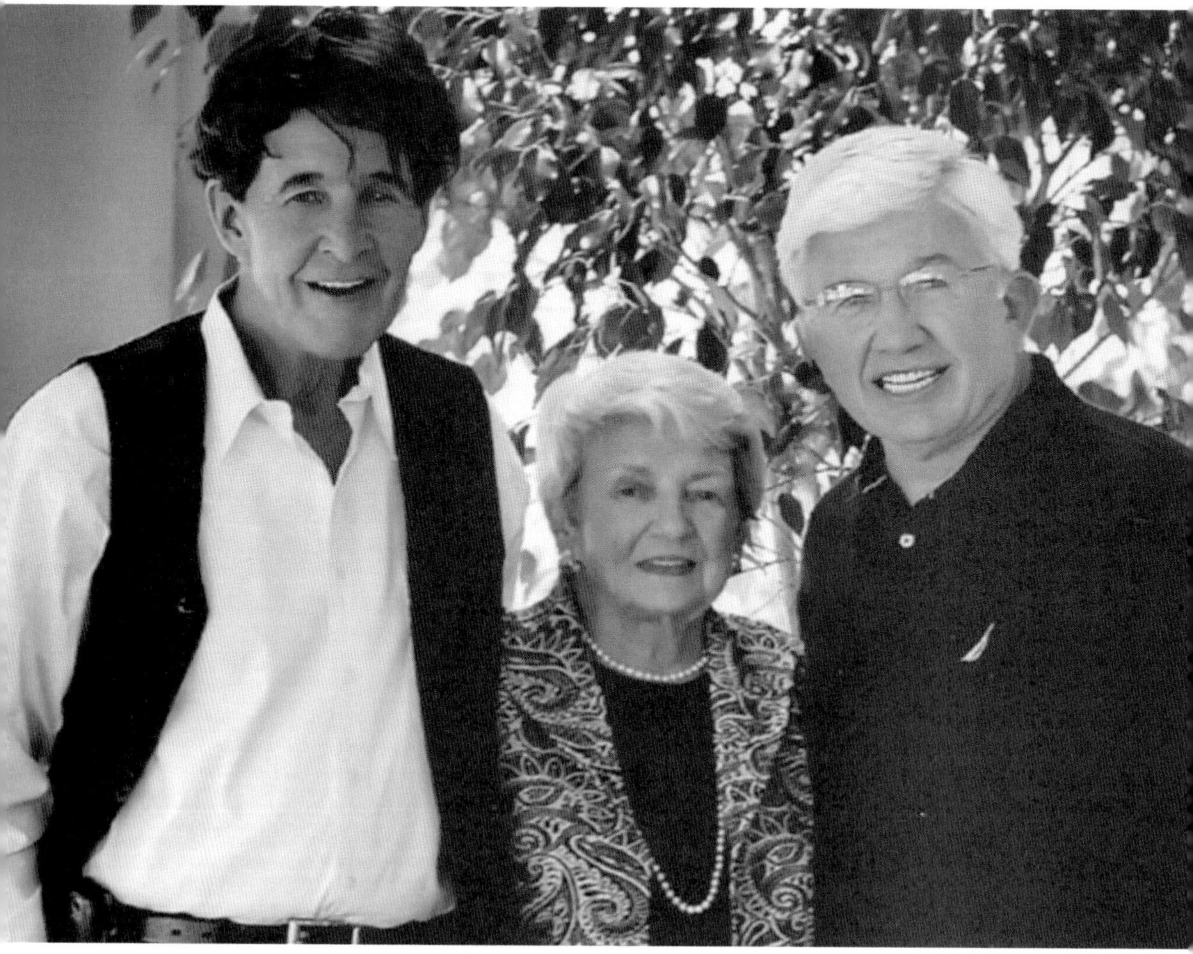

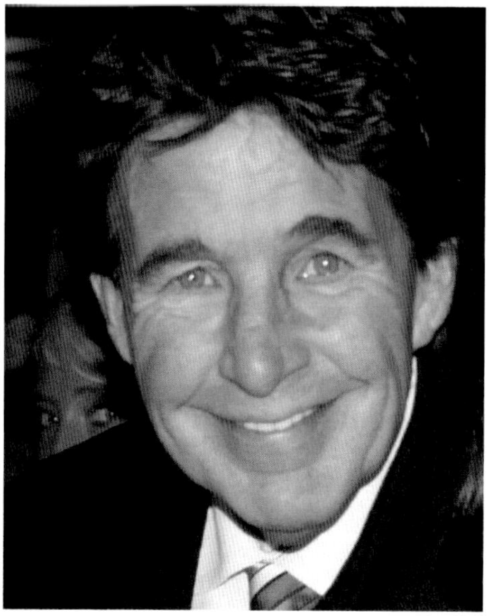

Happiness Is a Bar Owner

Though T.M. "Sully" Sullivan died March 31, 2010, River City's "Pied Piper of Good Cheer" lives on, thanks to a bottomless well of saloon stories about him, and the 14 area pubs—each with a different theme—he spawned in a 30-year barkeep career. He could even uncork a grin during the hottest boil of a political flap. Or open his cash drawer for someone in need.

Pictured above are T. Michael "Sully," mother, Colleen Kelleher Sullivan, and brother Patrick Sullivan; at left is the Sully himself. (Both, courtesy of Pat Sullivan.)

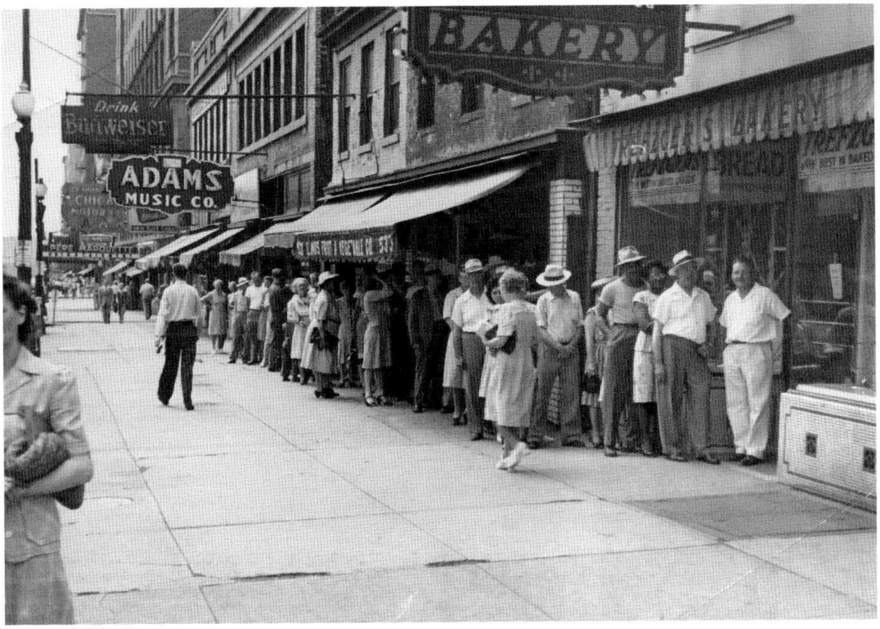

Peoria's Pastry Palace

Just in time for the outbreak of the Civil War in 1861, German Simon Trefzger opened his bakery on Fulton Street and snared a bid to provide succor for the nearby Union troops. For the next 132 years and four generations, the family enjoyed celebrity for its baked goods made from scratch. Trefzger's moved from downtown to North Prospect Avenue in 1953. Though the family sold its bake house in 1993, its traditions have continued, providing a sweet link of Peoria to its Civil War days.

Above, in July 1946, people are lining up for Trefzger's. Below is owner Jeff Huebner. (Above, courtesy of Jeff Huebner; below, courtesy of Karen Camper.)

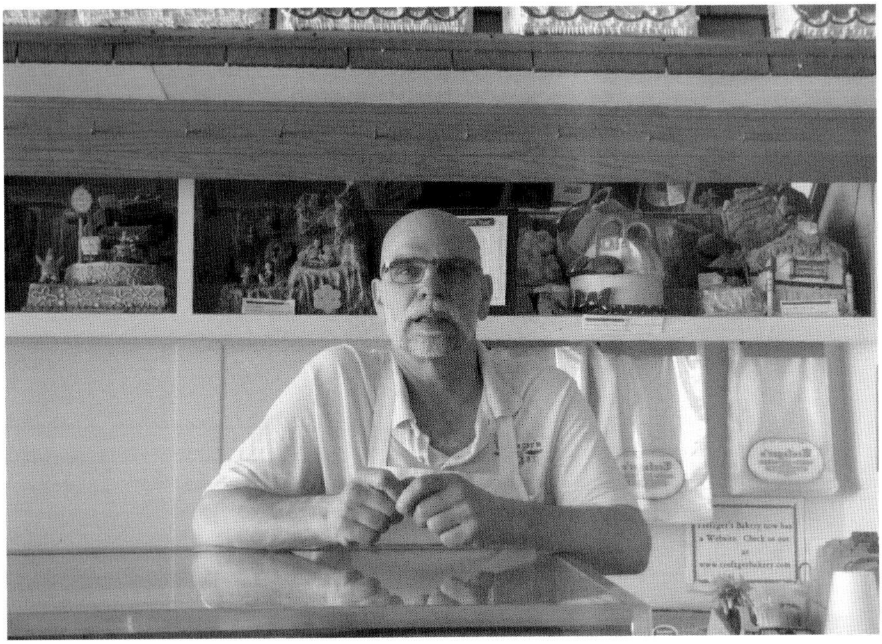

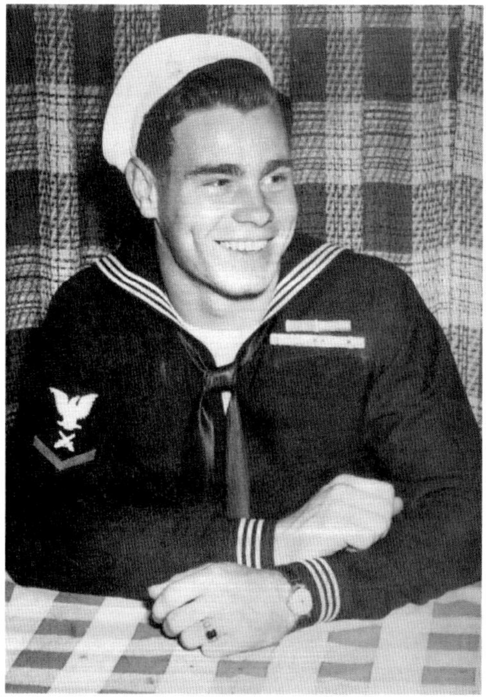

The Fin Man

Norman L. Tyler ("LaRue Norman Tyler" only on his September 12, 1926, San Jose, Illinois, birth certificate) grew up in Quincy before the 17-year-old enlisted in October 1943 with the Navy's Construction Battalion (Seabees). Showing fortitude and flat feet, he was one of the first 700 sailors to volunteer in late 1943 for the new, elite Underwater Demolition Teams (UDTs), the frogmen. He joined UDT-8 and history.

After "Advanced Agony" training at Fort Pierce, Florida, and Maui, Hawaii, along with two rounds of Marine boot camp, Tyler, now known as Tick-Tock, boarded the USS *George E. Badger* in August 1944 for the South Pacific.

Tick-Tock earned his fins on September 28 with 12 others of Team No. 8 during the most extraordinary recon in the annals of UDTs when they scouted the narrow, shallow channel between the islands of Peleliu and Ngesebus. It was a 6,000-yard round-trip gauntlet under relentless, raking Japanese machinegun crossfire. The frogmen (also known as the Naked Warriors since they only wore facemasks, swim trunks, and fins) swam the four-foot deep waters exposed and marginally protected by strafing US planes.

Miraculously, after the three-hour, 3.4-mile shooting-gallery grinder, there were no casualties; though Tick-Tock had scratches on his chest from scraping the channel's bottom while dodging gunfire.

He was unlucky at Leyte 20 days later, on October 18, when a large bullet from the heavy enemy shore barrage ripped through his left calf as he manned a recovery boat for his fellow frogmen. It ended his Navy career two days before General MacArthur splashed ashore at Leyte.

He returned to Peoria, where he graduated from Woodruff High (1946) and Bradley University (1952). He married in 1948 and raised three children, Brad, Cindy, and Karen. And he worked for his father's company in Peoria. He remained true to his self-imposed code as a combat swimmer—he never swam in calm waters.

He died in 1991.

As a charter member of World War II's deservedly fabled UDT frogmen whose small numbers (32 teams, 3,000 sailors) constituted 0.001 percent of the Navy, Norm Tyler's courage to persevere beyond mortal endurance sets the bar high, even for SEALs who followed. (Courtesy of Karen Schatsiek.)

CHAPTER FOUR

Infamy

Peoria and notoriety went hand-in-hand from sometime past its Fort Clark days until the mid-20th century, a period well over 100 years. It was a blue-collar Las Vegas that stayed wet during Prohibition with slot machines ever-present in dime stores and drugstores in the Roarin' Peoria heyday as a gambling sanctuary. And the bright red lights of Peoria never dimmed. They were well lit in the 1800s, too. In 1871–1872, Wyatt Earp, the future America's-most-famous lawman, was a dedicated "bummer" (pimp) in River City. Arrested three times before he saw the light, he lit out for Dodge City and never mentioned his Peoria days.

Jack Nahas fared better as a pimp from the 1930s to the 1970s. Nahas, who bragged he was Al Capone's chauffeur, wanted to own 1930s Peoria's dark side like Big Al in Chicago, but the Shelton Gang already had dibs and the muscle. One barroom ambush that landed him in the hospital convinced Nahas that it was better to work with girls.

Meanwhile, in city hall, Peoria's Mr. Mayor, Ed "Yo-Yo" Woodruff, played footsie with the Shelton Gang as long as his crime chums coughed up cash for the city coffers.

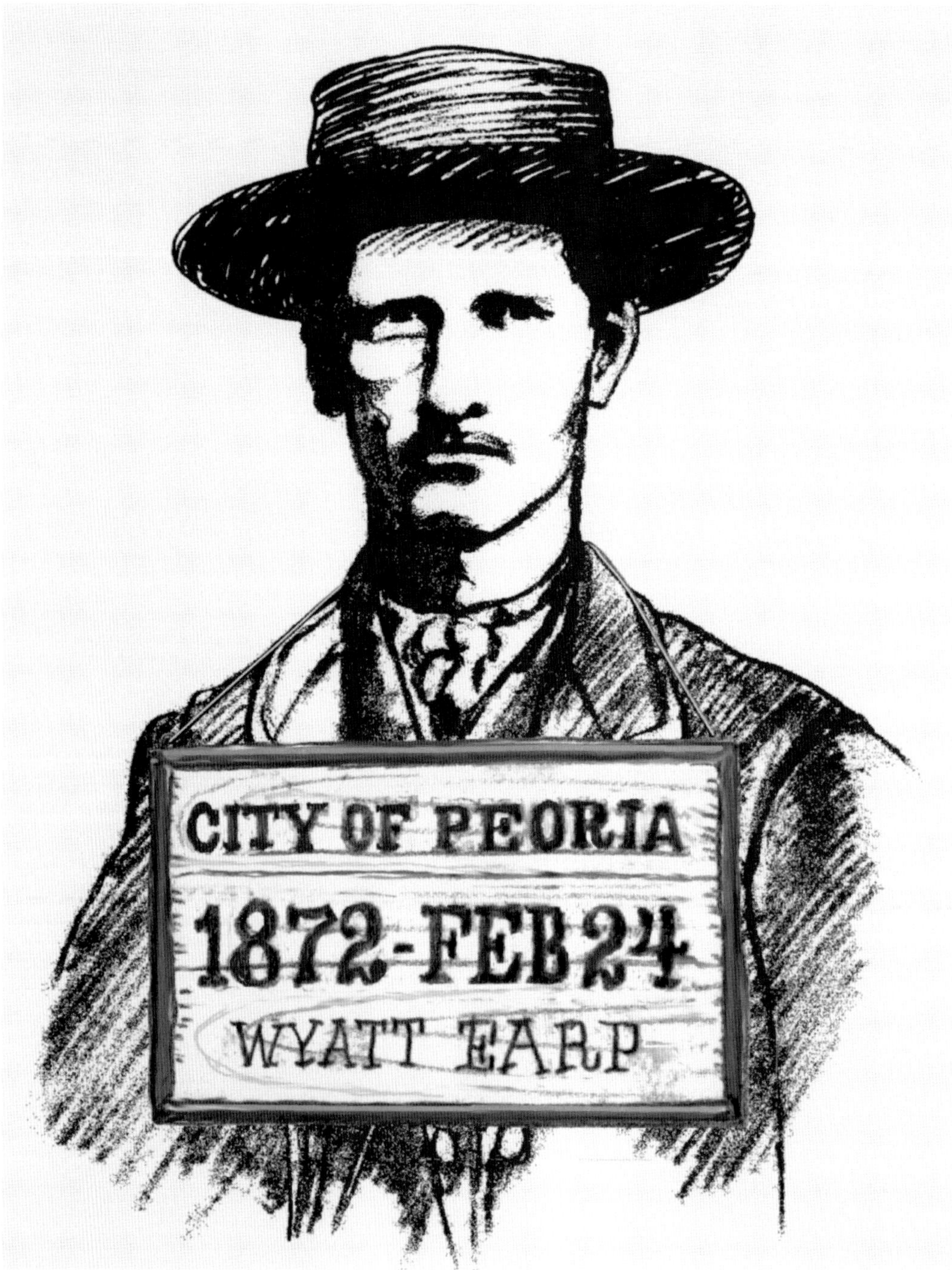

Whatta Bummer

America's most famous lawman, Wyatt Earp, was a bummer in 1871–1872 Peoria, finding himself three times on the business side of the jail bars. Nine years later, in 1881, Wyatt hit cowboy pay dirt at the gunfight at the O.K. Corral. Instead of thanking the Peoria police for scaring him straight, he never talked about doing time in River City. He died in Los Angeles in 1929. (Courtesy of Tim McGowan.)

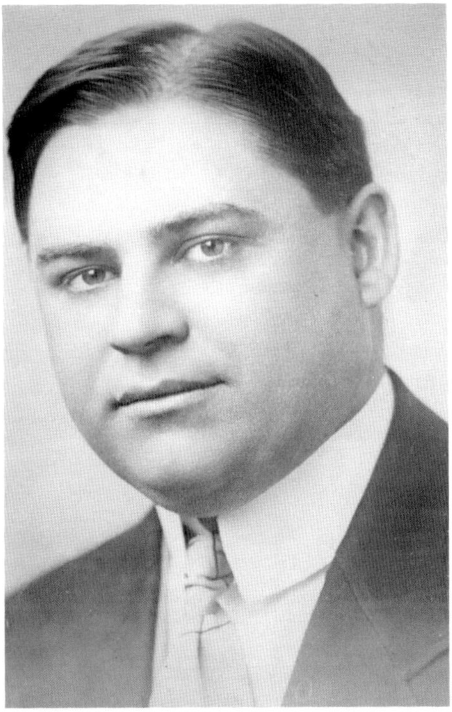

The Curse Birther

Peorian Harry H. Frazee (1881–1929) was a theatric impresario extraordinaire in Peoria, Chicago, and New York. The one-time Peoria Distillers ballplayer bought a new toy in 1916, the two-time defending World Series champion Boston Red Sox. In 1918, the Red Sox won again—their last in the 20th century. Soon, Frazee gored his team, sending his stars to the middling New York Yankees. He scored baseball's most outrageous trade on January 5, 1920, when he backloaded the Prima Bam-Donna Babe Ruth to the Yanks. It would take Boston 86 years (2004) to end the Curse of the Bambino while New York went on a galactic spree of 27 World Series championships.

Yankee-feeder Frazee is second from the right below in 1923 on day one at Yankee Stadium, the house Frazee packed. (Both, courtesy of the Library of Congress.)

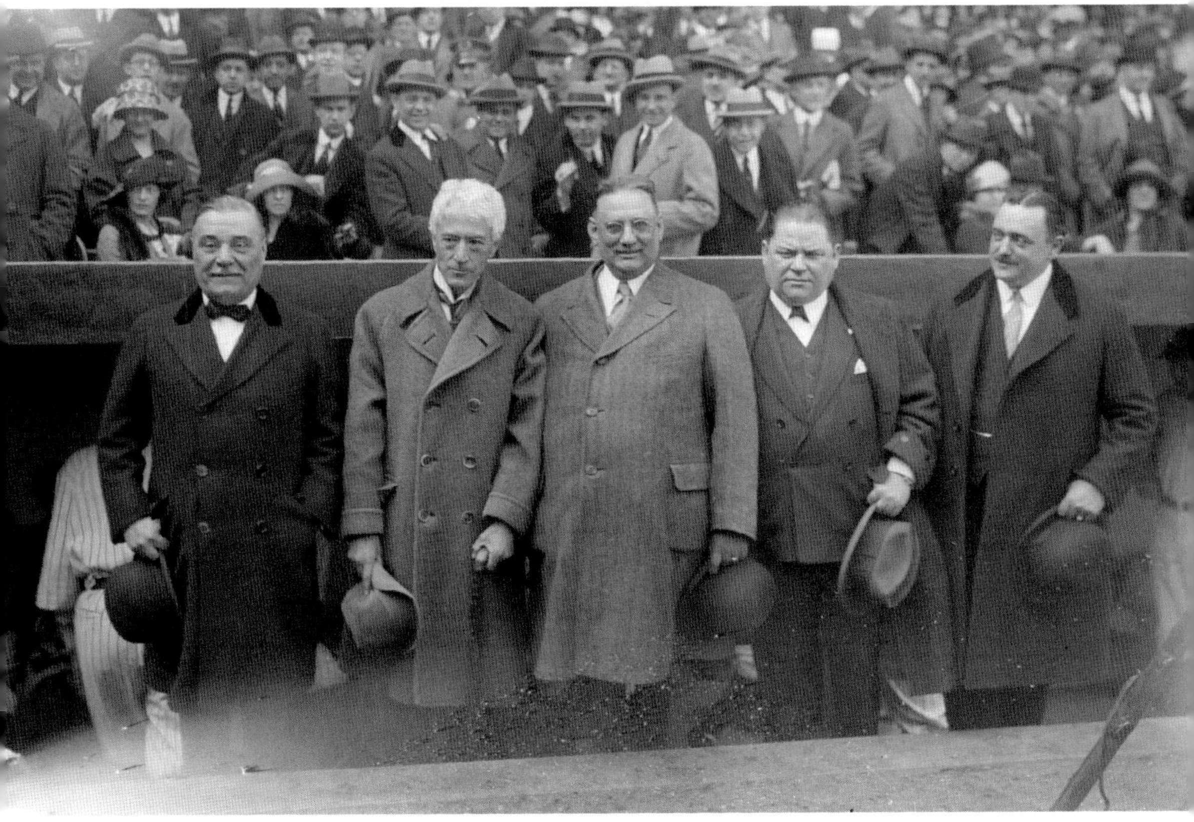

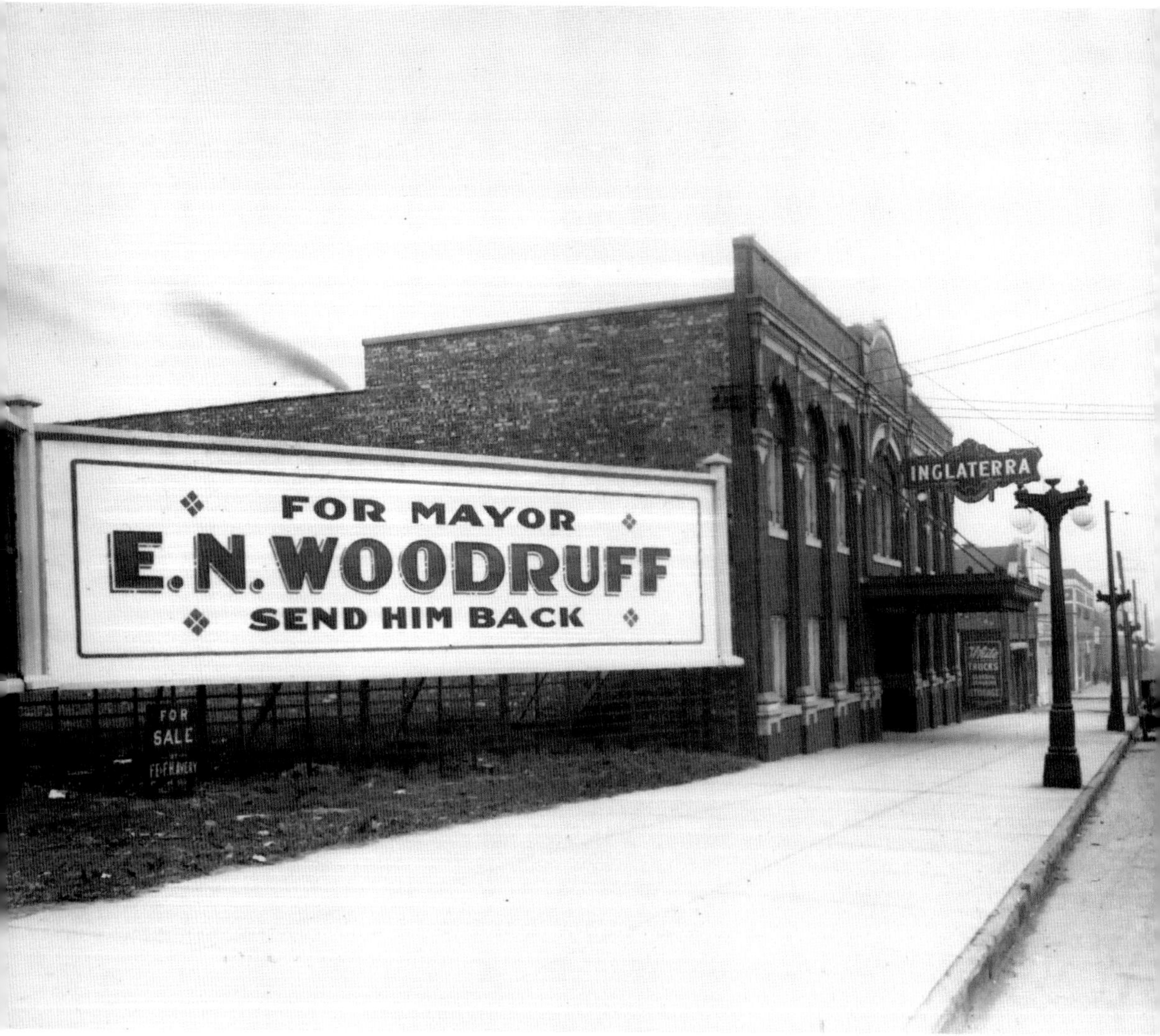

The Yo-Yo Man (ABOVE AND OPPOSITE PAGE)
Edward N. Woodruff (1862–1947) was Peoria's Mr. Mayor, having rapped the town's gavel for 24 mostly nonconsecutive years from 1903–1947. The "Ballot Box Bambino" ran a record "mayor-thon" 19 times, going 11-8, both city tops.

Peoria's love/hate relationship with the Yo-Yo Man had a lot to do with his chumminess with his crime pals, setting "fines" for everything illegal. As long as the murky cash made its way to city hall, the crooked mayor looked away. The good news was that he did not raise taxes. But Peorians, upset with their Sin City reputation, would boot him out every election cycle or two. Taxes would rise. And there would be vulpine Yo-Yo to the rescue—with a little help from his "friends."

Yo-Yo died December 1947, ending all hope of another campaign.

On the opposite page, Woodruff is seen receiving the hand-off from Mayor O'Brien in 1936. Above is Yo-Yo's oft-used billboard. (Above, courtesy of the Local History and Genealogy Collection, Peoria Public Library; opposite, courtesy Special Collections Center, Bradley University Library.)

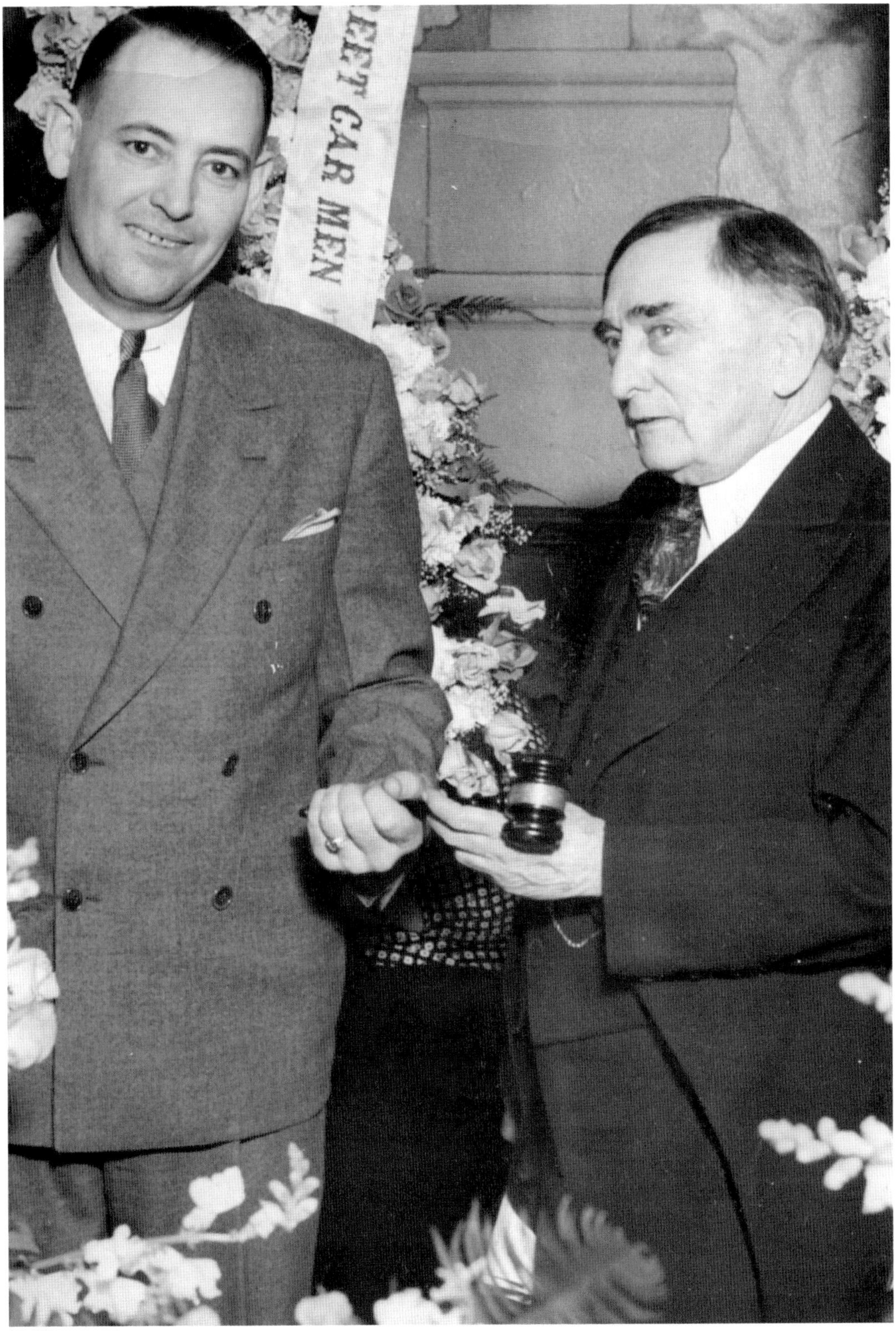
EET GAR MEN

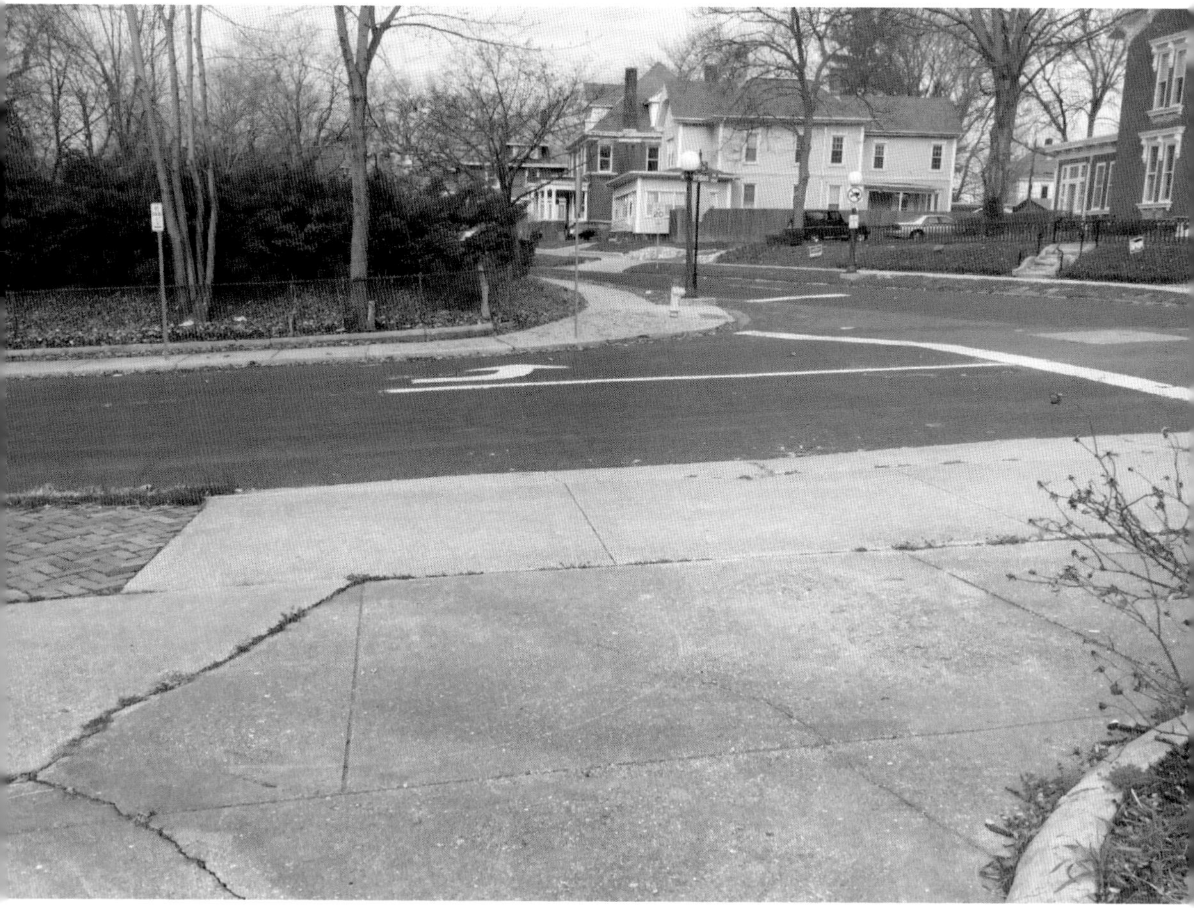

Moss Murder

George Plummer McNear Jr. came to Peoria in 1926 and bought the Toledo, Peoria & Western (TP&W) railroad. During the Depression, the hardworking boss, who demanded the same from his employees, had one of the few profitable railways. He clashed often with the unions. When the unions struck TP&W just after Pearl Harbor, McNear snubbed Pres. Franklin Roosevelt's plea for mediation. FDR then nationalized the Peoria railroad with the first use of the Plant Seizure Act.

It took the war's end for McNear to be back behind the wheel. But the strike continued. Strikebreakers on a February 6, 1946, run killed two strikers in Gridley, Illinois, and weren't convicted.

On March 10, 1947, near Moss Avenue, a shotgun bushwhacking killed McNear, the first American railroad president ever snuffed. His murder remains unsolved today.

Pictured on the right is McNear in 1938. Above is the ambush site at Sheridan Road and Moss Avenue. (Right, courtesy of Library of Congress; above, author's collection.)

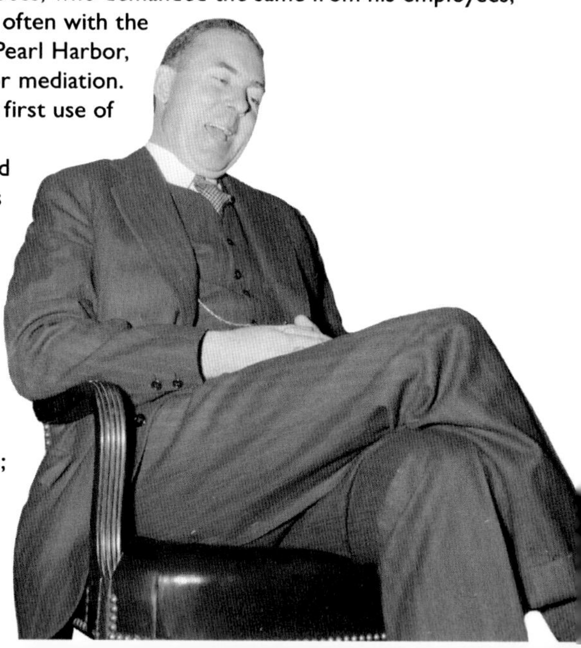

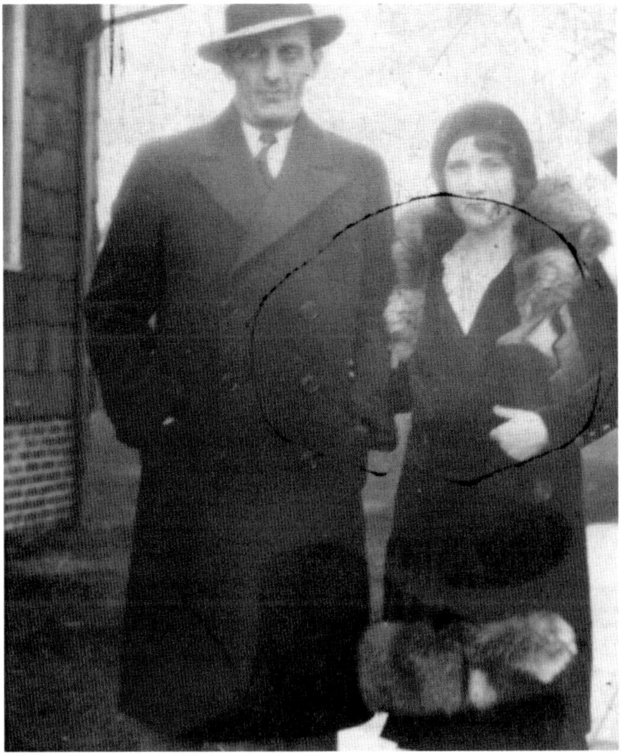

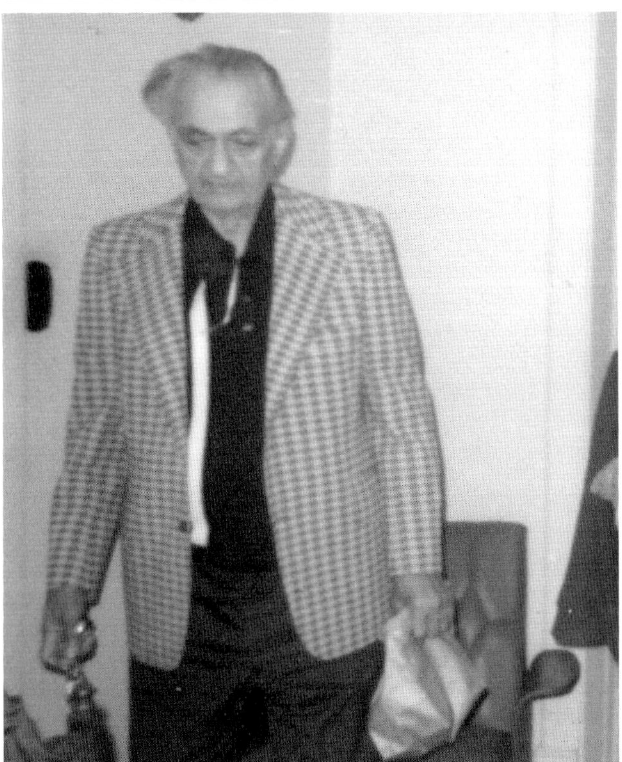

El Nasty, Capone's Wheelman
John "Jack" Nahas drove into 1937 Peoria, a two-bit hood intent on becoming River City's "Big Al." Unfortunately, the Shelton Gang had already grabbed the town's throat. After surviving a barroom ambush in 1945, Nahas, the one-time Capone driver, redoubled his efforts to be the city's top pimp. Convicted in 1972 of bribing a police officer, Nahas died of Lou Gehrig's disease without serving a day of his prison term. Nahas is pictured at top with his wife, Frida, and at bottom around 1974. (Both, courtesy of Peggy Leadley.)

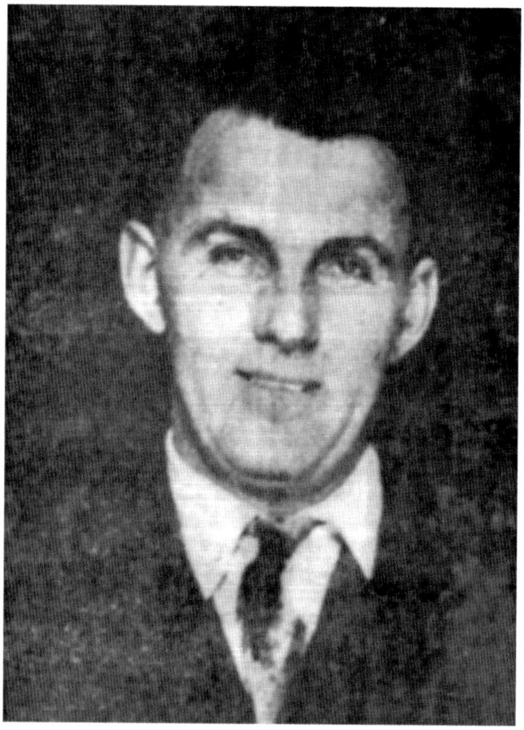

The Gunfight at the Linn Street Garage . . . Welcome to Sheltonville
Roarin' Peoria in the 1930s and 1940s was too much catnip for the mobs of Chicago and St. Louis. Whether it was those outsiders or local rivals, the October 1930 ambush at the Linn Street garage of Peoria gambling-heavy Clyde Garrison inspired Clyde's call to the downstate Shelton Gang for "Help." Though not part of Garrison's deal, the chance to own the netherworld of an entire city was too alluring for the bootleggin', strong-armin' wolf pack, led by Mr. Dandy Carl Shelton (pictured). The ungodly alliance between Garrison and the Sheltons worked, for a while, even with its queasiness of a garter snake cornered by a mongoose. By 1940, Garrison "retired" without a bullet exiting his head.

With the 1941 mayoral election of their chum-to-crime Ed "Dearie" Woodruff, the Shelton Gang would enjoy its greatest heyday. The city machine sizzled too, flushed by the dirty cash collected as "fees" for gambling and other vices. The rowdy downtown streets were as sleepless as those in New York City and—for Peorians who knew better than to tangle with the prickly Bernie Shelton—safe.

Fed up with the loosey-goosey reign of Dearie, the city in 1945 booted the Ballot Box Bambino in favor of Carl Treibel, who immediately severed the city hall–Shelton axis. Carl went farming in southern Illinois, leaving the daily run of the gang to his baby brother Bernie.

Bullets then started flying.

In 1946, Shelton associates Frank Kraemer, Joel Nyberg, and Phillip Stumpf all dropped from gunfire. On a Wayne County road in October 1947, kingpin Carl died in an ambush. In July 1948, a lone gunman from the bushy knoll behind Farmington Road's Parkway Tavern dropped Bernie Shelton to the ground, ending the Peoria era.

From May 1949 to June 1950, Big Earl Shelton and Little Earl Shelton survived several ambushes in their hometown of Fairfield. But the oldest Shelton, Roy, was not as lucky. On June 7, 1950, a sniper killed him with a single shot that, like a shooting arcade, clipped him clean off his tractor.

A 1950 article in the *Saturday Evening Post* called the Sheltons "America's Bloodiest Gang." Frank Sinatra in the mid-1950s mused about the Shelton saga as a movie, but his agent nixed the idea, given the chatter about alleged Sinatra mob ties. (Courtesy of the Local History and Genealogy Collection, Peoria Public Library.)

CHAPTER FIVE

Sports Heroes

Peoria has had an outstanding sports history in many fields of play at the national and international level. Throughout the years, basketball has been King Sport in River City. And it took coach A.J. Robertson to put Bradley on the map with his basketball powerhouses of the 1930s and 1940s, just as Knute Rockne had done with Notre Dame in the 1920s. Jack Brickhouse began his famed Chicago sportscasting career announcing Bradley basketball in the 1930s. A player on Coach Robertson's last team, Joe Stowell continued the Robby tradition as Bradley coach in the 1960s and 1970s. Smooth-shooting and assist-master Bobby Humbles energized the Braves in the mid-1970s.

Herbert Jamison was a record-setting sprinter who led Peoria High to the first Illinois high school state track championship (1893) and then won a silver medal at the first modern Olympics in Athens (1896). In 1960, Army cadet Ron Zinn, a race walker, became the first Olympian from West Point and the first cadet ever honored with a parade. He represented the United States again at the 1964 Olympics. Steve Shostrom founded the Steamboat Classic road races (1974) that have made Peoria a must-stop for Olympic hopefuls and other running stars.

Homegrown Jim Thome has hit more homers in Major League history than anyone born or raised in the Midwest; he was also only the sixth player in baseball to reach the 600-homer milestone. And he did it with humility. Joe Napoli averaged nearly .400 in three seasons at Bradley University and hit .490 his senior year to lead the nation. With the pros beckoning, he went to law school, came back to town, and championed his alma mater.

And journeyman outfielder George "Lucky" Whiteman bested the Babe as the hero of the 1918 World Series champ Boston Red Sox.

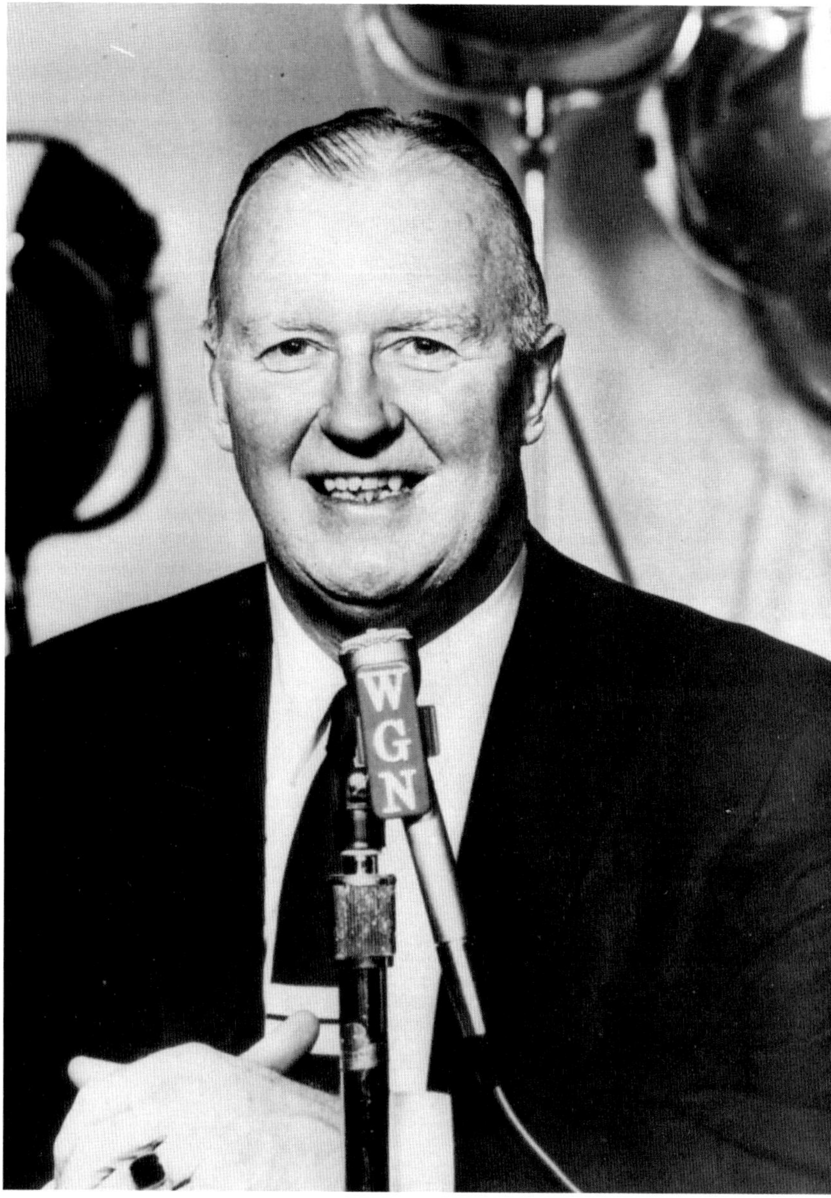

The Say Hey-Hey Kid

When the circus came into 1915 Peoria, its sideshow barker Will Brickhouse, age 39, blew in like a tornado and swept Daisy, a 15-year-old hotel clerk, into his vortex. She landed a year later, married to the carny, and a mother to their son John Beasley "Jack" Brickhouse, born January 24, 1916, at Methodist Hospital. Jack was two when Will the Wind, long gone from Daisy, died. Though he placed fifth out of six in a WMBD announcer contest, Brickhouse became the nation's youngest announcer in 1934. He went to WGN in 1940. For the next 41 years, he was Mr. Mic for Chicago sports and is remembered also for his brainchild *Marriage License Romances* show, on which he interviewed couples applying for licenses.

He is in 10 halls of fame, including Major League Baseball's. (Courtesy of Greater Peoria Sports Hall of Fame.)

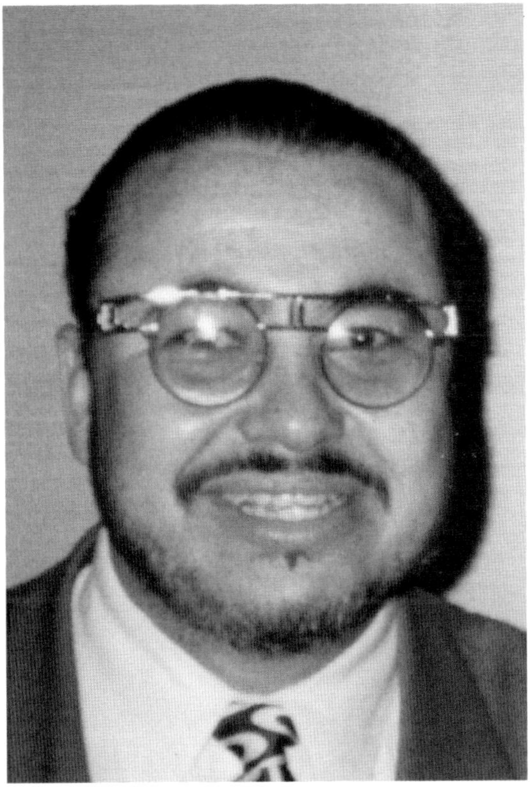

Peoria's BFF, Double D

Would any 1950s doctor think twice about spanking a newborn's bottom? Maybe, if that baby was Peorian Dana Davis, born September 25, 1956. That is the magnetism of smile prodigy Double D—everyone wanted to be his best friend.

He became the Happy Heart of Peoria.

According to Bob Humbles, a childhood best friend forever (BFF), the only child of Shirley "Jean" (Meischner) and William "Mercie" Davis had a strong stir to belong.

Though not a star—he was short and on the hefty side of lithe—he was enough of an athlete to play on Trewyn elementary and Manual High football, baseball, and basketball teams.

After a detour to Benedictine Junior College in Kansas so he could play football, he began at Bradley the next year, where he lit up the courtside as the Braves student manager, impressing Bradley basketball coach Joe Stowell enough to win a rare nontraditional athletic scholarship. Davis graduated with a business management degree in 1978.

He worked locally before fronting as tour manager for funk-blues idol Bootsy Collins in the 1980s, adding the entertainment world to the Peorian's universe of pals.

Besides involvement in numerous community activities, he founded, in the mid-1990s, the Mitchell J.J. Anderson All-Star Camp (née Hoops Hemisphere) with the Bradley icon and namesake. It was a celebrity-packed basketball summer camp for disadvantaged youths who also received free physicals.

Dana Davis knew how to get things done and never had to be asked twice. His modus operandi was off-stage and one-on-one.

He was a perfect fit when he joined the Memphis Grizzlies front office and, in 13 years, became team operations vice president; the team's billionaire owner Michael Heisley counted him as a best friend.

Dana Davis—the consensus BFF—died at age 56 in Memphis on October 3, 2012, of a heart attack triggered by diabetes. He left behind a mourning galaxy of best buds, including his beloved River City. (Courtesy of Bob Humbles.)

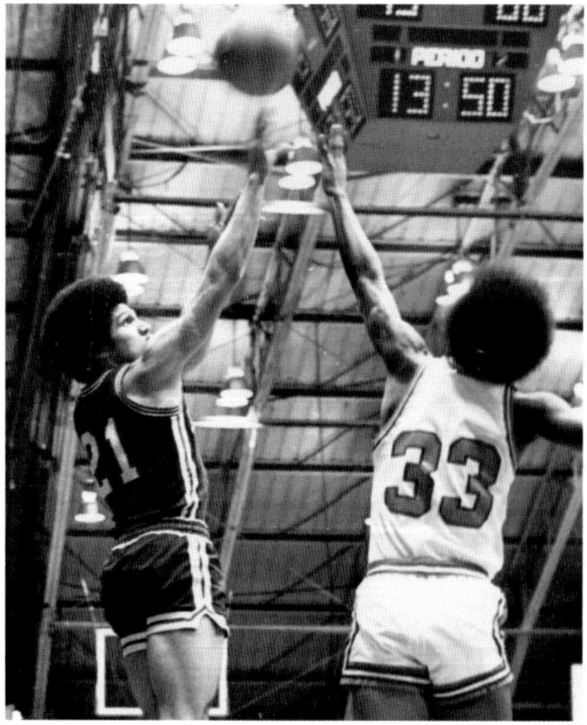

Court Master

For Bob "Bobby" Humbles, with his athletic career and business successes, he always pivots to his parents. "I'm blessed because of them."

The fourth of six children of Betty and Curtis learned the value of education, hard work, and the true toughness of poise. His first heroes were his two older brothers, Jim and Mike, who, with their cousin Henry Humbles, dazzled on Peoria playgrounds.

Humbles played basketball as a Lincoln School fourth grader, becoming a phenom by the sixth grade; he scored 56 points in a 104-8 rout of Norwood Elementary.

Entering Manual High in 1970, he was a sub for two years on the Illinois powerhouse Rams. Humbles had a memorable first game when he hit every shot he took—six for six from the field and two for two for free throws; Manual finished fourth in the state his sophomore year. Though the Rams struggled his last two seasons, Humbles starred, averaging 25 points per game and earning All-State honors as a senior. College offers piled high with the most serious coming from Louisiana State, Valparaiso, Kansas State, and Bradley. He opted for the Braves because coach Joe Stowell "called first."

Bradley, from 1974 to 1978, was déjà vu for Humbles: terrific teams his first two years followed by less-stellar squads the final two years. The smooth shooter finished as the 10th best scorer in the team's storied history and led the Braves in assists his junior and senior years. He was an inductee in both the Greater Peoria Sports and the Bradley Halls of Fame. Most Hilltop buffs consider the backcourt tandem of Bobby Humbles–Roger Phegley as the third-best guard set in Bradley basketball history.

Drafted in 1978 by the National Basketball Association's Golden State Warriors, he was one of the last rookies cut; he would spend the next several years playing the professional junior circuit before returning home to utilize his business degree. He worked for Widmer's Office for 13 years, and at age 28, began playing tennis. He has been a championship-caliber player at the Tri-County Tennis tournament ever since, proving that talent can cross courts.

Humbles became a State Farm agent in 1991 and shared a northwest Peoria office with Dean Taylor, the company's first black agent in downstate Illinois. As popular in business as in sports, he provides soft-spoken smooth assists to his clients. (Courtesy of Bob Humbles.)

Return to Cinder

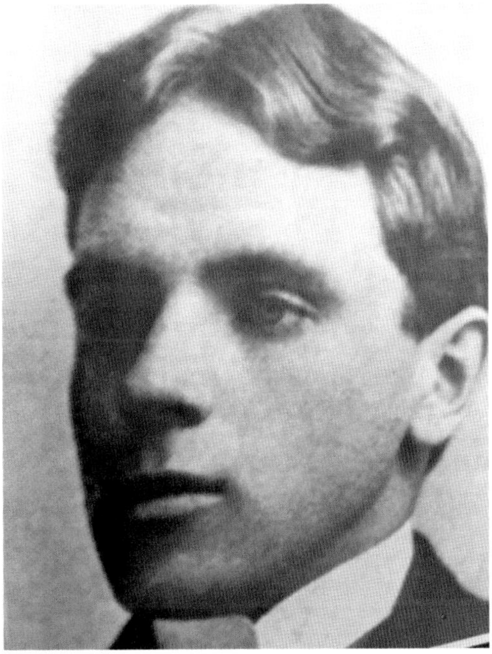

Herbert Jamison (1876–1938) grew up well fixed with torchy speed. At the 1893 first-ever Illinois schoolboy state track meet, he won three sprinting races to lead Peoria High to the championship. He was a charter member of the US Olympic team in 1896 as a Princeton junior. With his favorite event, the 200 meters, off the venue, he ran second at the 400 meters, winning the silver medal—the only medal ever won by a River City Olympian.

He married moneyed Caroline Grier, had four children, went into the insurance business, and set the social scene as a local Gatsby until the Great Depression.

In June 1938, Jamison leaped from the Franklin Street Bridge into the eternal plod of the Illinois River—a Greek tragedy in full circle. Below is the 1896 first US Olympic team—Herb Jamison is at lower left. (Right, courtesy Greater Peoria Sports Hall of Fame; below, courtesy of Bob Bonn.)

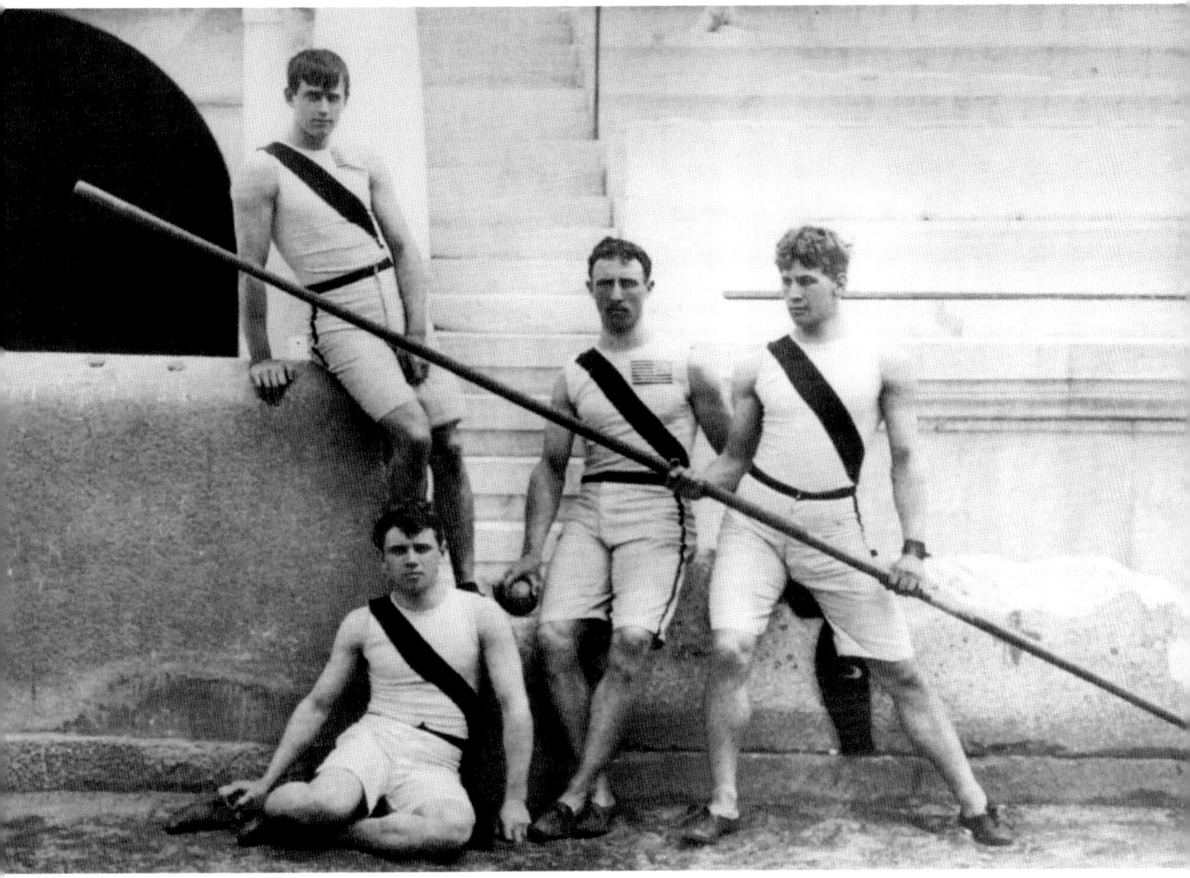

Joltin' Joe Peoria

Brooklyn-born Joe Napoli's love of baseball came from his father, Rudolph, and Santa Claus; as a youngster, he would receive a ball and a glove every Christmas. First coached by his dad, he learned the basics early and well. At Brooklyn Technical High School, he hit .433 to win the Tommy Holmes Award given to the best hitter in the New York area.

For Napoli, with a mechanical engineer dad, play-for-pay would have to take a backseat to academia. His first stop was New York University. Living in Greenwich Village and owning a Buick Roadmaster convertible didn't allow enough time to go to class. And he dropped out. His dad reviewed Joe's options, which were to go into the military or get a job. Napoli chose the Air Force, and for the next four years, he honed his skills with military ball, hitting .350 or better (in 1956 he hit .396) and winning all-star honors in leagues that included Major Leaguers. He also won looks from colleges, receiving offers from many schools, including Arizona State and Bradley. The Midwest won.

At Bradley, he excelled as a business major and at whacking the ball. In his three varsity years, the third baseman averaged a still-standing record of .392. In his senior year in 1960, he hit an atmospheric .490—the first and only Bradley Brave to lead the country in hitting. And all the while he led an active campus life. He then weighed his post-collegiate options, which were to try out for the San Francisco Giants, go to Dartmouth College for business graduate work, or go to John Marshall Law School. Being in his mid-20s would grind against a long professional ball career, so the Flatbush Flash opted for law and hung up his cleats.

He came back to a Peoria he regarded as his hometown to practice law after graduating from John Marshall in 1964. He also reconnected with Bradley as a hands-on booster of both their athletic and academic programs. He cofounded the Bradley Chief Club and became a sports agent for a number of renowned Bradley stars. Napoli taught classes from 1964 to 1989 and encouraged every student to aim high, especially to law school.

Bradley and River City have recognized his talent by electing him to the Bradley and Greater Peoria Sports Halls of Fame. He is pictured below demonstrating his "big league cut." (Courtesy of Brandy Napoli.)

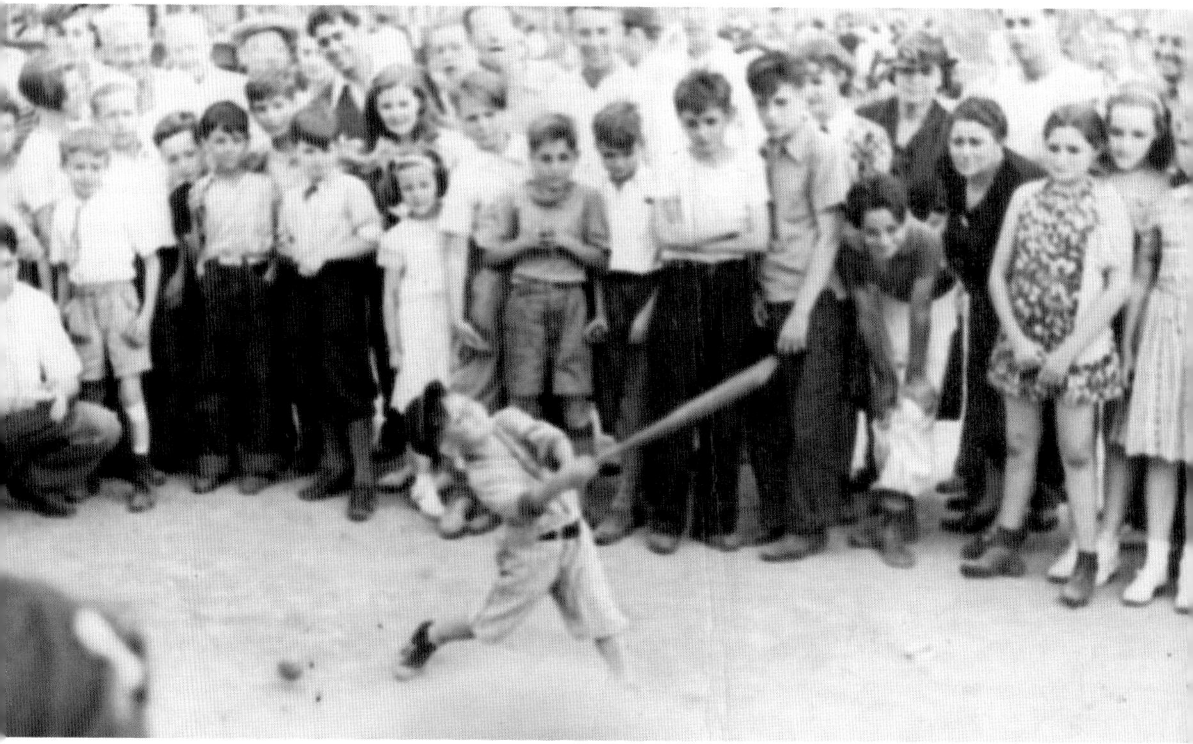

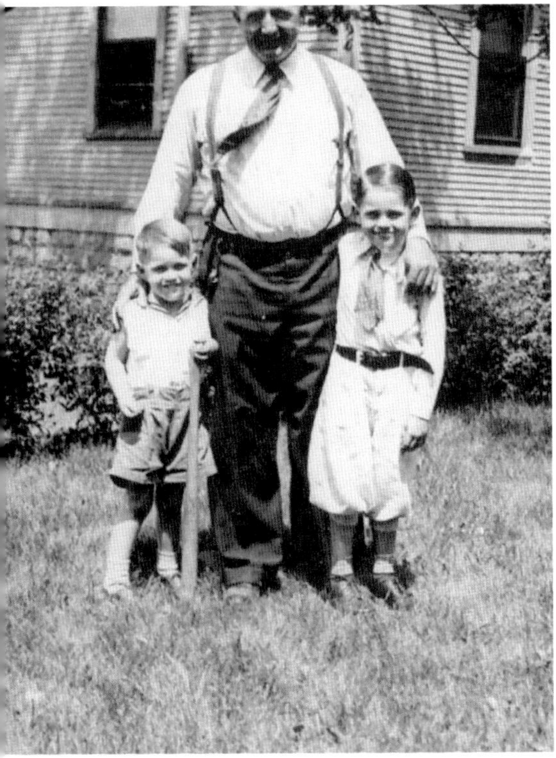

A.J. Robertson, Bradley's Daddy

Alfred James Robertson (A.J., or Robbie) put Peoria's Bradley University on the national map through sports (basketball) much as fellow coach and friend Knute Rockne had done at Notre Dame (football). The South Haven, Minnesota, native, known at the University of Montana as "Ribs" for his fat-free physique, was a three-sport star in football, basketball, and baseball (his favorite) who came to Bradley's hilltop in 1920 to coach the same three sports and become athletic director of a near still-born athletic department. He would remain and thrive at those posts for the rest of his life until he died in 1948, age 56.

Though his least pet, he made basketball the stud of Bradley athletics, becoming the school's winningest coach.

He's considered one of the greatest three-sport coaches in college history.

At left, A.J. is pictured with his sons Jim and Corky in the 1930s. Below, before the Fieldhouse Fall, are three generations of A.J., including grandson Bill, great-grandson James, and son Corky. (Left, courtesy of Bill Robertson, below, author's collection.)

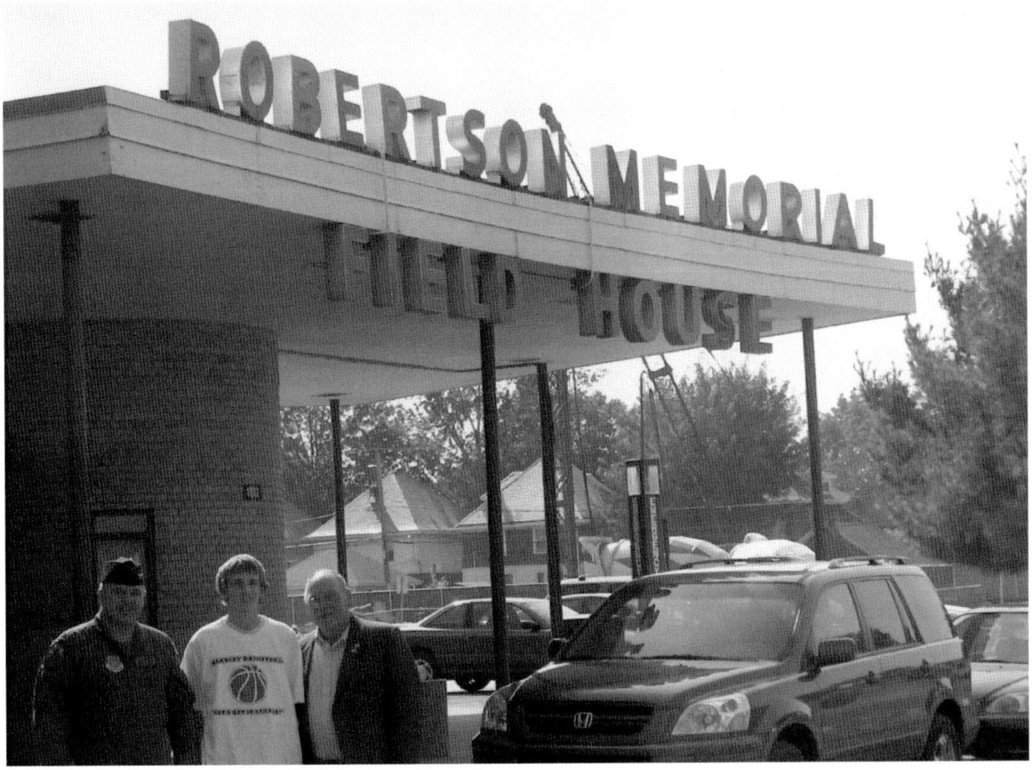

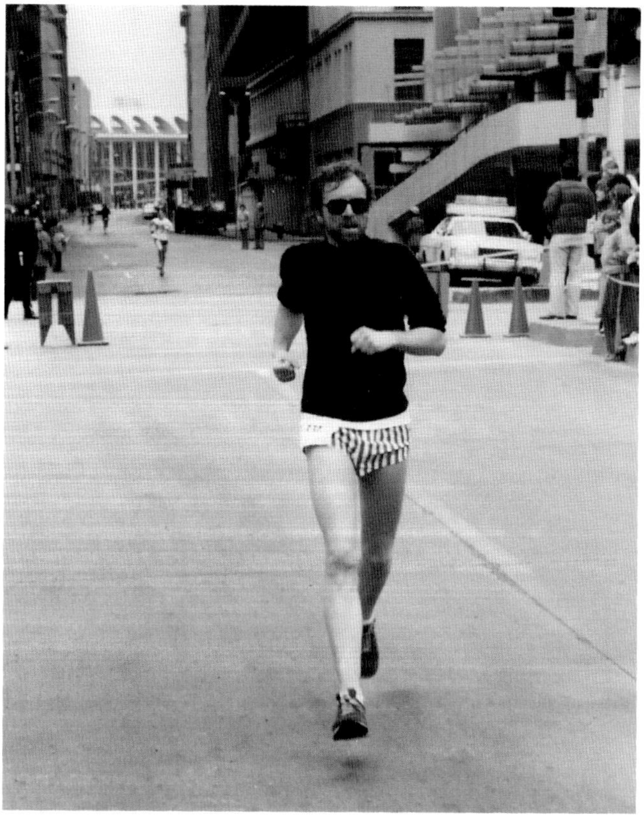

The Fleet Streeter

Chicagoan Steve Shostrom played basketball and baseball at Fenger High and MacMurray College and viewed running as dreary conditioning only. While at the University of Illinois Law School, his favorite professor introduced him to long-distance racing. The professor later steered him in 1967 to the Peoria office of the National Labor Relations Board.

Within a few years, Shostrom would become Mr. River City Strider, the first from Peoria to run in the Boston Marathon (1973); six months later, he unleashed his inner teammate as a cofounder of the Illinois Valley Striders, destined to be one of the largest in the Midwest. In 1974, he founded Peoria's Steamboat Classic, which became an international road-race favorite, featuring the world's fastest 4-mile and the 15-kilometer, the toughest in Illinois. In 1977, in response to the town's overwhelming interest, he opened Running Central on Main Street, a non–Big Box specialty store.

Meanwhile, Steve Shostrom kept up a hectic pace, zipping through 70-plus marathons, including 18 Boston Marathons. His administrative skills were recognized by the running world for his ability to bring Olympians and runners from 50-plus countries to Peoria. He was the Road Runners Club of America Midwest director (1981–1986). He won the 1991 Road Race Management Director of the Year award. He was a founding member of the Peoria Area Sports Commission and was named its 1997 Commissioner of the Year. The Greater Peoria Sports Hall of Fame inducted him in 1998 after honoring him with the 1983 Neve Harms Meritorious Service award for his activities with youths.

Though many honors have come his way, he says his 1980 marriage to Joy Kessler was the best.

Proving that he had not forgotten the game of his youth, he was a founding member of the Moonlight Basketball League that encouraged youth ball playing over gang doings.

He retired from law in 2002 and no longer runs, except in his dreams, where he is paradoxically "always winning, but always getting lost."

Pictured is Steve Shostrom fleet streeting in the St. Louis Marathon. (Courtesy of Joy Kessler.)

Out of Peoria

Joe Stowell learned to diagram sentences in grammar school, and later, X's and O's as a basketball coach. His competitive ethos evolved as a youngster watching the 1930s Bradley Braves basketball squads of the legendary A.J. Robertson; he later played as a sophomore for Coach Robbie's last team, in 1947–1948. After his playing days ended with a Bradley diploma in 1950, he coached preparatory basketball, first at Armington, Illinois, and then in Peoria before returning to his alma mater as an assistant coach in 1956, the same year he earned a Bradley master's degree.

He became head coach in 1965 and began the "Robbie chase," in which he would become the second-winningest Bradley basketball coach ever with 197 wins in 13 seasons (ending in 1978)—next to the immortal's 312 wins in 26 seasons. During his ride, it was a Viper-palooza at Robertson Memorial Fieldhouse where his feisty teams won a heady 79 percent of their home games, going 151-41. Stowell's floor-burned Braves dived for every loose ball heading for the sideline hinterlands of their raised court, something most opponents would not dare. As the women's basketball head coach for two years in the early 1980s, the Lady Braves mirrored their fiery coach, winning 33 games and, in 1982–1883, leading the nation in scoring.

He traded his whistle at the Hilltop for a WMBD radio mic, providing color for Bradley games from 1985 until 2010.

Yet, during his radio stretch, his hardwood daydreamin' never stopped. He coached around the globe, 23 countries in all—more than any other US university coach or professor. And for his inexhaustible basketball knowledge and stamina, the hoarse-voiced goodwill ambassador received job offers in several countries, but turned them down, preferring to keep his wife, Marilyn, and their family of four boys (Joe Jr., Jerry, and twins Jim and Jon) in River City.

After all, he knew nothing beats driving the lane in Peoria.

Here, "hailing" from a camel, Egyptian Olympic coach Joe goes for a ride. (Courtesy of Jim Stowell.)

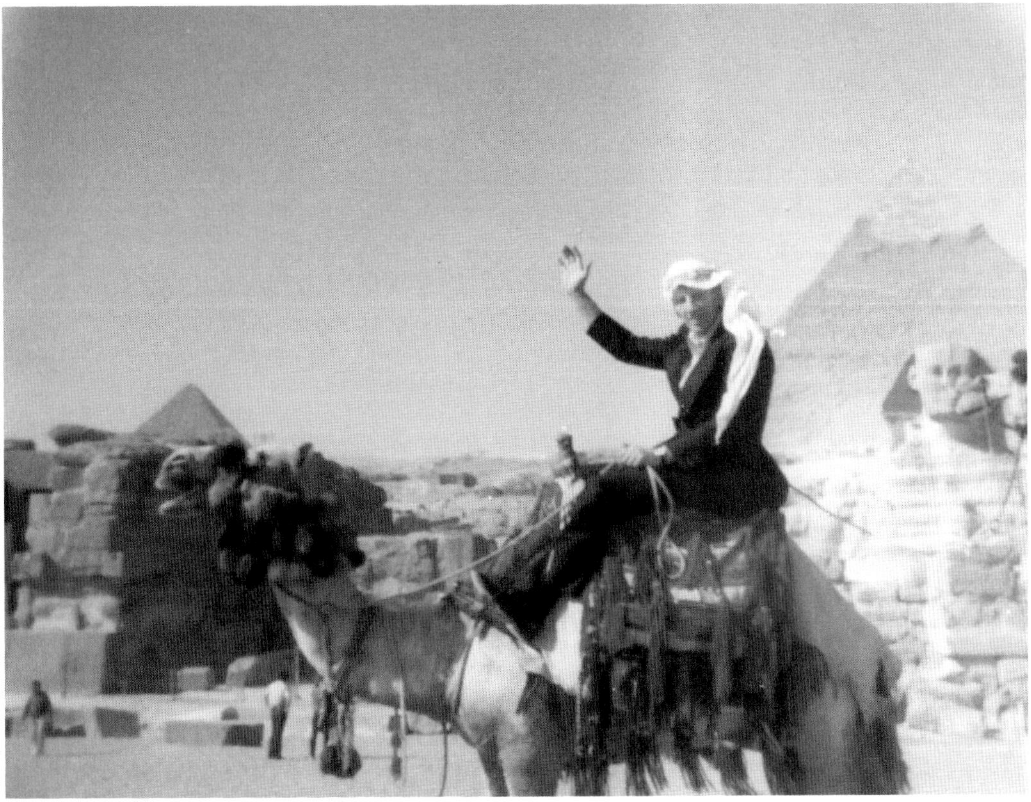

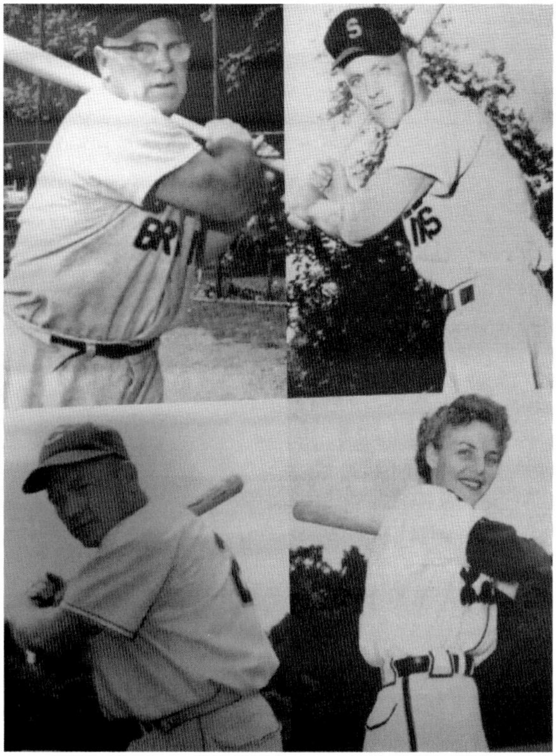

A League of Their Own

In a way, the ever-increasing launching of baseballs and softballs over the fence by three generations of Peoria's Thome family mirrored the cycle of rocketry propulsion of the 1960s NASA programs of Mercury-Gemini-Apollo. For the Thome clan, it started with Chuck Sr. (Mercury); followed by his duo of hard-hitting sons Art and Chuck Jr. (Gemini), along with their national softball hall of famer sister Carolyn; and then came Chuck Jr.'s powerful son Jim (Apollo) who would become only the sixth player in Major League history (19,000-plus players) to hit over 600 home runs, many of which were breathtaking rips of cowhide covers.

Team Thome for years owned the nation's oldest amateur fastball league, central Illinois's hypercompetitive Sunday Morning League. Chuck Sr., a Ruthian slugger (1923–1959), remains the league's all-time homer champ with 14 more dingers than the runner-up; he could also hit for an average that included a 1935 batting title. His son Art won his first batting title at age 15 and added three more in his 20-year career (1942–1962). Not to be outdone, Chuck Jr. (1953–1968) had a league best average in 1964, giving the family of third basemen six batting crowns. Chuck Jr. also was a nationally recognized whiz at fast pitch softball, playing outfield on the 1967 World Softball Champion Harrelson Motors team (72-3) out of Moline, Illinois.

Lefty Carolyn Thome, on the distaff side, starred for the Caterpillar Dieselettes, starting as a 15-year-old, and, later, for the powerhouse Pekin Lettes, the nation's oldest continuous fast pitch softball women's team. A five-time All-American outfielder in the 1950s, she usually led her teams in hitting, powering them into 10 national tournaments in her 15-year career. Known as Cotton for her platinum-blond hair, she was an early inductee to the National Softball Hall of Fame (1962). Later, she added the Illinois and Greater Peoria Sports Halls of Fame to her laurels.

Into the 21st century, Cotton is still the Lettes' all-time leader in homers (almost a Thome given) and doubles; she is also second lifetime in stolen bases—a bow to her "Cotton Hustle" persona.

Hall of Famers pictured here are, clockwise from top left, Chuck Sr., Art, Carolyn, and Chuck Jr. (Courtesy of the Greater Peoria Sports Hall of Fame and the Peoria Civic Center.)

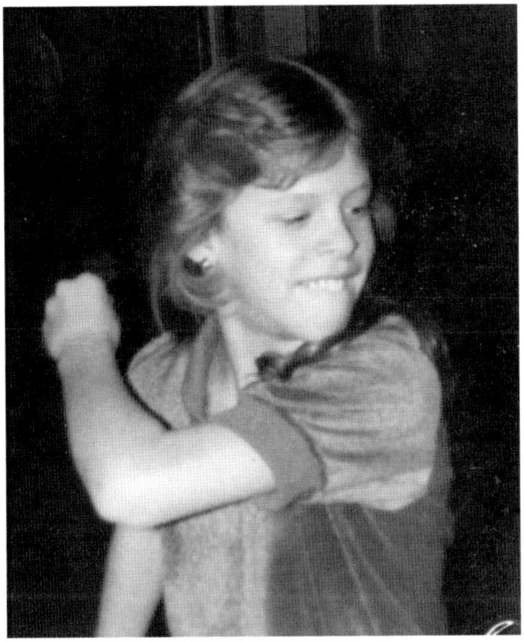

River City Rocketeer

Jim Thome has belted more Major League home runs (612) than anyone ever born or raised in the Midwest.

And even though his diamond achievements allow him to stand shoulder-to-shoulder or higher with baseball's elite stars, his humility remains admired and rarified in contrast to the diva flambino-style that has wracked big-time baseball.

The baby (his twin, Jennifer, is three minutes older) of five children of Chuck Jr. and Joyce Thome had to scratch to be noticed athletically with his two older brothers, Chuck III and Randy, who were bigger standouts in baseball and basketball. (Sisters Lori and Jennifer, though, gave him a pass.) Jim first played baseball on Peoria's concrete tennis courts, hitting tennis balls thrown by his dad, himself a legendary local ballplayer. He batted right-handed until his brother Randy told him to go lefty. At Limestone High, Thome, undersized compared to his brothers, played decently on the baseball and basketball teams but wasn't a star. No sniffs from the pros led Thome to local Illinois Central College for a year. In 1989, he hung around until the 13th round of the draft, also known as bargain bin time, when the Cleveland Indians claimed him.

Away from home for the first time, his 1990 St. Petersburg rookie league season yawned, hitting .236 with no four-baggers. Yet, that offseason back in Peoria showed the true pluck of his resolve as his regimen of long days of offloading trucks at Caterpillar and workouts led to a more muscle-slapping physique. That, and the fateful collaboration with Indians hitting coach Charlie Manuel catapulted Thome to Cleveland in September 1991. In the next 13 seasons, he would become the greatest slugger in Indian history and only the second Cleveland player honored with a statue—the other being Bob Feller.

When Ruth hit a homer for a hospital-bound child, the story splashed everywhere. With little herald, Thome bested the Bam when his nephew in the hospital asked him to hit three homers in the next two games. He did.

Ever the Rocketeer, Thome launched skyward 612 taters in 21 Big Show seasons that ended in 2012—the greatest slugger ever from the Midwest.

Adding weight to a sure-bet hall of fame enshrinement, Chuck Jr. would say, "As a dad, I could not imagine a career any better than my son's."

Who says nice guys can't finish first?

Pictured is the rare righty swing of Jim Thome. (Courtesy of Chuck Thome Jr.)

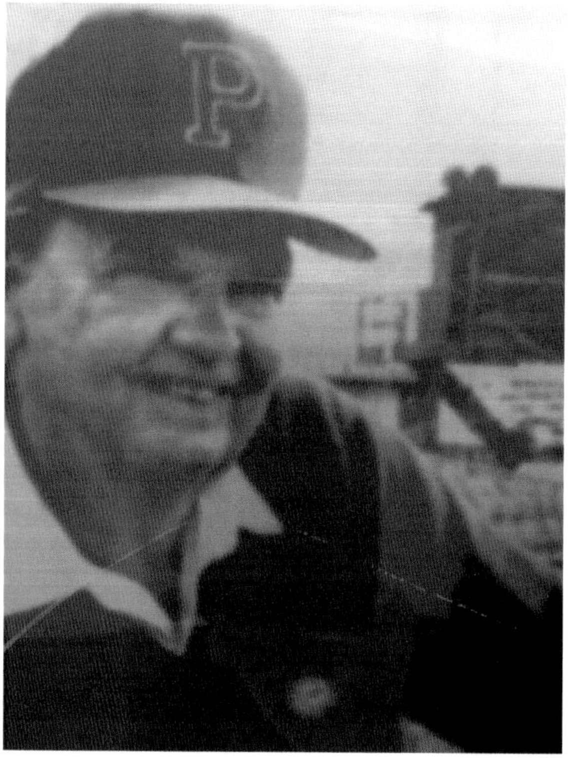

Cheer On

Harry A. "Pete" Vonachen, a member of Bradley University's class of 1949, had the moxie to turn a sports fan's dream into reality when, in 1984, he bought his hometown's minor league team, the Peoria Chiefs, and, as he had in business, made it thrive with his own firebrand-style of community activism. Mr. Peoria Baseball has had many honors, but none have been cherished more than being a pal to all, including Chicago Cubs big-pipes Harry Carey and Peorian Jack Brickhouse. (Left, courtesy of the Greater Peoria Sports Hall of Fame; below, courtesy of Karen Camper.)

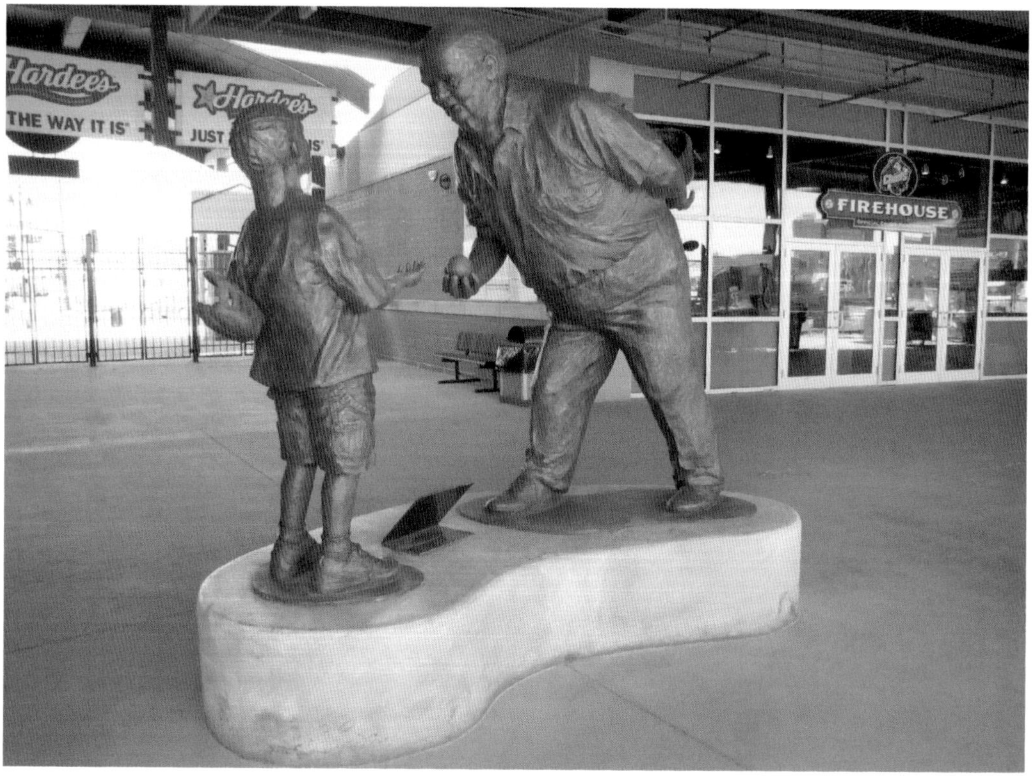

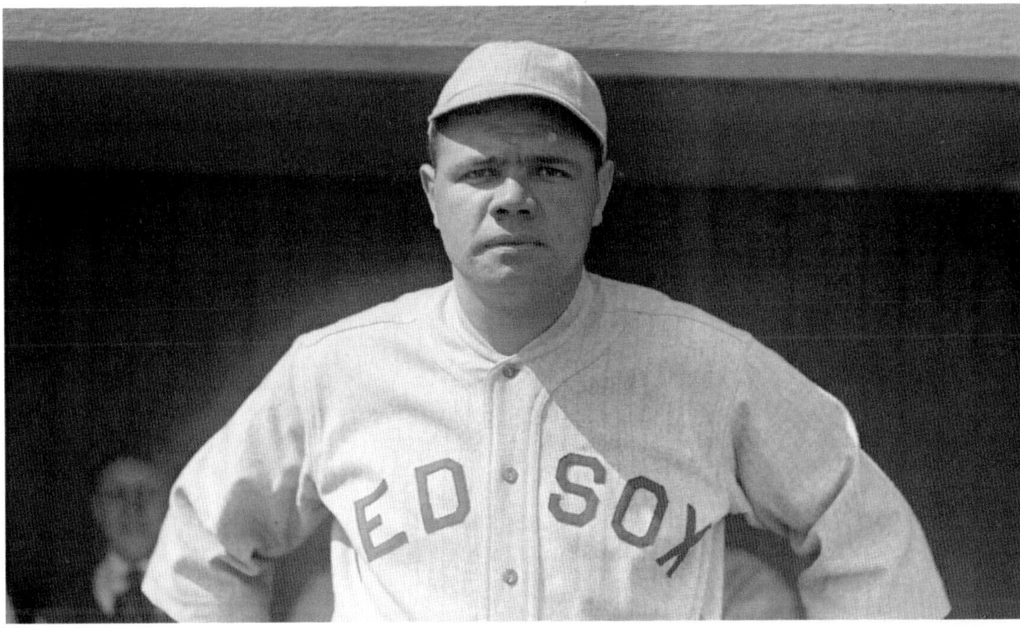

Lucky, the Babe Beater

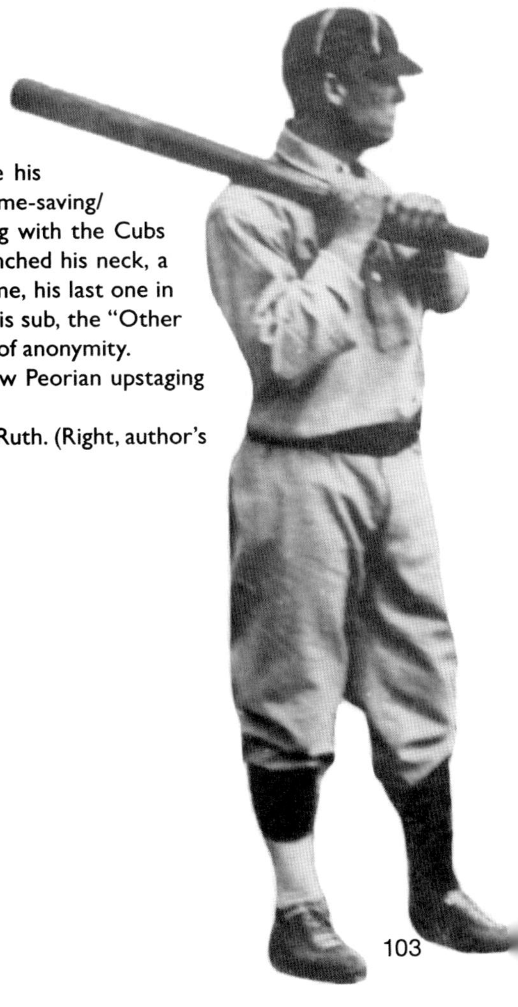

George "Lucky" Whiteman (1882–1947) may have been Boston's Glitterless George in 1918, but many thought the journeyman outfielder was the most valued player for the World Series–winning BoSox. He factored in eight key scores against the Cubs and starred in the outfield where his catches led to Beantown wins, including "The Catch," the game-saving/series-winning somersaulting grab came in the eighth inning with the Cubs threatening to score. Lucky came up with the ball but wrenched his neck, a freak accident for the former diving acrobat. He left the game, his last one in the Major Leagues, to thunderous cheers by Fenway fans. His sub, the "Other George," known as the Babe, trotted out in a rare moment of anonymity.

Owner Harry Frazee probably drank to that one: a fellow Peorian upstaging the Babe.

Above is the "Other George" on the 1918 Red Sox—Babe Ruth. (Right, author's collection; above, courtesy of Library of Congress.)

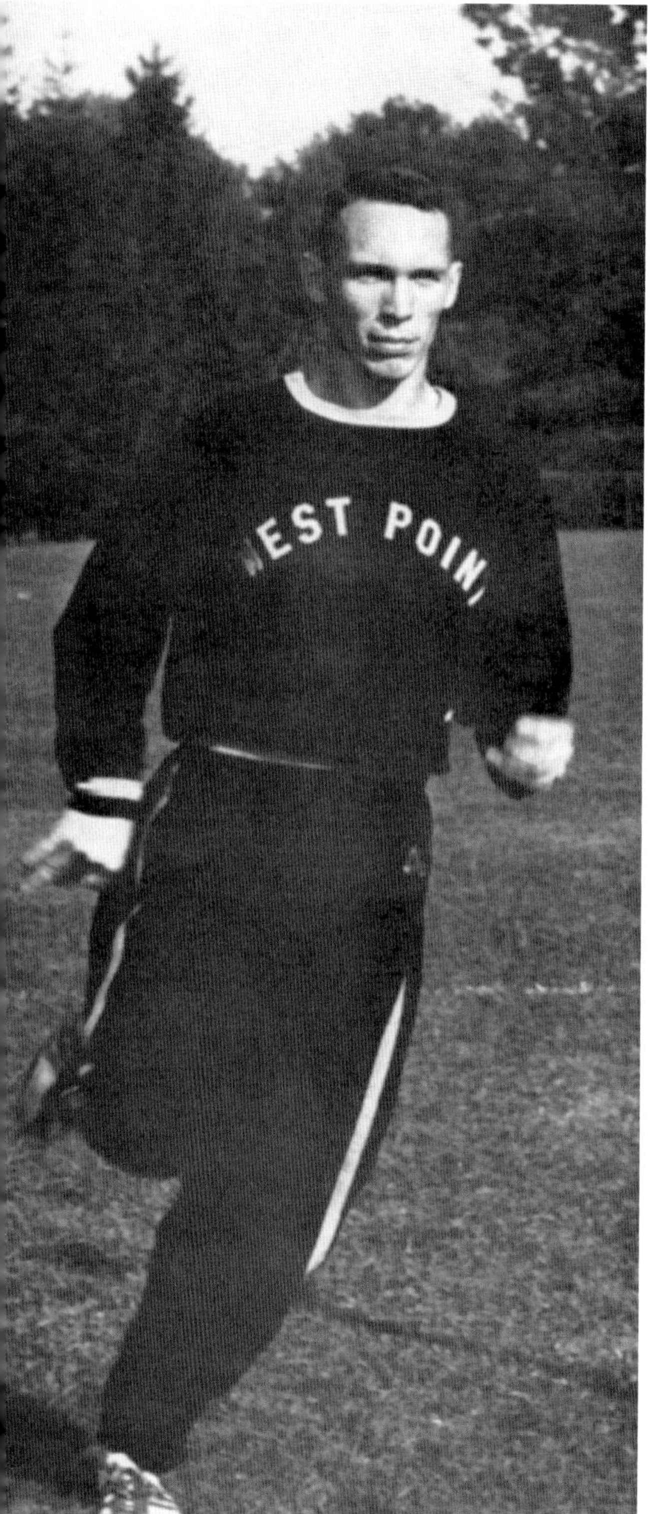

The Walkabout

Peoria native Ronald Lloyd Zinn's grit to never quit, as he often said, came from his waitress mother who sacrificed it all for him. His family moved from Peoria to the Chicago south suburb of Orland Park when he was 14. He applied himself both in academics, becoming a West Point cadet (class of 1962 with fellow Peorian Wayne Downing), and in sports, becoming a race walker. Within a year of learning the odd-duck gait of speedwalking, the former cross-country runner and wrestler made the 1960 US Olympic team, a first-ever Olympic cadet. He placed 19th in the 20-kilometer at Rome, which showed the domination of the Russians and Europeans. West Point honored his return with a parade—the only cadet ever so honored. At the 1964 Tokyo Olympics, Zinn, by now an Army officer whose marching style clashed with his hip-rolled walker stride, took sixth and became the first American walker to beat a Russian; it capped a remarkable streak of 12 national titles from 1960 to 1964 and a 1963 Pan Am Games bronze medal.

Ronald Lloyd Zinn reported to Vietnam at the end of 1964. On July 7, 1965, Captain Zinn's platoon came under fire near Saigon and during the fight he took fire and died as he tried to help his wounded squad leader. Spurred by his captain's sacrifice, Milton Olive went above and beyond, receiving the Medal of Honor.

Ron Zinn was one of the first officers killed in Vietnam.

At the time of his death, he held eight national records. While names can fall from the collective conscience, Wall, New Jersey, celebrates the Peoria walker with its annual Captain Ron Zinn Memorial Races. Additionally, the USA Track & Field Association annually honors the top female and male walkers with the Ron Zinn Memorial Awards.

Cadet Zinn is pictured here in a rare run. (Courtesy of Army Athletes.)

CHAPTER SIX

Atmospheric Icons

Peoria never had a shortage of celebrity. As a king-maker during the Vaudeville days, the town set the tone for America's entertainment tastes. The Golden Age of Radio took Vaudeville's handoff, with Peorians dominating the airwaves from the 1920s to the 1950s, thanks to Charles Correll (*Amos 'n' Andy*), Marian and Jim Jordan (*Fibber McGee and Molly*), and Fr. Fulton Sheen (*The Catholic Hour*). Comedy from River City continued as the Habitat for Humor later in the 20th century with laugh lords Richard Pryor and Sam Kinison. Songwriter hall of famer Richard Whiting made melody magic for movies, becoming the great catch for fabled lyricists during Hollywood's great musical era. Dan Fogelberg exemplified soft rock from the 1970s onward. Philip José Farmer stirred cosmic dust in science fiction, defying convention. Spig Wead fell and then soared as a screenwriter while Johnston McCulley made swashbuckling history. Betty Friedan gave a name to the thing without a name and started a movement. Lonnie Stewart beautified the world with his art.

Lydia Moss Bradley went from dirt to riches and championed education. Robert Ingersoll, the great late 1800s orator, took the gloves off and made debate a blood sport. Meanwhile, Joseph Greenhut ensured whiskey flowed throughout the globe with the Octopus.

The Duryea brothers put America on the move with the country's first car; they spawned an entire new industry, too. Octave Chanute looked to the heavens and foresaw a sky full of planes.

John Shalikashvili came from bomb-cratered Poland to unbombed Peoria, and ran the Army table to become a four-star general and chairman of the Joint Chiefs of Staff in 1993—showing that the American dream does indeed live in Peoria.

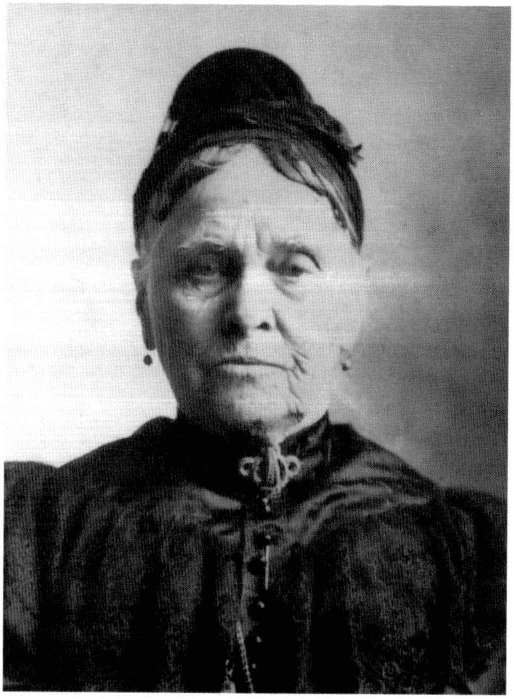

Flipping a Fortune

Lydia Moss Bradley was a modern woman in frontier times. Born in the Ohio River spit of Vevay, Indiana, in 1816, the farmer's daughter intuitively knew how to make money grow; after enjoying an orphaned colt her father had given her, she later flipped the pony for 40 acres of timber that she then cleared, selling the lumber. She made a hefty turn from the deal. Lydia Moss also met sawmill owner Tobias Bradley; they would marry in 1837. Ten years later they moved to Peoria, a place rippling with possibilities.

At first, it was the "Tobias Touch"—with his wife nearby—that made the Bradleys a fortune in business and real estate.

Yet along with their wealth rode tragedy—the six Bradley children all died young; the oldest lived to 14. The death of Tobias in a carriage accident in 1867 cinched the circle of heartbreak for her.

The Lydia Moss Bradley saga could have ended there since, by any era's standards, she was rich.

But all that had happened so far was only a run-up.

Raised on self-reliance and repulsed by sloth, she abhorred the notion of being a "shawl on the porch." She held her grief in as she assumed management of the family monies. By daily keeping her laced gloves on the money pulse and through her prudent decisions, she grew her worth from $500,000 to nearly $3 million at her passing in 1908 at age 91.

She would become one of America's richest women; few, if any, owned more New World land. She was also the first woman to sit as a member of the board of directors of an American national bank, the First National Bank, the very one Tobias had served as president and one of its founders.

As she went from dirt floors to fortune, Lydia Moss Bradley embodied noblesse oblige. Among her good works, she donated land to the Order of St. Francis for a hospital; built the Bradley Home for Aged Women; gave land for a park named after her daughter Laura; championed the idea of a city park system, a first in Illinois; and established her greatest and enduring gift, Bradley University, née Bradley Polytechnic Institute.

She founded the institution in 1897 in memory of her children and husband. Her educational endowment was the largest by any woman in the world. (Courtesy of Special Collections Center, Bradley University Library.)

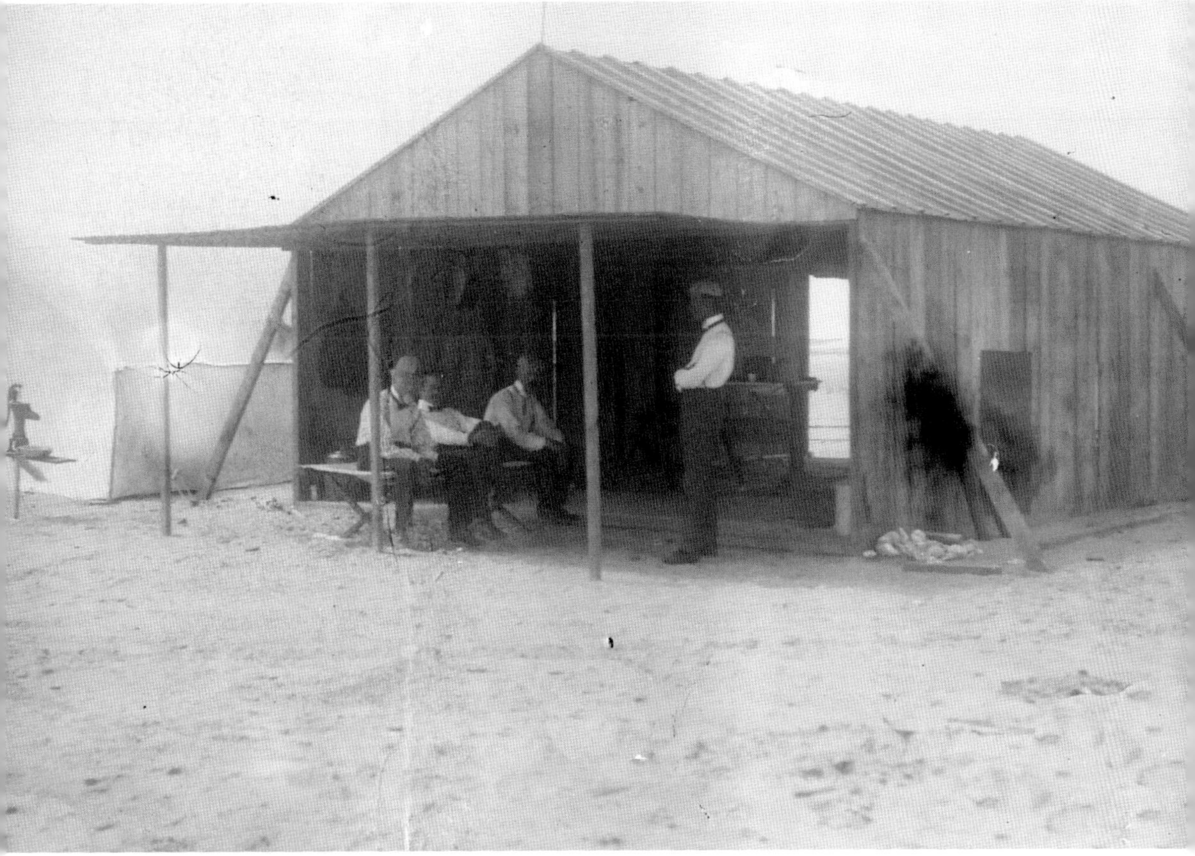

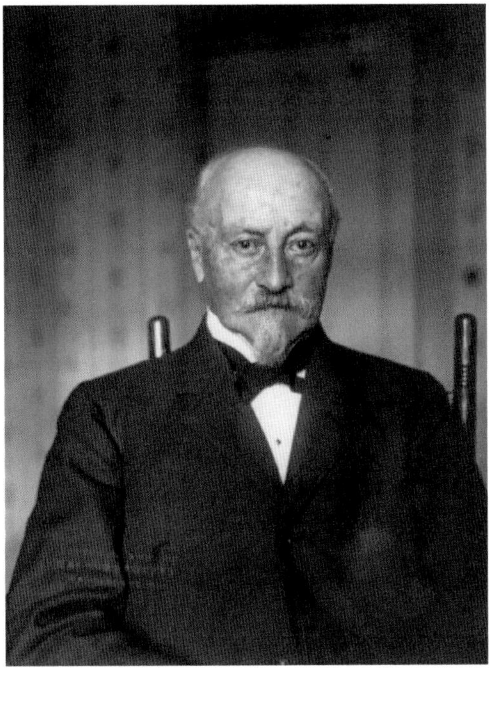

High Octave

Though known as the Father of Aviation, Paris-born Octave Chanute was a self-taught engineer who, among many ventures, built the first railroad bridge over the Illinois River at Peoria (1856), his home for a decade in the mid-1800s.

He looked toward the heavens with the possibility of manned flight in the late 1880s and began building gliders. After watching sparrows descend, he advocated "tail down" landings for aircraft (if he had watched spooked cats jump and land, he might have foreseen the helicopter). He argued for collaboration and against a roped-off sky, and published the classic *Progress in Flying Machines* (1894). The Wright brothers used his glider design for their 1903 prototype airplane.

Chanute and his wife from Peoria, Annie, are buried at Springdale Cemetery.

At left is Chanute, Father of Flight. Above, Chanute, seated at far left, is pictured at Kitty Hawk, helping the Wright brothers. (Both, courtesy of the Library of Congress.)

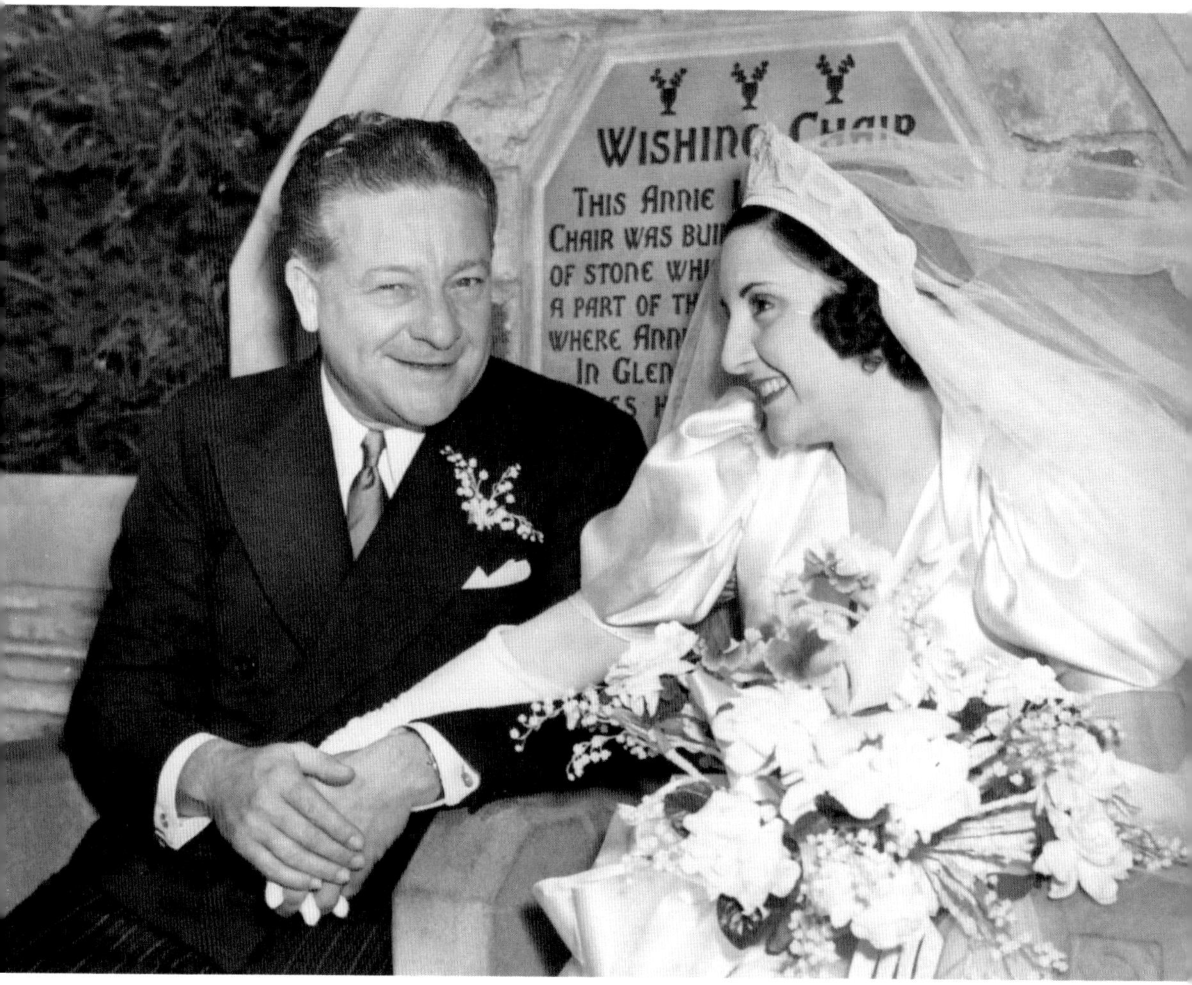

Amos 'n' Andy

Peorian Charles Correll was a laborer until he joined a 1920s road show and teamed up with Freeman Gosden of Richmond, Virginia. That led, in 1925, to a 34-year radio run as *Amos 'n' Andy*, radio's first megahit. In 1930–1931, 40 million listeners (one third of America) tuned in for the daily 15-minute skits about two Southern blacks who came to Chicago hoping for a better life. Writers Gosden and Correll imbued their characters with traits common to all Americans, especially the belief in the American Dream.

The show ended in the early 1950s after 4,000 episodes. Correll ("The Man of 200 Voices") resides in several national halls of fame.

It was not a bad life for a one-time Peoria bricklayer. (Courtesy of Local History and Genealogy Collection, Peoria Public Library.)

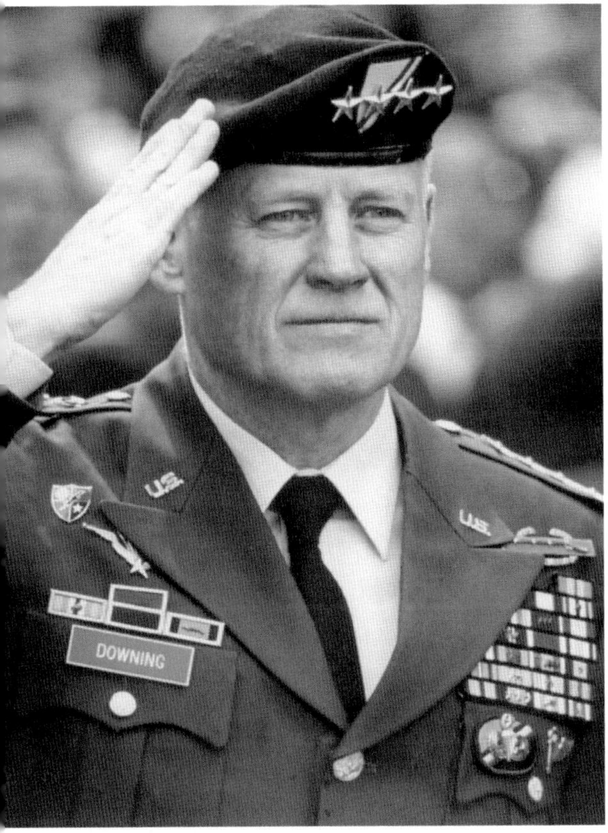

Terror Fighter Supreme

Four-star general Wayne Downing led by example. As commander-in-chief of US Special Forces Command, General Downing had written the book on counter-terrorism. After the 1996 Saudi Khobar Towers attack, General Downing warned that a "persistent, not intermittent, terrorism threat exists" and concluded that there was an "undeclared war against the United States."

After 9/11, he served as the nation's counter-terrorism chief, advising President Bush. He finished his tour in 2002, returning to Peoria, his retirement command post and not a golf course.

Instead, he founded West Point's Combatting Terrorism Center, used his 1972 Tulane MBA to serve on corporate boards (including the Order of St. Francis), served as NBC's military commentator, and taught.

During a swim, he contracted bacterial meningitis and died on July 18, 2007. America lost its great Point Man.

At left is Gen. Wayne Downing. Below is Cadet Downing's favorite picture—"Feeding the Animal." (Both, courtesy of Jim Heldman.)

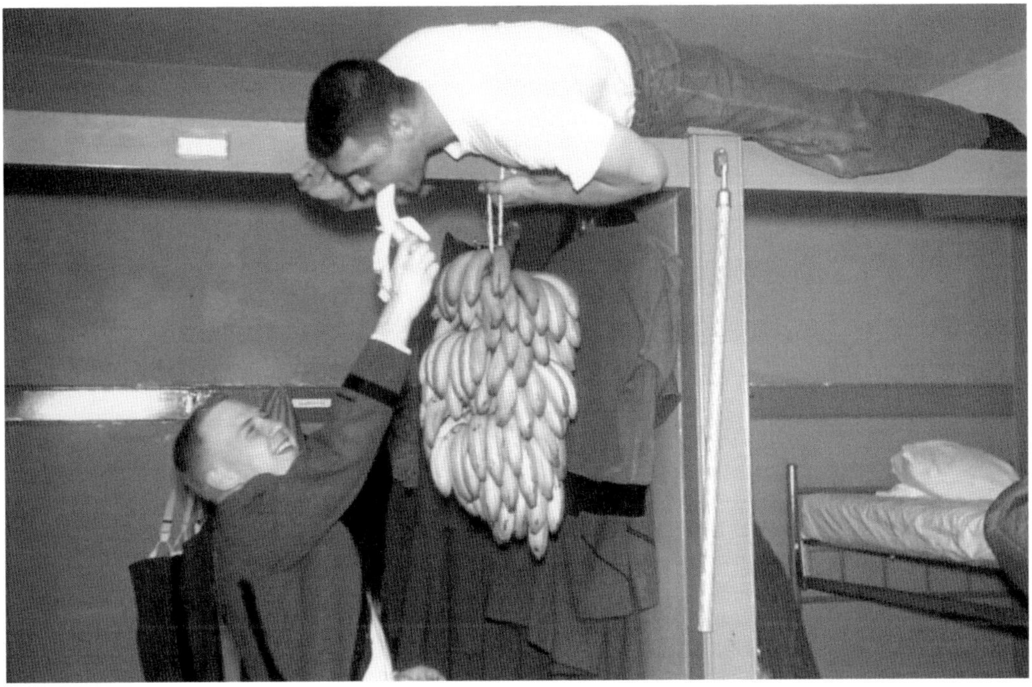

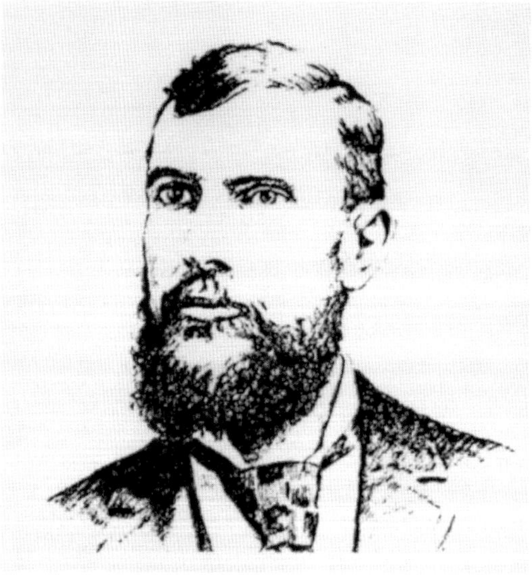

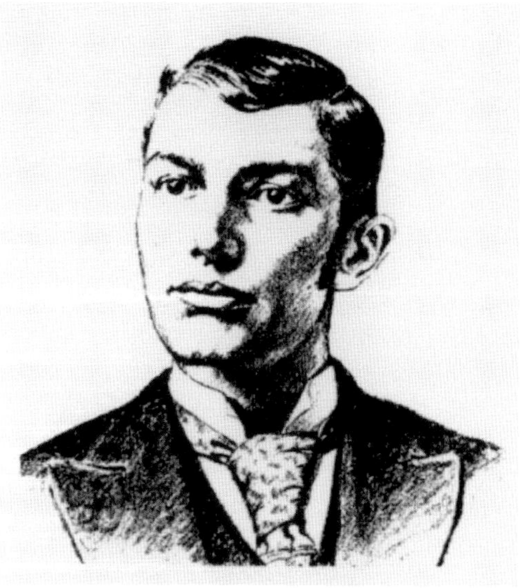

No Horseless Remorse

Ironic that it took the gas-powered car to jettison 19th-century urban America's polluting scourge: the horse.

In the late 1800s, cities faced ever-greater heapings of horse droppings fouling their streets. There were dire predictions of pony poo piled as high as third-floor Manhattan windows by 1930 and a run on nose plugs.

Enter the Peorialand Duryea brothers, Charles (1861–1938) and J. Frank (1869–1967), who developed America's first auto, the anti-horse, in 1893; the beginning of Manifold Destiny. They also pioneered an entire industry, launching the country's first two car companies with Peoria as the home of the second firm. What Charles designed, Frank could build. The Duryea auto won America's first auto race, the 1895 Chicago, besting the Benz cars.

Henry Ford the brothers were not; they made only a few cars.

Charles Duryea is pictured above left with J. Frank Duryea. Below, Charles Duryea is at the helm of the 1895 Chicago winner. (Both above, courtesy of Special Collections Center, Bradley University Library; below, courtesy of the Library of Congress.)

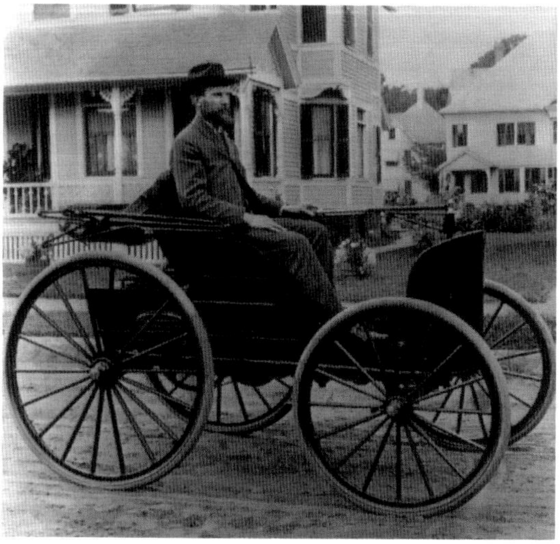

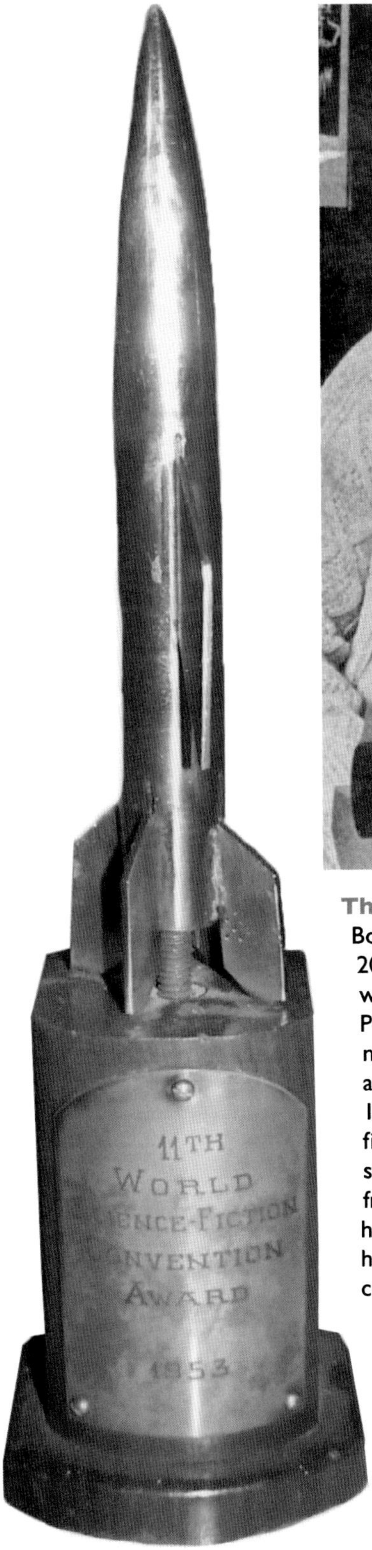

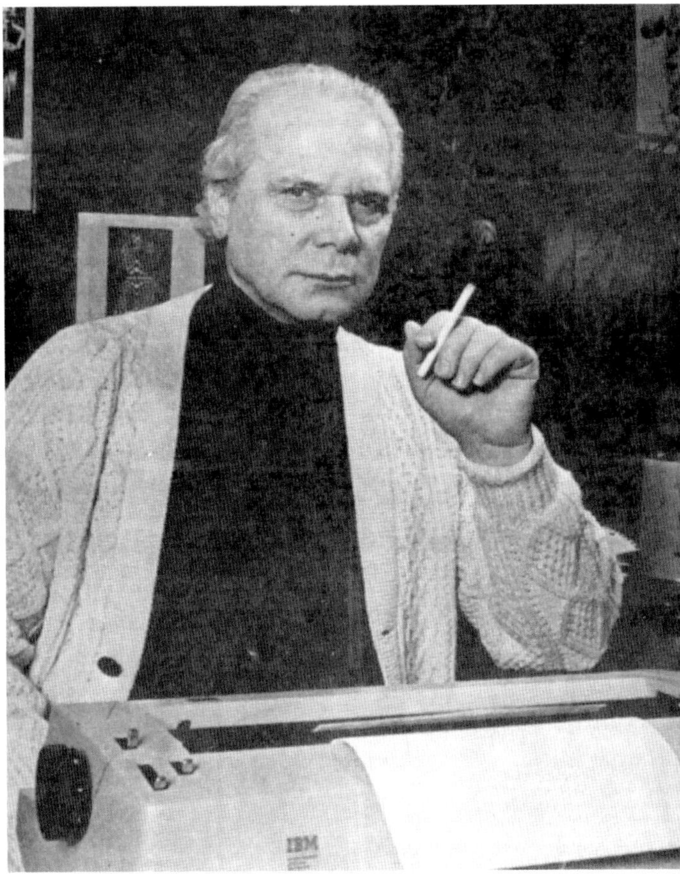

The Brando of Science Fiction

Born in North Terre Haute, Indiana, Philip José Farmer (1918–2009), the science-fiction icon, spent most of his life in Peoria writing about universes beyond the earth's tether. He was a 1938 Peoria High and a 1950 Bradley Polytechnic graduate. In 1952, his novella *The Lovers* detailed sex between a space alien and a human, a science-fiction taboo, and netted Farmer the Pulitzer-esque 1953 Hugo Newcomer of the Year award. The Brando of science fiction rolled his shoulders through 45 novels and hundreds of short stories and poems. He was easily the most prolific writer from Peoria. When asked why he stayed in the town of his youth, he said, "Peoria's as good a place as any to watch the world go to hell in a handbasket," or rocket toward distant galaxies. (Above, courtesy of the Local History and Genealogy Collection, Peoria Public Library; left, author's collection.)

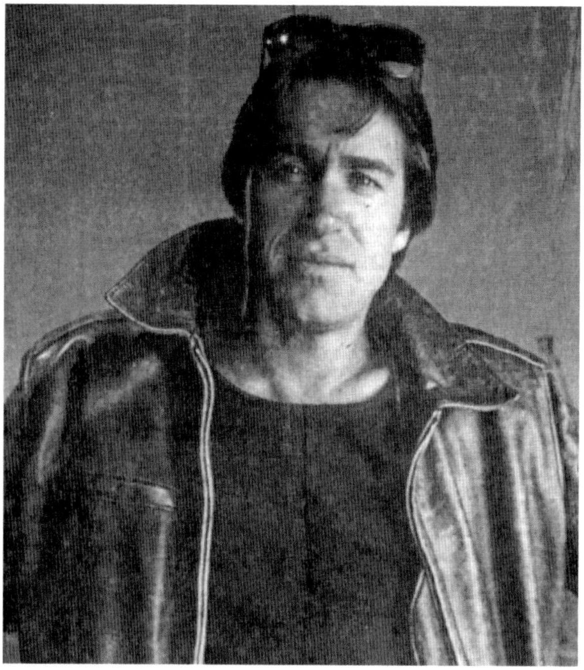

For the Good Rhymes

In the time of the Iron Butterfly, he was unplugged from the prairie.

His worldwide burst came in the mid-1970s, when music tamped down its amps and opened its mics to the soft-rock balladeer.

And few on the planet ever did it better than Peorian Dan Fogelberg.

Born August 13, 1951, into a musical family, the youngest of three sons of Margaret (a classically trained vocalist) and Lawrence (a popular high school/Bradley band director) began a full-on, pre-kindergarten training on the piano and then guitar. By 16, the songwriter showed all the tags of his future success with "Maybe Time Will Let Me Forget," recorded in 1967 with his second band, the Coachmen.

The 1969 Woodruff High grad left for the University of Illinois, Urbana-Champaign, studying theater before switching to art. He also brought his six-string, which soon overwhelmed his palette and impressed Irving Azoff, a local booking agent, who saw him as the ticket to Big-Time Los Angeles.

It was 1971 when West Coast met west Illinois with the world just offstage.

While his first album, 1972's *Home Free* (with "The River," an Illinois River reflective), caught a following and good reviews, he "arrived" with *Souvenirs* (1974), a platinum herald for his next six albums. Dan Fogelberg was in Peoria during 1975 helping his ailing father and writing *Captured Angels*, a platinum outing in which he played most of the instruments himself.

The world soon recognized him for his extraordinary lyrical songwriting that stirred intense, personal feelings within his listeners. For example, from 1981's critically admired double-platinum *Innocent Age* album, "Same Old Lang Syne" recalled a poignant Christmas-eve chance meeting with an old flame at a Peoria foodmart. Ever since the song's first spin, it has had heavy holiday airplay worldwide. Fogelberg, in an interview, said he did not know if he "will ever write a better song than that."

Dan Fogelberg kept recording until his last album, 2003's *Full Circle*, which celebrated the full diversity of his musical excursions, dating back to his toe-in-the-water *Home Free*.

On December 16, 2007, he died of prostate cancer, age 56. He left a cache of memorable songs melodically written and sung.

Three granite boulders, each etched with an ethereal lyric, stand at the Peoria riverfront in tribute to native son Dan Fogelberg, who sat by "The River" and dared to dream. (Courtesy of the Local History and Genealogy Collection, Peoria Public Library.)

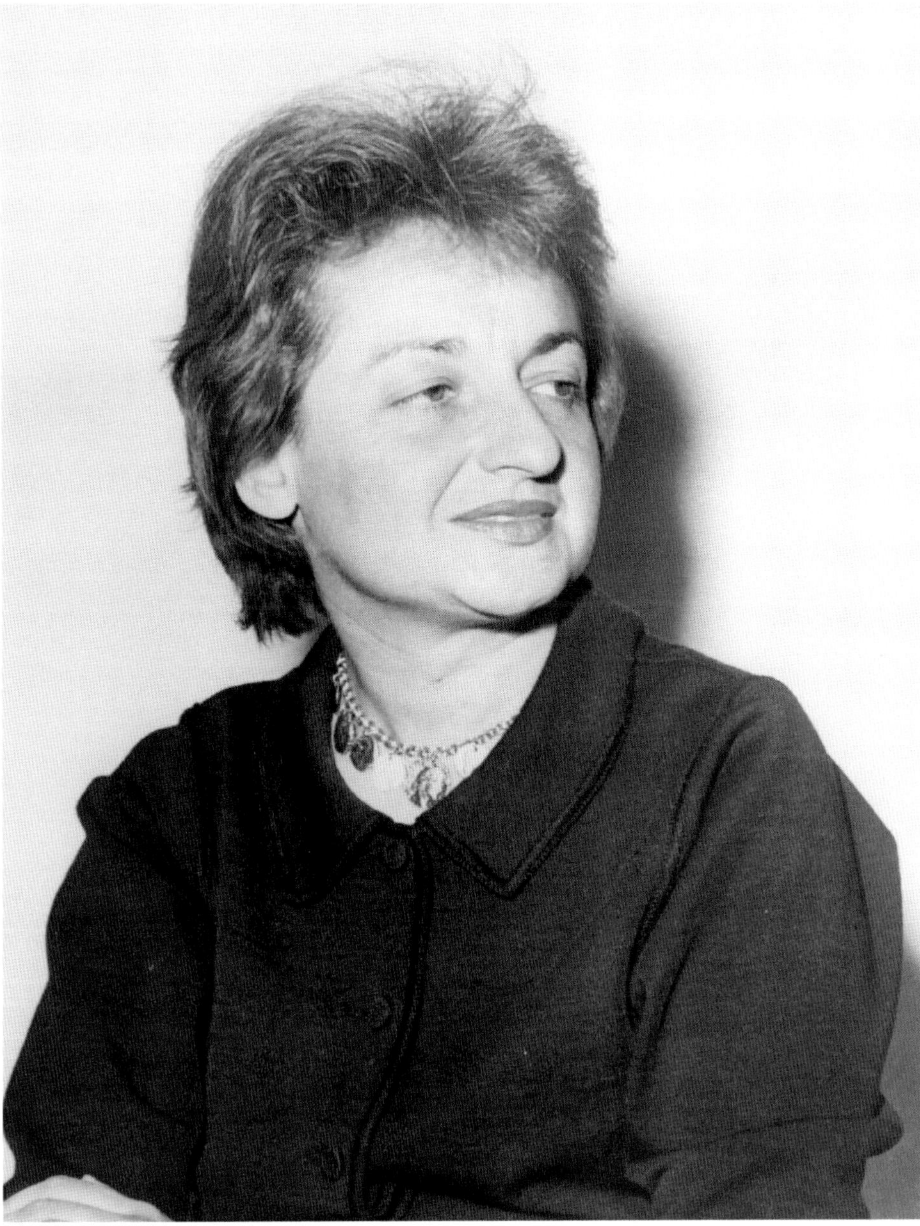

Illinois Valley Girl

Born on February 4, 1921, in Peoria to Harry and Miriam Goldstein, feminist icon Betty Friedan was the oldest of three children who lived in comfort on the West Bluff's Farmington Road overlooking Laura Bradley Park. Early on, Betty pushed for excellence. In 1938, she was among six valedictorians at Peoria High School. She graduated from Smith College in 1942 before writing for radical union publications. She married theater producer Carl Friedman in 1947 and, like her mother, had three children. Exhuming visions of her sighing, unfulfilled housewife-mother's angst, Friedan wrote about the "problem without a name" in *The Feminine Mystique*—the 1963 book that spawned the Feminist movement. She also founded NOW, the National Organization of Women, and served as its first president. (Courtesy of the Library of Congress.)

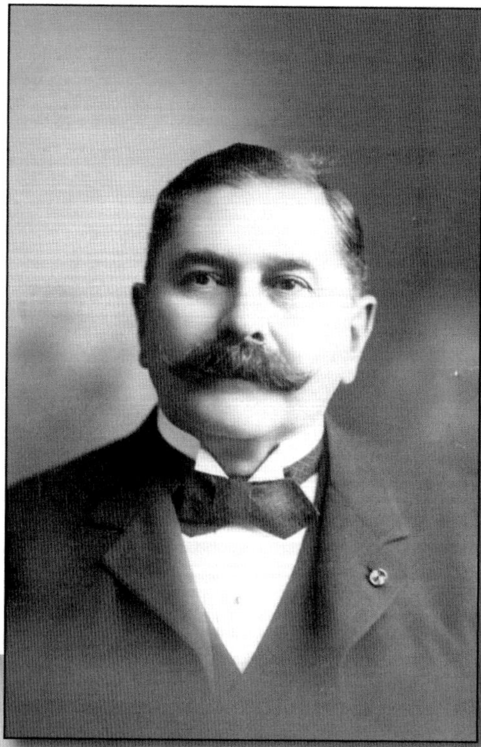

Cheers Leader

He made Peoria "Tipple Town USA" in the late 1800s as the King of the Whiskey Barons. Austrian-native Joseph Greenhut came to Peoria in the 1870s from Chicago. He added kick to the town's booze boom by building the Great Western Distillery, the world's largest, in 1881 and by forming the Distillers' and Cattle Feeders' Trust (1887), also known as "the Octopus." "Head Hooch" Greenhut and his *spiritus frumenti* pals would call the price on 85 percent of the world's whiskey.

As one of the world's richest men, he spent his wealth lavishly on himself and the city, donating numerous *objects d'art* and underwriting civic causes.

But the Gay 1890s brought federal antitrust action against the Octopus, and Greenhut left for a New Jersey estate. He died in 1918.

Shown below is the home of the world's former Head Hooch. (Left, courtesy of Local History and Genealogy Collection, Peoria Public Library; below, author's collection.)

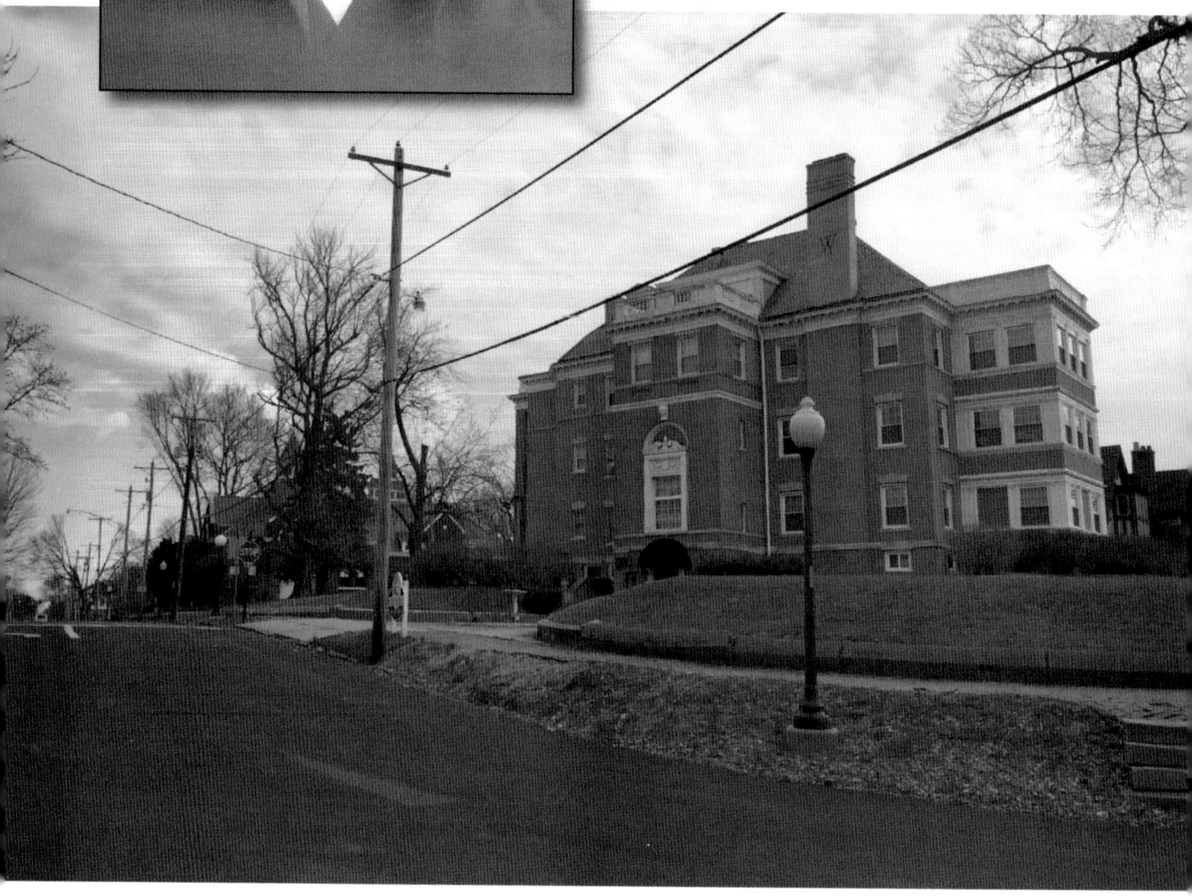

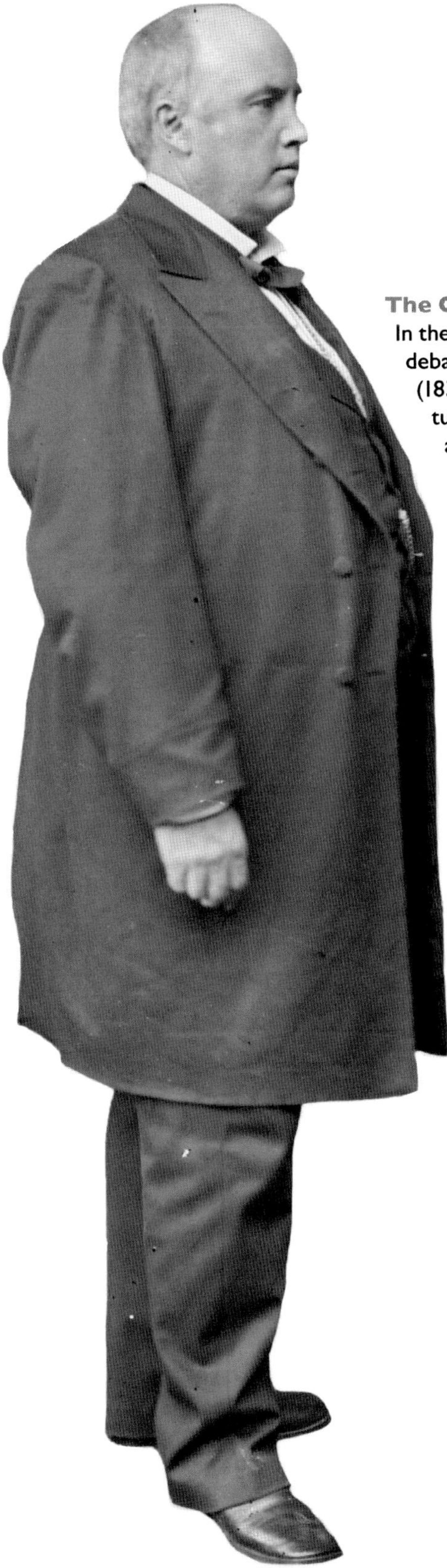

The Oratio

In the 1800s, America's number one spectator sport was the debate. (Think Lincoln-Douglas.) It took Robert Ingersoll (1833–1899), an attorney in Peoria from 1857 to 1877, to turn debate into a cage fight. A minister's son turned agnostic, he became one of the greatest orators of the 19th century with the skills he learned during his River City days. A superb phrase-ginner who first gained distinction in politics, he zealously sank his teeth deep into religious issues, championing secularism. Pictured below is Ingersoll's "baseball card." (Left, courtesy of the Library of Congress; below, courtesy of the Local History and Genealogy Collection, Peoria Public Library.)

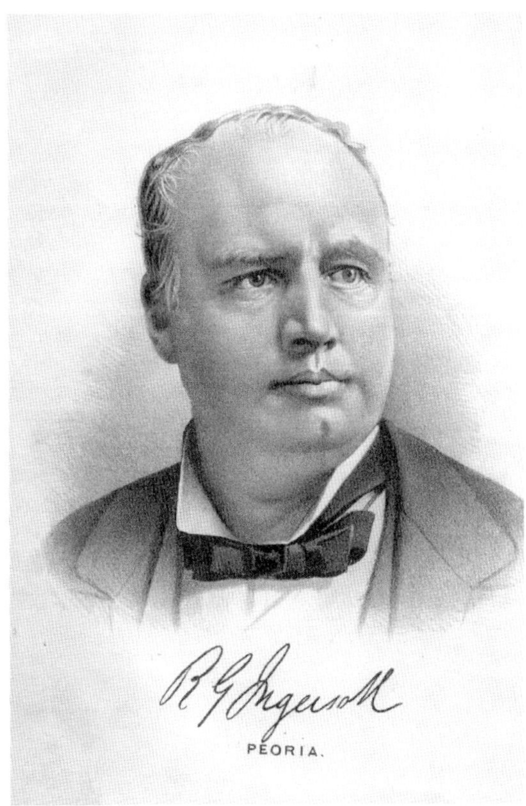

Fibber McGee-West Bluff Kid.

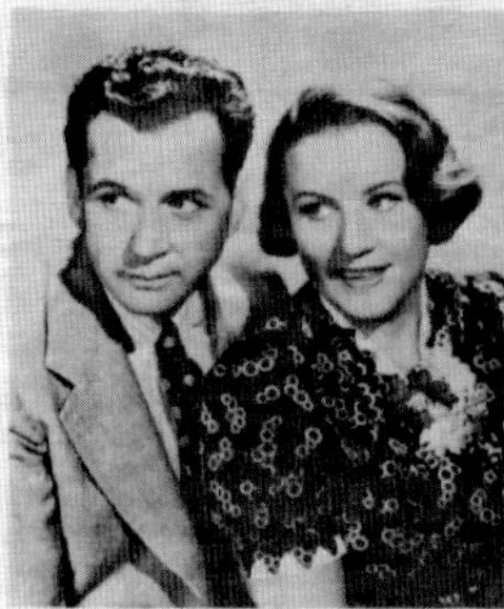

Jim & Marion Jordan in the 1930's

As you may remember, in the February issue of the Word we brought you part one of the story of a West Bluff resident who became a famous radio personality-Fibber McGee, known to his Peoria friends and relatives as Jim Jordon. As part one ended Jim and Marion Jordon, after years of struggle, had moved to Chicago and landed a job with NBC radio.

The year was 1931. Five days a week, the Jordans starred in a show called "Smackout". It was about a small-town

Johnson Wax continued to sponsor the show throughout its run on radio, until the Jordans retired in 1950. Even in those days of single-sponsor shows, this was an unusually durable relationship. The Fibber McGee and Molly Show's success owes a lot to their luck in being sponsored by a company that gave them the time and the freedom to grow. Quinn developed a remarkable talent for writing radio comedy and the Jordans soon became highly skilled comedians. By 1947 their show was the top-ranked show in radio and, if you remember, there was some formidable competition-Lum and Abner, Amos and Andy, Jack Benny, Fred Allen and Duffy's Tavern.

The show revolved around the McGees in their home with the famous closet at "79 Wistful Vista" where a varied assortment of friends and neighbors regularly dropped in. Any small premise was sufficient to get the show rolling. Fibber might be reminiscing about the good old days in Peoria, or they might be cleaning up after opening the hall closet...

FIBBER: Gotta straightn out that closet one of these days, Molly. I don't see that electric cord anyplace...Oh, my gosh!

MOLLY: Now what?

FIBBER: Look! My old mandolin-remember?

Church groups praised the clean gentle and patriotic comedy. "We don't like-I m don't like-humor that sugge repulsive," Marion once st refused to use mother-in "...because we liked each thers." In 1948, they receiv LLD's from St. Joseph's Collegeville, Indiana for the Christian philosophy" and ability" of their comedy. they were awarded the Anci Hibernians Award for, "... family entertainment.

What did success mea personal lives of the Jordans? were very much like the cha played and it certainly didn't Glimpses into the Jordan's after becoming successful s be unchanged other tham their generosity and kindness at least two West Bluff purchased others for variou (One of the homes they occupied by Maggie and C discovery was the original looking into this story.) The good business sense and investments allowed them wealthy long after the big s gone.

Interesting insight into t family life and philosophy wa in a 1937 issue of Radio Guid The reporter interviewed th

Laughter's Their Best Legacy

Fibber McGee and Molly were the heyday couple of the Golden Age of Radio who made America chuckle during two of the 20th century's worst disasters: the tag team of the Great Depression (1929–1939) and World War II (1939–1945). They were also the whimsy of real-life married Peorians Marian (née Driscoll) and Jim Jordan—preteen sweethearts who met at a St. John's Church choir practice in 1908.

Though hitched by music, with Marian playing piano and Jim at the mic, their fame came with laughs. Jim's nephew, Leo Jordan, would say decades later that "the only thing that'd satisfy them was an audience."

They married on August 31, 1918, after a draft board member assured Jim he would not be drafted into World War I. Five days into their honeymoon, Jordan received his draft notice with France in the wings. Six weeks later, the war ended on November 11, 1918.

The Jordans spent the next few years in Peoria (a Vaudeville mecca) on the Midwest circuit and started their family with Kathryn (1920) and James (1923). Then, in 1924 Chicago on the dare of a lifetime from his brother Byron, Jim and Marian performed for the first time on radio, winning WIBO's audition show and a $10-per-week contract.

It took 11 years of a dizzying army of shows and discovering their comedic voices (eventually 147 of them) to become Fibber McGee and Molly. In 1931, they teamed up with cartoonist/writer-wannabe Don Quinn, who would help write their first national program, *Smackout*, the pappy of Fibber. It was Quinn who coined "Fibber" after Jordan had won the 1935 National Liar's Contest; "Molly" came from Irving Berlin's 1911 song "Molly O! Oh, Molly."

"McGee" was easy; the Jordans were Irish.

Fibber aired in 1935; a pioneering situational family comedy set in the fictional Wistful Vista followed Fibber, a prairie Pinocchio whose silo-sized whoppers his wife, Molly, skewered without drawing blood. Molly's "Taint funny, McGee," deflating a Fibber-bombast, overflowed into American jargon. Steeped in Middle American humor with quirky, recurring characters (many voiced by the Jordans), the series surged in the 1940s, becoming the top radio show in 1943. It remained on radio's top shelf until the series ended in 1959.

Marian Jordan died in 1961. Jim Jordan died on April 1, 1988—April Fool's Day. Somewhere that day in the heavens, perhaps, echoed a misty "Taint funny, McGee." (Courtesy of the Local History and Genealogy Collection, Peoria Public Library.)

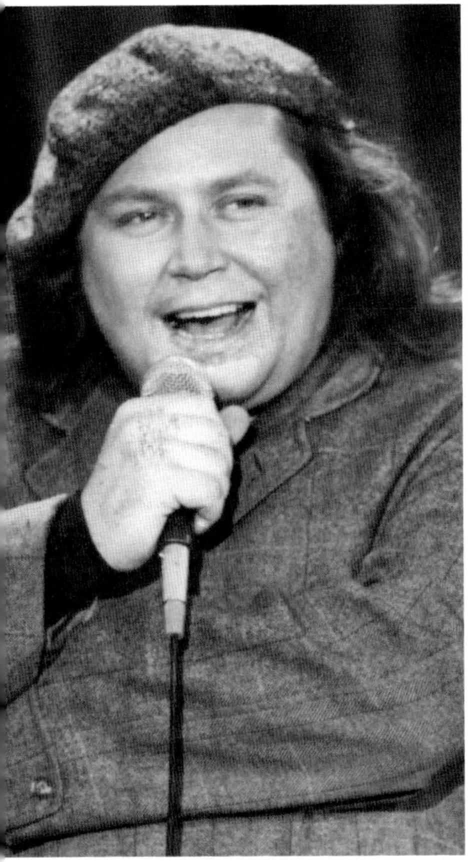

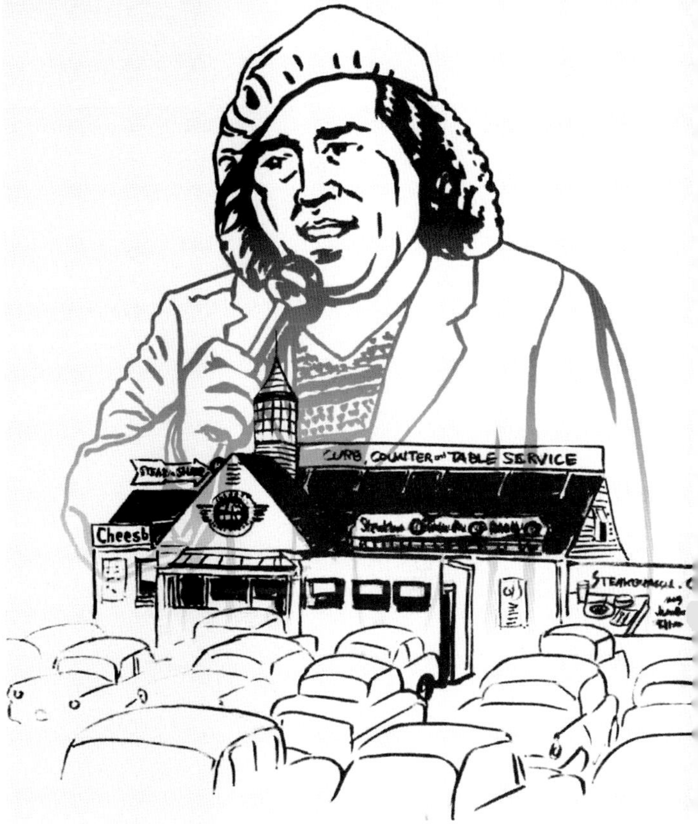

Peoria's Big Bel

Yakima-born, Peoria-raised Samuel Burl Kinison Jr. (1953–1992) was the third of four boys of Pentecostal reverend Sam Kinison Sr. and wife Marie. They lived in the Warner Home projects when five-year-old Sam suffered a serious brain injury from a truck hitting him, changing him from "sweet to ornery," according to older brother Bill. In 1959, the family moved to an East Peoria church's basement.

His father died in 1972, and Samuel Burl Kinison Jr. felt "the call," becoming a minister like his older brothers. He questioned his faith in 1978 and turned to comedy.

Twice named Funniest Man in Texas, he moved to Hollywood and got his break on HBO's *Young Comedians* in 1985. The Scream-meister, with a yen for Steak 'n Shakes, set records wherever he performed.

In 1992, he died in a car crash.

Pictured above on the right is his favorite haunt, the East Peoria Steak 'n Shake. (Left, courtesy of *Peoria Journal Star*; right, courtesy of Tim McGowan.)

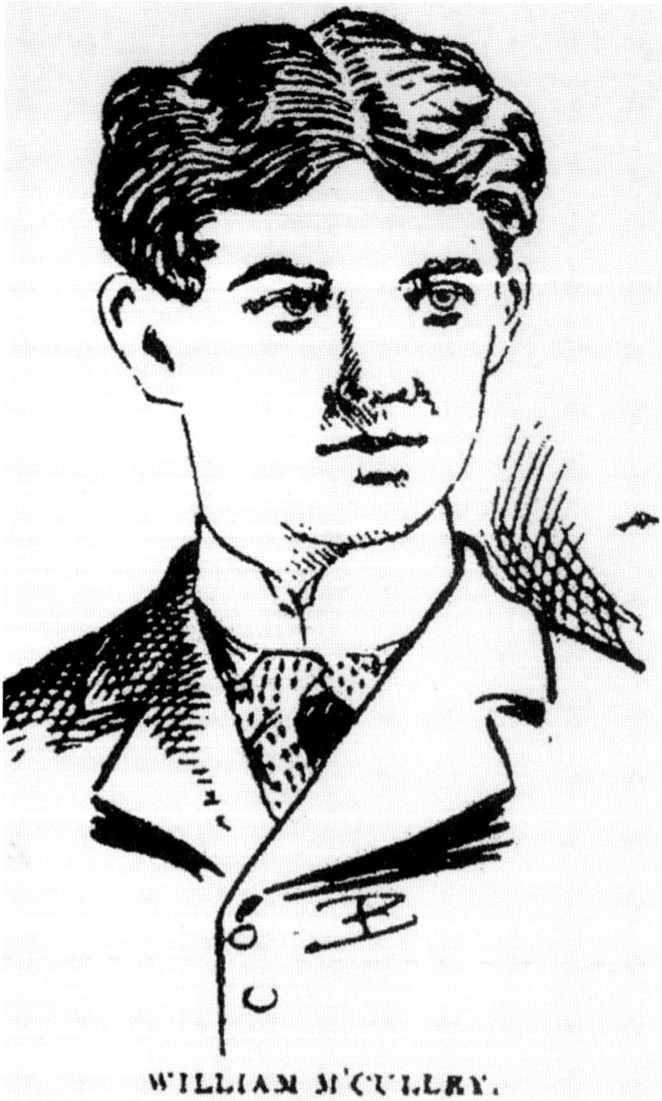

The Z-nom (ABOVE AND OPPOSITE PAGE)
No one would have mistaken him for the actors who have played his creation, Zorro. In his later years, (William) Johnston McCulley resembled an ostrich with glasses.

No matter.

No leading man could ever lug the typewriter of the writer who grew up in Chillicothe, Illinois, and began as a Peoria reporter who wrote the fabled 60-plus Zorro yarns that began in 1919.

He died in 1958.

But, for a pulp moment in 1909 River City, he was the swashbuckling McCulley—the brigand-reporter who swept up a swooning young woman, leaving the city gasping at the *Peoria Star* January 14 headline: "(Peoria) Journal writer flees city in company of Olga Patterson—Deserts his wife for smiles of buxom young lady."

The great fictioneer could not have tapped a more potboiling slug line.

A young W. Johnston McCulley is pictured above in 1901. (Above, courtesy of Gary Fyke, Chillicothe Historical Society; opposite page, artwork by Peter Poplaski; courtesy of Chillicothe Historical Society.)

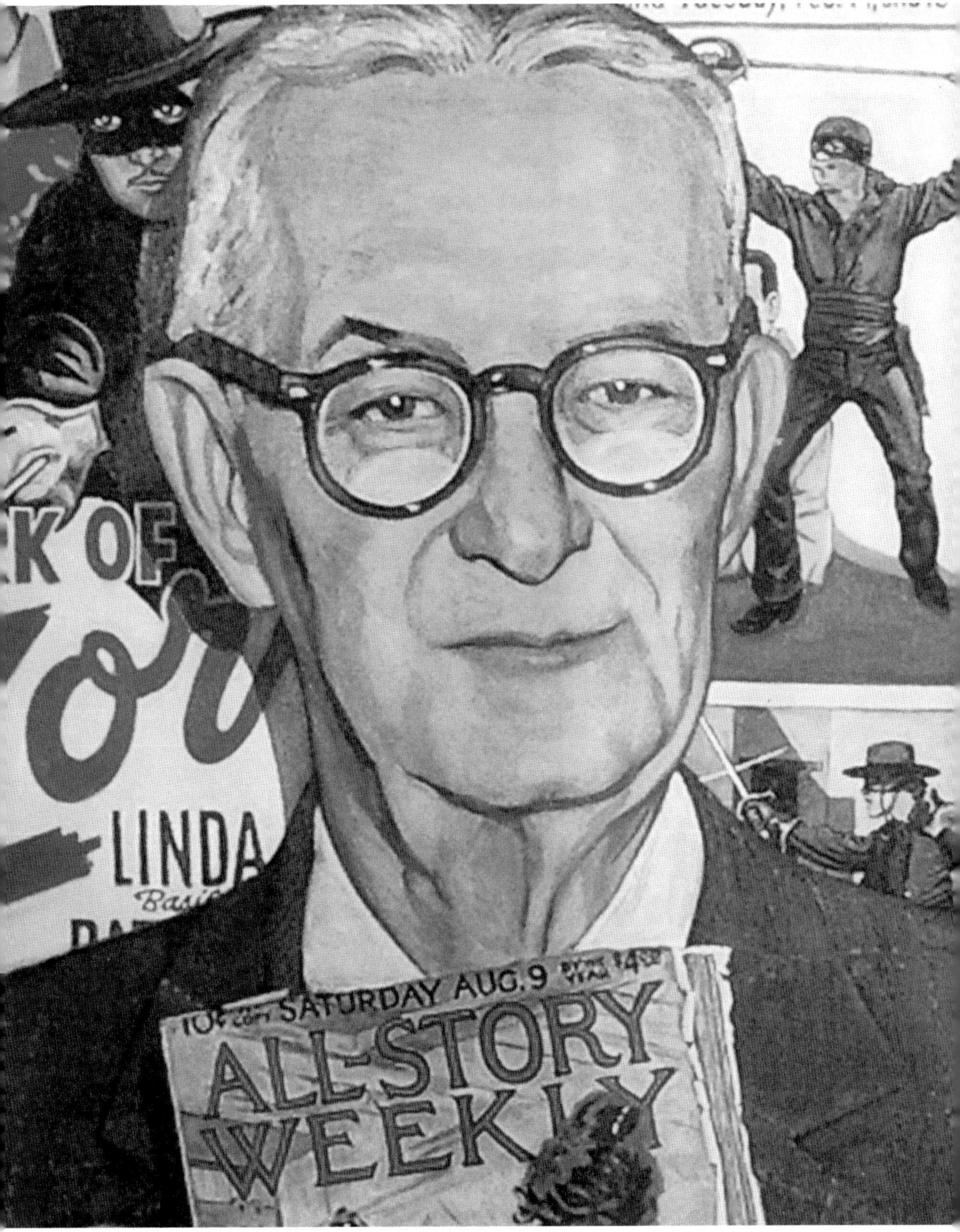
K OF
LINDA
SATURDAY AUG. 9
ALL-STORY
WEEKLY

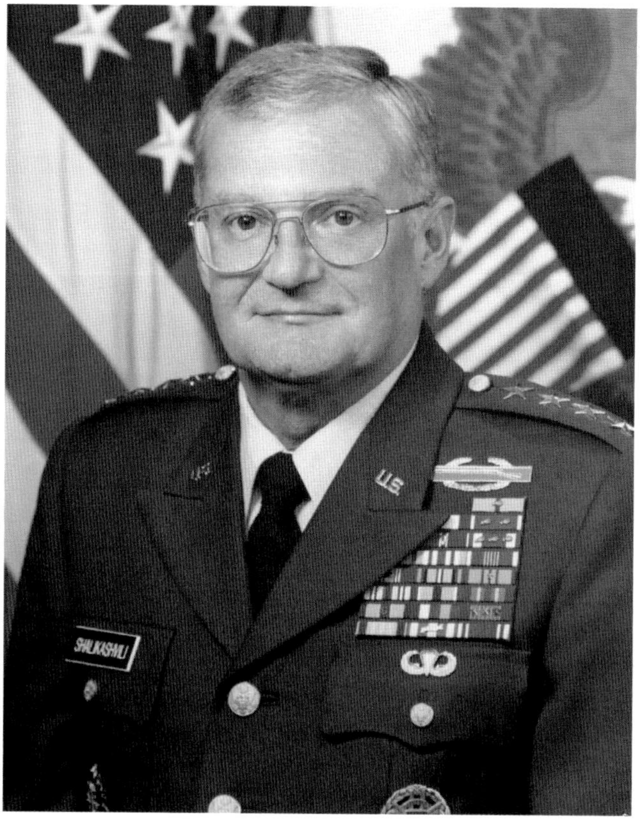

The Peoria Chief

Thanks to a River City woman who had married Shalikashvili's second cousin, 16-year-old John "Shali" Shalikashvili arrived in a prosperous (and unbombed) 1952 Peoria that was light years from his native Warsaw, the most wracked European city of World War II. He and his family—mother, Maria, father, Dmitri, brothers Othar and Gale—had as their guardian angel George L. Luthy, a monied banker. Soon, with determined hard work, the former war-chased refugees assimilated into the mosaic of Middle America. Shali, at the height of his epic life, often said, with tongue in cheek, that he learned English while watching John "Duke" Wayne movies; those films would later pale when compared to Shali's real life.

He graduated with honors from Peoria High in 1954, and in his watershed year of 1958, graduated from Bradley University with a bachelor's degree in mechanical engineering, became a US citizen, and received an Army draft notice. The latter set in motion his life course. Starting at the bottom rank of private, Shali spectacularly ran the table, retiring as the nation's top military officer—the chairman of the Joint Chiefs of Staff in 1997. He broke convention for a chairman when President Clinton tapped him to succeed Gen. Colin Powell in 1993: the first immigrant, the first draftee (private), and the first graduate of Officer Candidate School rather than a military academy. America's 13th chairman quietly rattled military conventions and broke the staid leadership mold. Yet, Shali was not the first general in his family—his maternal grandfather was a cavalry general in the Czarist army in Petersburg, Russia.

General Shalikashvili's tenure followed the end of the Cold War as the world spun from doomsday to global boomlets of conflict, a time akin to the arcade game Whac-A-Mole. As Chairman Shali said, "There were never less than ten active operations overseas on any given day."

After he retired, the four-star general became a visiting professor of international studies at Stanford University. He died at Fort Lewis, Washington, where he was once commander.

Shali's life was a heck of an American story—with a Peoria bedrock. (Courtesy of the Department of Defense.)

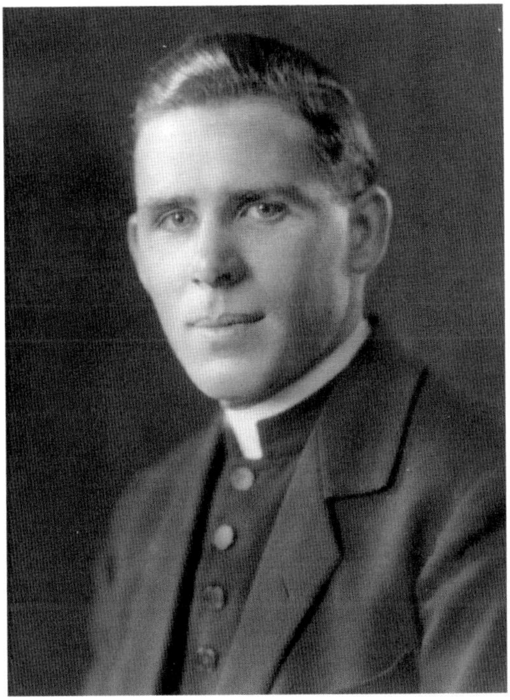

The Peoria Prelate

At age five, Peter John Sheen (1895–1979) moved with his family from his birthplace in El Paso, Illinois, to Peoria; it set in motion a life that would affect tens of millions. His intellect beamed early, starring as the top student at St. Mary's Cathedral School and as the class of 1913 valedictorian at Spalding Institute. As a schoolboy, he changed his first name to Fulton as a paean to his maternal grandfather.

Next stop: priesthood.

Fulton J. Sheen realized his dream in 1919 with his ordination into the Peoria Diocese at St. Mary's Cathedral. Father Sheen continued his academic climb, culminating with a super-doctorate from Belgium's University of Louvain in 1924. Other theology and philosophy honors from Europe's academics followed; many were a first for an American. With an appointment to Oxford looming, Bishop Dunne recalled the Peoria wunderkind home to serve as assistant pastor at the worn St. Patrick's church. During the nine months he served, he filled the pews and steeped the moribund parish with hope. Satisfied that Father Sheen had passed the test of humility, the bishop released him back to academia; the St. Pat's posting would be Fulton Sheen's only pastoral call.

It marked the end of his time in Peoria.

He returned to Catholic University in Washington, DC, to teach. There, his fellow academics discovered his oratory brilliance, and in 1930, he became the voice of radio's *The Catholic Hour*; something he would continue for the next 22 years, taking the national listenership from a few hundred thousand to four million. In 1952, Bishop Sheen began a six-year TV run of *Life Is Worth Living*. He garnered an Emmy for Outstanding Personality, over such Hollywood hefties as Milton Berle and Frank Sinatra, by mixing religious and secular topics into a witty homily on life. He became an American megastar. Conversions to Catholicism increased more than at any other time in US history. After the successful television run, Pope Paul VI named Bishop Sheen as the archbishop to the Titular See of Newport (Wales) in 1969. Archbishop Sheen died in New York City in 1979.

In 2004, from the Peoria diocese that begat Archbishop Sheen's remarkable religious life, the long trek for canonization began. On July 28, 2012, Pope Benedict XVI declared the Peorian "venerated," a robust step toward sainthood. (Courtesy of the Local History and Genealogy Collection, Peoria Public Library.)

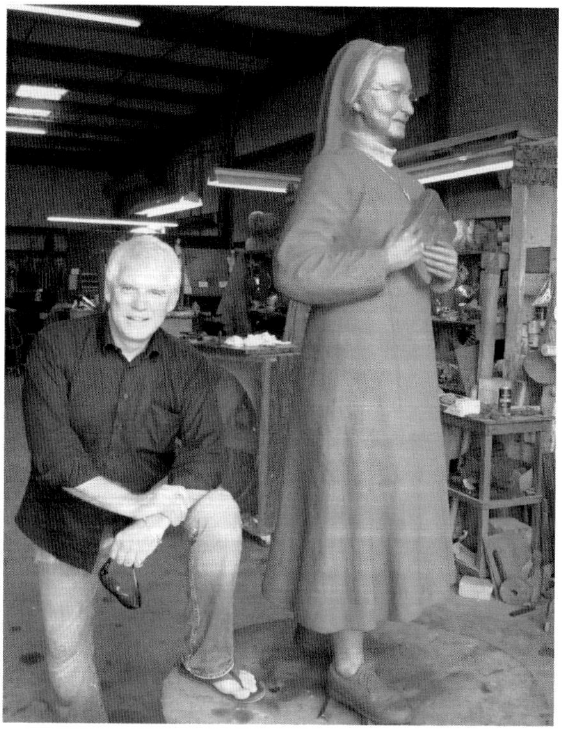

Blackie and the Boy

Lonnie Stewart is a world-class Peoria artist whose stylish paintings and sculptures capture the real nub of his subjects, many of whom are globally famous.

Yet, as a five-year-old living in rural Delong outside Galesburg, his dream of riding horses almost overtook his art career—except for the reality of watching his blind horse Blackie crash into the side of the family barn. Blackie's death scotched all fantasy of a life other than as an artist; he redoubled his efforts to develop his precocious knack at portraiture. In a grade school without art classes, Barbara Hopkins stepped up and provided lessons for the youngster. His first painting was of a forlorn teacup in a garden. Later, as a student at Galesburg's Churchill Junior High, he designed the school's flag—his first public artwork that's still in use. After graduating from Galesburg High, Stewart continued his studies at Knox College, the Chicago Art Institute, and in Florence, Italy, where another notable sculptor, Peorian Fritz Triebel, once had studied in the 1880s.

Soon, the world would become his canvas as he has lived the words of the early Greek painter Appelles: *Nulla dies sine linea*, "No day without a line." Besides his extraordinary hands, he has applied unflagging research to his subjects, the crux of each piece. From his first commissioned sculpture, *Trone Angel* (1984), at Galesburg's East Linwood Cemetery, his works have included the likes of Mother Teresa, Pope John Paul II, King Constantine, Pres. Ronald Reagan, Princess Diana, and Princess Sarah Ferguson among scores of others. His artwork also has included an array of animals, though he has drawn the line at having "critter-sittings in his living room."

With the luxury to live anywhere, Stewart works close to his prairie past; a Peoria Warehouse District studio serves as his primary launchpad to the world. He maintains a Charleston, South Carolina, home and workshop as well.

Without harking trumpet-fare and true to a Heartland ethos, he has donated innumerable pieces for charities. His plans to establish art scholarships for promising high school seniors will be his way to pass the paintbrush to the future.

Lonnie Stewart poses here with one of his favorite statues—Sister Canesia. The statue now graces the entryway to Peoria's St. Francis Hospital. (Courtesy of Lonnie Stewart.)

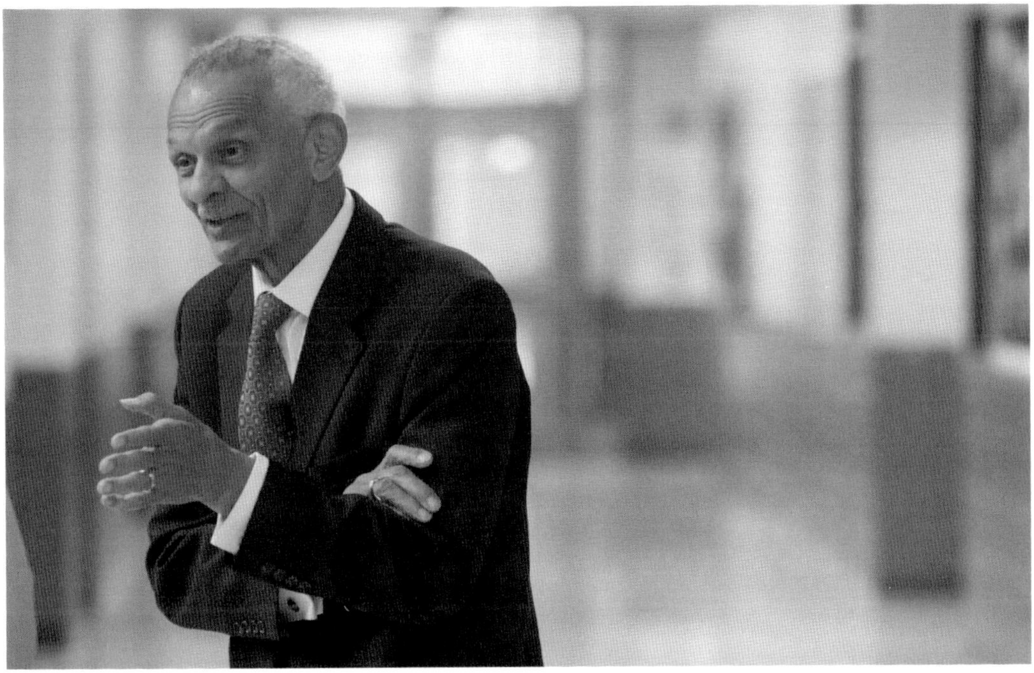

C.T. Vivian and the Peoria Counters

By the time six-year-old Cordy Tindell (C.T.) Vivian left his Boonville, Missouri, birthplace in 1930 with his mother and grandmother, he had seen the family home razed by a firebug and their farm lost to the Great Depression. The two women had suffered enough racial bile that they had a vision for the youngster—they wanted him educated in an integrated school system in a town with a college.

Macomb, Illinois, had both.

Still, it was not the perfect bucolic burg, but it was better than Boonville. And in America, bigotry was inescapable. Vivian graduated from Macomb High (1942) and went to the local Western Illinois University, majoring in sociology but leaving short of a degree.

It was the mid-1940s and time for C.T. to meet his future. He went to Peoria, a town steeped in abolitionist history.

There, he worked as assistant boys' director of the Carver Community Center. While Peoria was not a "Sundown Town" that kept blacks at bay, it had some Jim Crow tendencies, especially at its eateries. Vivian in 1947 led peaceful campaigns against segregated lunch counters, where he would stand in line and wait his turn. His dignity overpowered bigotry, and River City dining became a matter of choice and not of skin color.

Within the civil rights movement, Vivian's pioneering efforts spurred hopes of American segregation's defeat through nonviolence.

By 1953, Vivian had become the NAACP Peoria chapter vice president after promoting non-janitorial jobs for blacks at the Caterpillar plants. In the same fateful year, he married fellow Carver staffer Octavia Geons. They had six children and remained married for 58 years until her death in 2011.

Vivian, in 1954, heeded the call and delivered his first sermon at the Mount Zion Baptist Church. The next year, he left his Foster-Gallagher Mail Order Company job and Peoria. With the financial support of Mount Zion and Helen Gallagher, he enrolled at Nashville's American Baptist Theological Seminary.

He carried his Peoria lessons to the national and international scenes as a reckoning force for equality among all people.

On November 22, 2013, Dr. C.T. Vivian received the nation's highest honor, the Presidential Medal of Freedom, for his legendary impact on civil rights in America.

Dr. C.T. Vivian is shown in Peoria, the site of earlier reckonings. (Courtesy of *Peoria Journal Star.*)

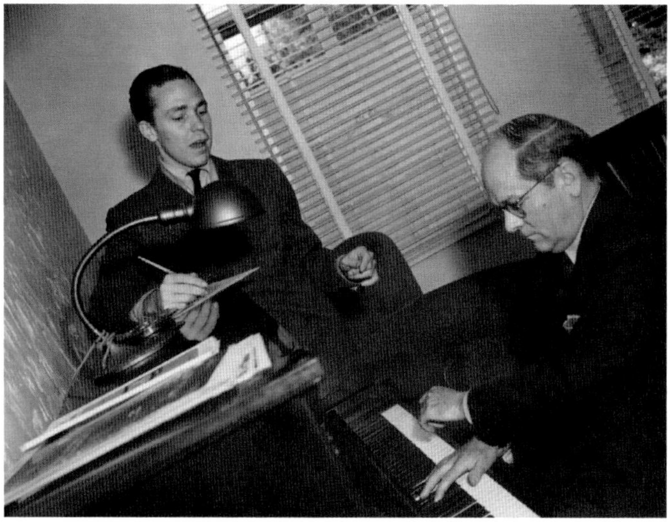

Hooray for Pe-OR-i-A!

Songwriter hall of famer Richard Whiting wrote some of the most memorable tunes during the golden age of musicals and was the "Big Get" for the era's great lyricists, including Oscar Hammerstein and Johnny Mercer. Starting in 1914, the young pianist riffed hundreds of melodies for the movies. His haunting "Till We Meet Again" (1918) became World War I's number one song.

His 1921 "Ain't We Got Fun," embodied the Roarin' Twenties.

In the 1930s, Whiting scored 50 notable movie ditties, including Shirley Temple's "On the Good Ship Lollipop" and, with Johnny Mercer, the Academy Award anthem "Hooray for Hollywood" in 1938, the year he died.

Above, Whiting is pictured at the piano with Johnny Mercer around 1938. Below is the eighth-grade class at Franklin School in 1906. Richard Whiting is fourth from the left in the first row. (Courtesy of the Johnny Mercer Collection, Georgia State University.)

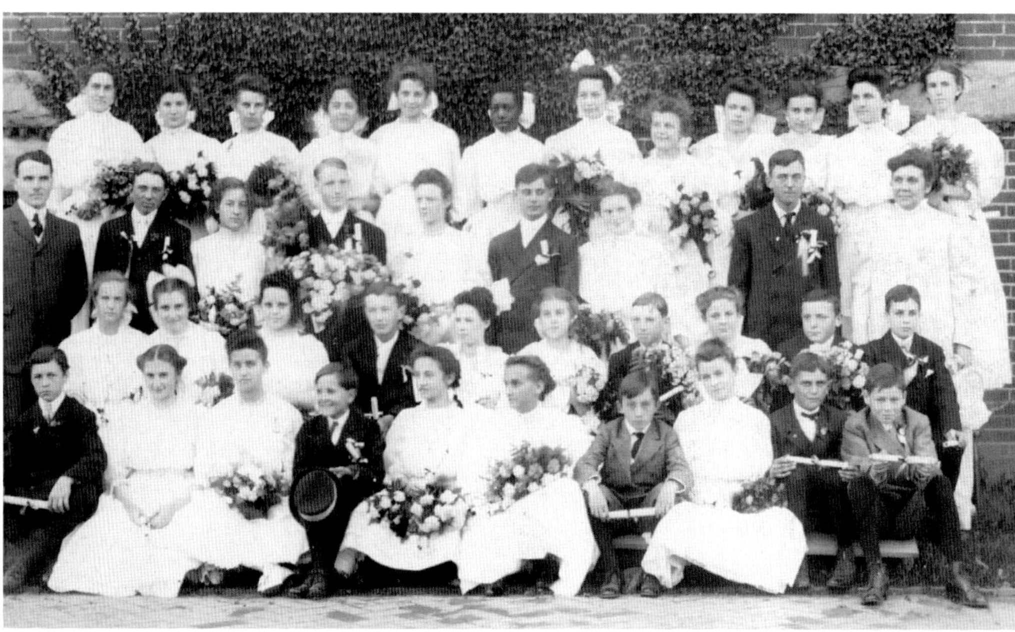

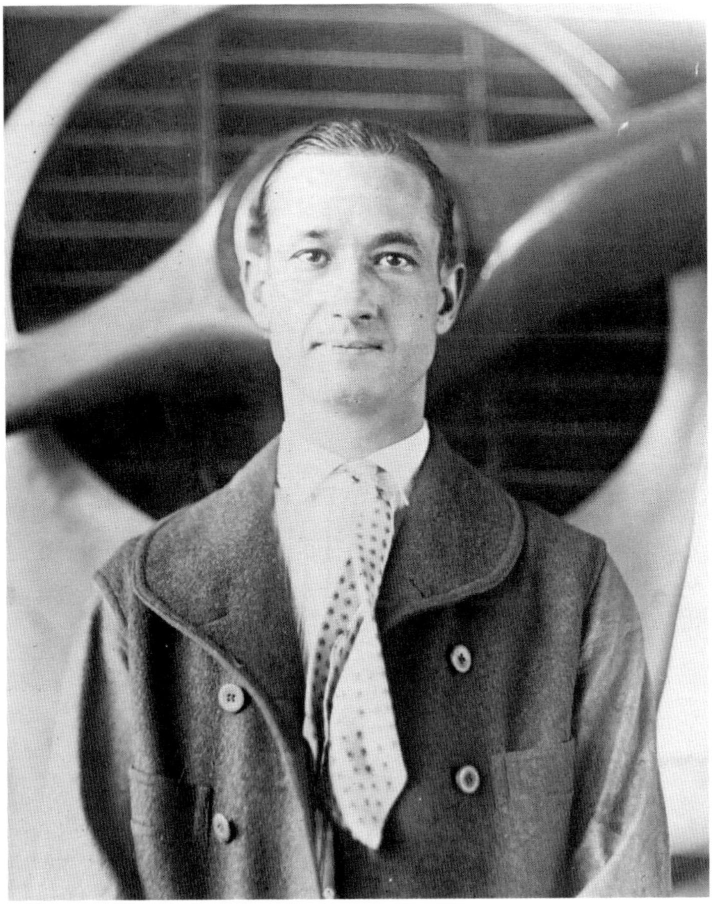

Spig Wings It

Born into Peoria gentry, Frank W. "Spig" Wead (1895–1947) foresaw naval aviation as the future and promoted it, especially after a crippling accident. The 1916 Naval Academy graduate served on a minelayer in World War I and became a racing aviator who set records in the early 1920s, usually against legendary Army pilot Jimmy Doolittle. One night in 1927, when his daughter cried out, he tripped down the stairs and suffered a debilitating neck injury; it may have ended his days in the cockpit, but it launched a writing career.

For the next 20 years, he wrote Navy-muscled flying stories in magazines, chiefly for the *Saturday Evening Post*, and a couple of novels, including *Ceiling Zero*, which he rolled into a play and then a 1936 film. He'd prove his greatest strength as a screenwriter, whistling through 36 screenplays. In 1938, he scored a rarity of two Oscar nominations in the same year for writing *Test Pilot* (original story) and *The Citadel* (screenplay). He wrote *They Were Expendable*, the 1945 film considered one of the finest about war. Without question he was Navy Air's best friend.

But the attack at Pearl Harbor proved too much catnip for the dynamo, who pressed for his reentry into the Navy despite being able to walk only with leg braces and canes. He had assignments mostly in the strategic Pacific planning arena at the US War Department. However, before he retired in late 1944, he saw combat in the Marianas while aboard the aircraft carrier USS *Yorktown*.

He died in 1947 in Santa Monica, California, and is buried at Peoria's Springdale Cemetery.

Hollywood celebrated Spig in the 1957 biopic *The Wings of Eagles* with John Wayne, no less, playing the sea flyer from Peoria. Frank Wead, River City's greatest screenwriter, could not have scripted it better. (Courtesy of the Library of Congress.)

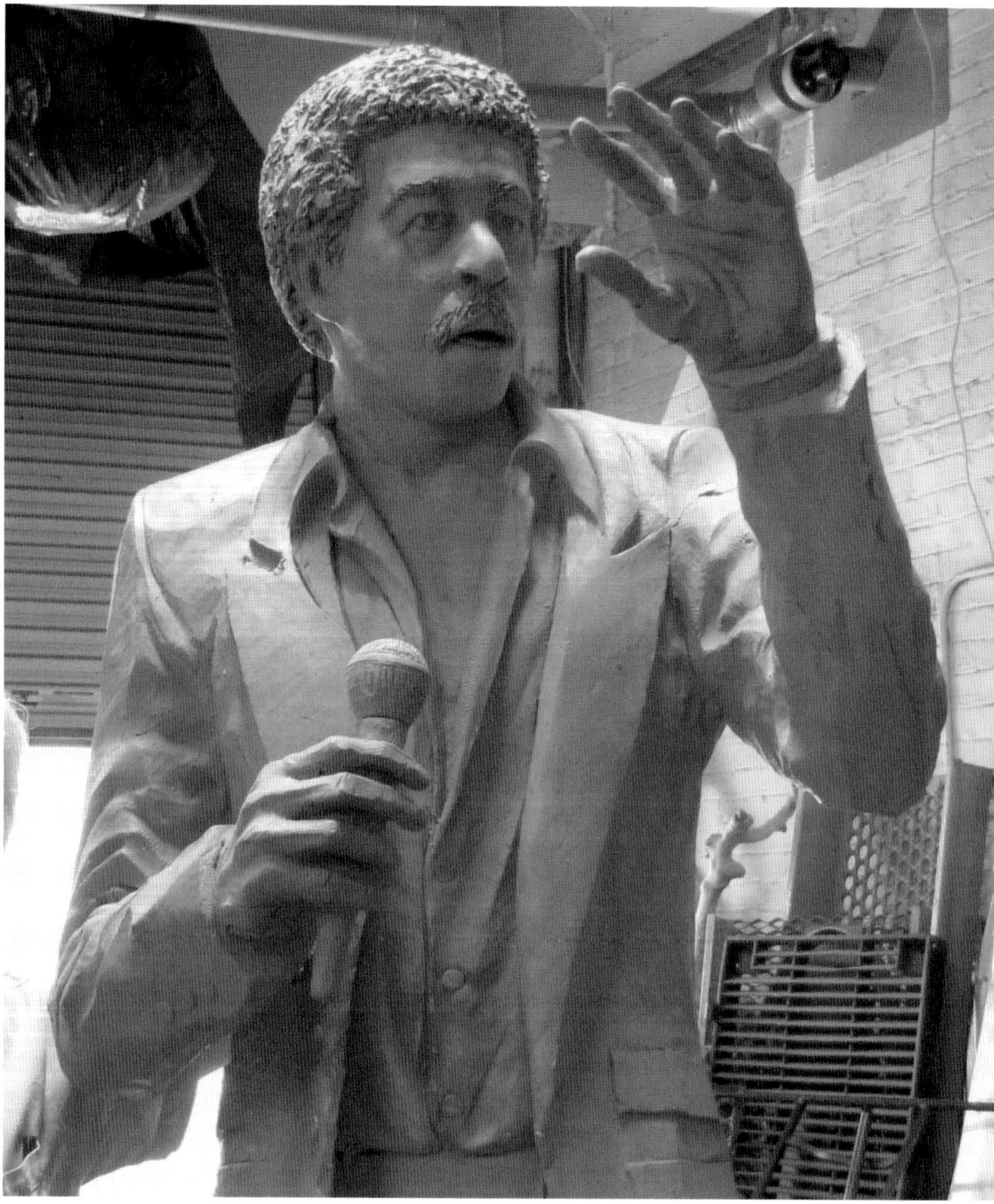

A Standup Peorian

Born to a red-light lady and her peddler, Richard Pryor did not let an appalling childhood keep him from sitting atop the regal fart-seat as the acknowledged King of Comedy. Thanks to Juliette Whittaker, he had his first comic turn in the Carver Community Center's *Rumplestiltskin*, and funny became his way out.

Pryor's first national starburst came in 1963 as a Bill Cosby-Lite.

He returned in the early 1970s as "that cat from (Peoria's) Washington Street," and ignited, as comedian Dick Gregory said, the "Peoria in all of us" by bridging white and black humor into human hilarity. His personal life, though, was a mess of unhinged wolfing of drugs, booze, and sex.

Diagnosed with multiple sclerosis in 1986, the Sultan of Skits died in 2005. Preston Jackson created this Richard Pryor statue. (Courtesy of Karen Camper.)

INDEX